MEDIA AND COMMUNICATIONS - TECHNOLOGIES, POLICIES AND CHALLENGES

ELECTRONIC COMMUNICATIONS PRIVACY ACT

OVERVIEW AND ISSUES FOR CONSIDERATION

MEDIA AND COMMUNICATIONS - TECHNOLOGIES, POLICIES AND CHALLENGES

Additional books in this series can be found on Nova's website under the Series tab.

Additional e-books in this series can be found on Nova's website under the e-book tab.

MEDIA AND COMMUNICATIONS - TECHNOLOGIES, POLICIES AND CHALLENGES

ELECTRONIC COMMUNICATIONS PRIVACY ACT

OVERVIEW AND ISSUES FOR CONSIDERATION

MARISSA G. HAUL
EDITOR

nova publishers
New York

For permission to use material from this book please contact us:
Telephone 631-231-7269; Fax 631-231-8175
Web Site: http://www.novapublishers.com

Library of Congress Cataloging-in-Publication Data

ISBN: 978-1-62948-826-4

Published by Nova Science Publishers, Inc. † New York

CONTENTS

PREFACE

The statutory framework for the communications sector largely was enacted prior to the commercial development and deployment of digital technology, Internet Protocol (IP), broadband networks, and online voice, data, and video services. These new technologies have driven changes in market structure throughout the communications sector. In a technologically dynamic sector, the statutory framework cannot be modified every time there is a significant technological change. The challenge therefore is to create statutory language that is flexible enough to continue to foster articulated public policy objectives in the face of technological change, without artificially favoring either legacy technology or new technology. This book focuses on updating the statutory framework for communications for the digital age. The authors also provide statements and testimonies from hearings on lawful access to stored content, and geolocation privacy surveillance.

Chapter 1 – Provides an overview of the Electronic Communications Privacy Act (ECPA). ECPA consists of three parts. The first, sometimes referred to as Title III, outlaws the unauthorized interception of wire, oral, or electronic communications. It also establishes a judicial supervised procedure to permit such interceptions for law enforcement purposes. The second, the Stored Communications Act, focuses on the privacy of, and government access to, stored electronic communications. The third creates a procedure for governmental installation and use of pen registers as well as trap and trace devices.

Chapter 2 - Statement of Judiciary Committee Chairman Bob Goodlatte. "Hearing on Electronic Communications Privacy Act (ECPA) Part 1: Lawful Access to Stored Content" before the House Judiciary Committee, Subcommittee on Crime, Terrorism, Homeland Security, and Investigations, dated March 19, 2013.

Chapter 3 – Statement of Elana Tyrangiel, Acting Assistant Attorney General, Office of Legal Policy, Department of Justice. Hearing on "Electronic Communications before the House Judiciary Committee, Subcommittee on Crime, Terrorism, Homeland Security, and InvestigationsPrivacy Act (ECPA) Part 1: Lawful Access to Stored Content", dated April 25, 2013.

Chapter 4 – Testimony of Richard Littlehale, Assistant Special Agent in Charge of the Technical Services Unit, Tennessee Bureau of Investigation. Hearing on "Electronic Communications Privacy Act (ECPA) Part 1: Lawful Access to Stored Content" before the House Judiciary Committee, Subcommittee on Crime, Terrorism, Homeland Security, and Investigations. dated March 19, 2013.

Chapter 5 – Statement of Orin S. Kerr, Fred C. Stevenson Research Professor, George Washington University Law School. Hearing on "Electronic Communications Privacy Act (ECPA) Part 1: Lawful Access to Stored Content" before the House Judiciary Committee, Subcommittee on Crime, Terrorism, Homeland Security, and Investigations, dated March 19, 2013.

Chapter 6 - Testimony of Richard Salgado, Director, Law Enforcement and Information Security, Google, Inc.. Hearing on "Electronic Communications Privacy Act (ECPA) Part 1: Lawful Access to Stored Content" before the House Judiciary Committee, Subcommittee on Crime, Terrorism, Homeland Security, and Investigations, dated March 19, 2013.

Chapter 7 - Statement of Judiciary Committee Chairman Bob Goodlatte. "Hearing on Electronic Communications Privacy Act (ECPA), Part 2: Geolocation Privacy and Surveillance" before the House Judiciary Committee, Subcommittee on Crime, Terrorism, Homeland Security, and Investigations, dated April 25, 2013.

Chapter 8 - Statement of Mark Eckenwiler, Senior Counsel, Perkins Coie, LLP. Hearing on "Electronic Communications Privacy Act (ECPA) Part 2: Geolocation Privacy and Surveillance" before the House Judiciary Committee, Subcommittee on Crime, Terrorism, Homeland Security, and Investigations, dated April 25, 2013.

Chapter 9 - Statement of Peter A. Modafferi, Chair, Police Investigative Operations Committee of the International Association of Chiefs of Police. Hearing on "Electronic Communications Privacy Act (ECPA) Part 2: Geolocation Privacy and Surveillance" before the House Judiciary Committee, Subcommittee on Crime, Terrorism, Homeland Security, and Investigations, dated April 25, 2013.

Chapter 10 - Statement of Catherine Crump, Staff Attorney, American Civil Liberties Union. Hearing on "Electronic Communications Privacy Act

(ECPA) Part 2: Geolocation Privacy and Surveillance" before the House Judiciary Committee, Subcommittee on Crime, Terrorism, Homeland Security, and Investigations, dated April 25, 2013.

Chapter 11 - Testimony of Matt Blaze, Professor, University of Pennslyvania. Hearing on "Electronic Communications Privacy Act (ECPA) Part 2: Geolocation Privacy and Surveillance" before the House Judiciary Committee, Subcommittee on Crime, Terrorism, Homeland Security, and Investigations, April 25, 2013.

In: Electronic Communications Privacy Act ISBN: 978-1-62948-826-4
Editor: Marissa G. Haul

Chapter 1

PRIVACY: AN OVERVIEW OF THE ELECTRONIC COMMUNICATIONS PRIVACY ACT*

Charles Doyle

SUMMARY

This report provides an overview of federal law governing wiretapping and electronic eavesdropping under the Electronic Communications Privacy Act (ECPA). It also appends citations to state law in the area and the text of ECPA.

It is a federal crime to wiretap or to use a machine to capture the communications of others without court approval, unless one of the parties has given his prior consent. It is likewise a federal crime to use or disclose any information acquired by illegal wiretapping or electronic eavesdropping. Violations can result in imprisonment for not more than five years; fines up to $250,000 (up to $500,000 for organizations); civil liability for damages, attorneys' fees and possibly punitive damages; disciplinary action against any attorneys involved; and suppression of any derivative evidence. Congress has created separate, but comparable, protective schemes for electronic

* This is an edited, reformatted and augmented version of the Congressional Research Service Publication, CRS Report for Congress R41733, dated October 9, 2012.

communications (e.g., email) and against the surreptitious use of telephone call monitoring practices such as pen registers and trap and trace devices.

Each of these protective schemes comes with a procedural mechanism to afford limited law enforcement access to private communications and communications records under conditions consistent with the dictates of the Fourth Amendment. The government has been given narrowly confined authority to engage in electronic surveillance, conduct physical searches, and install and use pen registers and trap and trace devices for law enforcement purposes under ECPA and for purposes of foreign intelligence gathering under the Foreign Intelligence Surveillance Act.

INTRODUCTION

This is an outline of the Electronic Communications Privacy Act (ECPA).[1] ECPA consists of three parts. The first, sometimes referred to as Title III, outlaws the unauthorized interception of wire, oral, or electronic communications.[2] It also establishes a judicial supervised procedure to permit such interceptions for law enforcement purposes.[3] The second, the Stored Communications Act, focuses on the privacy of, and government access to, stored electronic communications.[4] The third creates a procedure for governmental installation and use of pen registers as well as trap and trace devices.[5] It also outlaws such installation or use except for law enforcement and foreign intelligence investigations.[6]

BACKGROUND

At common law, "eavesdroppers, or such as listen under walls or windows, or the eaves of a house, to hearken after discourse, and thereupon to frame slanderous and mischievous tales, are a common nuisance and presentable at the court-leet; or are indictable at the sessions, and punishable by fine and finding of sureties for [their] good behavior."[7] Although early American law proscribed common law eavesdropping, the crime was little prosecuted and by the late nineteenth century had "nearly faded from the legal horizon."[8] With the invention of the telegraph and telephone, however, state laws outlawing wiretapping or indiscretion by telephone and telegraph operators preserved the spirit of the common law prohibition in this country.

Congress enacted the first federal wiretap statute as a temporary measure to prevent disclosure of government secrets during World War I.[9] Later, it proscribed intercepting and divulging private radio messages in the Radio Act of 1927,[10] but did not immediately reestablish a federal wiretap prohibition. By the time of the landmark Supreme Court decision in *Olmstead*, however, at least forty-one of the forty-eight states had banned wiretapping or forbidden telephone and telegraph employees and officers from disclosing the content of telephone or telegraph messages or both.[11]

Olmstead was a Seattle bootlegger whose Prohibition Act conviction was the product of a federal wiretap. He challenged his conviction on three grounds, arguing unsuccessfully that the wiretap evidence should have been suppressed as a violation of either his Fourth Amendment rights, his Fifth Amendment privilege against self-incrimination, or the rights implicit in the Washington state statute that outlawed wiretapping.

For a majority of the Court, writing through Chief Justice Taft, Olmstead's Fourth Amendment challenge was doomed by the absence of "an official search and seizure of his person, or such a seizure of his papers or his tangible material effects, or an actual physical invasion of his house or curtilage[12] for the purposes of making a seizure."[13]

Chief Justice Taft pointed out that Congress was free to provide protection which the Constitution did not.[14] Congress did so in the 1934 Communications Act by expanding the Radio Act's proscription against intercepting and divulging radio communications so as to include intercepting and divulging radio or wire communications.[15]

The Federal Communications Act outlawed wiretapping, but it said nothing about the use of machines to surreptitiously record and transmit face to face conversations.[16] In the absence of a statutory ban the number of surreptitious recording cases decided on Fourth Amendment grounds surged and the results began to erode *Olmstead*'s underpinnings.[17]

Erosion, however, came slowly. Initially the Court applied *Olmstead*'s principles to the electronic eavesdropping cases. Thus, the use of a dictaphone to secretly overhear a private conversation in an adjacent office offended no Fourth Amendment precepts because no physical trespass into the office in which the conversation took place had occurred.[18] Similarly, the absence of a physical trespass precluded Fourth Amendment coverage of the situation where a federal agent secretly recorded his conversation with a defendant held in a commercial laundry in an area open to the public.[19] On the other hand, the Fourth Amendment did reach the government's physical intrusion upon private property during an investigation, as for example when they drove a "spike mike" into the common wall of a row house until it made contact with a heating duct for the home in which the conversation occurred.[20]

The spike mike case presented something of a technical problem, because there was some question whether the spike mike had actually crossed the property line of the defendant's town house when it made contact with the heating duct. The Court declined to rest its decision on the technicalities of local property law, and instead found that the government's conduct had intruded upon privacy of home and hearth in a manner condemned by the Fourth Amendment.[21]

Each of these cases focused upon whether a warrantless trespass onto private property had occurred, that is, whether the *means* of conducting a search and seizure had been so unreasonable as to offend the Fourth Amendment. Yet in each case, the object of the search and seizure had been not those tangible papers or effects for which the Fourth Amendment's protection had been traditionally claimed, but an intangible, a conversation. This enlarged view of the Fourth Amendment could hardly be ignored, for "[i]t follows from ... *Silverman* ... that the Fourth Amendment may protect against the overhearing of verbal statements as well as against the more traditional seizure of papers and effects."[22]

Soon thereafter the Court repudiated the notion that the Fourth Amendment's protection was contingent upon some trespass to real property in *Katz v. United States.*[23] Katz was a bookie convicted on the basis of evidence gathered by an electronic listening and recording device set up outside the public telephone booth that Katz used to take and place bets. The Court held that the gateway for Fourth Amendment purposes stood at that point where an individual should to able to expect that his or her privacy would not be subjected to unwarranted governmental intrusion.[24]

One obvious consequence of Fourth Amendment coverage of wiretapping and other forms of electronic eavesdropping is the usual attachment of the Amendment's warrant requirement. To avoid constitutional problems and at the same time preserve wiretapping and other forms of electronic eavesdropping as a law enforcement tool, some of the states established a statutory system under which law enforcement officials could obtain a warrant, or equivalent court order, authorizing wiretapping or electronic eavesdropping.

The Court rejected the constitutional adequacy of one of the more detailed of these state statutory schemes in *Berger v. New York.*[25] The statute was found deficient because of its failure to require:

- a particularized description of the place to be searched;
- a particularized description of the crime to which the search and seizure related;
- a particularized description of the conversation to be seized;
- limitations to prevent general searches;
- termination of the interception when the conversation sought had been seized;
- prompt execution of the order;
- return to the issuing court detailing the items seized; and
- any showing of exigent circumstances to overcome the want of prior notice.[26]

Berger helped persuade Congress to enact Title III of the Omnibus Crime Control and Safe Streets Act of 1968, a comprehensive wiretapping and electronic eavesdropping statute that not only outlawed both activities in general terms but that also permitted federal and state law enforcement officers to use them under strict limitations designed to meet the objections in *Berger*.[27]

A decade later another Supreme Court case persuaded Congress to supplement Title III with a judicially supervised procedure for the use of wiretapping and electronic eavesdropping in foreign intelligence gathering situations. When Congress passed Title III there was some question over the extent of the President's inherent powers to authorize wiretaps—without judicial approval—in national security cases. As a consequence, the issue was simply removed from the Title III scheme.[28]

After the Court held that the President's inherent powers were insufficient to excuse warrantless electronic eavesdropping on purely domestic threats to national security,[29] Congress considered it prudent to augment the foreign intelligence gathering authority of the United States with the Foreign Intelligence Security Act of 1978 (FISA).[30] The FISA provides a procedure for judicial review and authorization of electronic surveillance and other forms of information gathering for foreign intelligence purposes.

Two other Supreme Court cases influenced the development of federal law in the area. In *United States v. Miller*,[31] the Court held that a customer had no Fourth Amendment protected expectation of privacy in the records his bank created concerning his transactions with them. These third party records were therefore available to the government under a subpoena ducestecum rather than a more narrowly circumscribed warrant.[32] In *Smith v. Maryland*,[33] it held that no warrant was required for the state's use of a pen register or trap and trace device, if the device merely identified the telephone numbers for calls made and received from a particular telephone. No Fourth Amendment search or seizure occurred, the Court held, since the customer had no justifiable expectation of privacy in information which he knew or should have known the telephone company might ordinarily capture for billing or service purposes.[34]

In 1986, Congress enacted the Electronic Communications Privacy Act (ECPA).[35] ECPA consists of three parts: a revised Title III;[36] the Stored Communications Act (SCA);[37] and provisions governing the installation and use of pen registers as well as trap and trace devices.[38] Congress has adjusted the components of ECPA and FISA, over the years. It has done so sometimes in the interests of greater privacy; sometimes in the interest of more effective law enforcement or foreign intelligence gathering; often with an eye to some combination of those interests. Prominent among its enactments are:

- the USA PATRIOT Act; [39]
- the Intelligence Authorization Act for Fiscal Year 2002;[40]
- the 21st Century Department of Justice Appropriations Authorization Act;[41]
- the Department of Homeland Security Act;[42]
- the USA PATRIOT Improvement and Reauthorization Act;[43] and
- the Foreign Intelligence Surveillance Act of 1978 Amendments Act of 2008 (2008 FISA Amendments Act).[44]

TITLE III: PROHIBITIONS

In Title III, ECPA begins the proposition that unless provided otherwise, it is a federal crime to engage in wiretapping or electronic eavesdropping; to possess wiretapping or electronic eavesdropping equipment; to use or disclose information obtained through illegal wiretapping or electronic eavesdropping; or to disclose information secured through court-ordered wiretapping or electronic eavesdropping, in order to obstruct justice.[45]

Illegal Wiretapping and Electronic Eavesdropping

First among these is the ban on illegal wiretapping and electronic eavesdropping that covers:

- any person who
- intentionally
- intercepts, or endeavors to intercept,
- wire, oral, or electronic communications
- by using an electronic, mechanical, or other device
- unless the conduct is specifically authorized or expressly not covered, e.g.,
  - one of the parties to the conversation has consented to the interception,
  - the interception occurs in compliance with a statutorily authorized (and ordinarily judicially supervised) law enforcement or foreign intelligence gathering interception,
  - the interception occurs as part of providing or regulating communication services,
  - certain radio broadcasts, and
  - in some places, spousal wiretappers.[46]

Person

The prohibition applies to "any employee, or agent of the United States or any State or political subdivision thereof, and any individual, partnership, association, joint stock company, trust, or corporation."[47]

Intentional

Conduct can only violate Title III if it is done "intentionally," inadvertent conduct is no crime; the offender must have done on purpose those things which are outlawed.[48] He need not be shown to have known, however, that his conduct was unlawful.[49]

Jurisdiction

Subsection 2511(1) contains two interception bars—one, 2511(1)(a), simply outlaws intentional interception; the other, 2511(1)(b), outlaws intentional interception when committed under any of five jurisdictional circumstances with either an implicit or explicit nexus to interstate or foreign commerce.[50] Congress adopted the approach because of concern that its constitutional authority might not be sufficient to ban instances of electronic surveillance that bore no discernable connection to interstate commerce or any other of Congress's enumerated constitutional powers. So it enacted a general prohibition, and as a safety precaution, a second provision more tightly tethered to specific jurisdictional factors.[51] The Justice Department has honored that caution by employing subparagraph (b) to prosecute the interception of oral communications, while using subparagraph (a) to prosecute other forms of electronic eavesdropping.[52]

Interception

Interception "means the aural or other acquisition of the contents" of various kinds of communications by means of "electronic, mechanical or other devices."[53] Although logic might suggest that interception occurs only in the place where the communication is captured, the cases indicate that interception occurs as well where the communication begins, is transmitted, or is received.[54] Yet, it does not include instances when an individual simply reads or listens to a previously intercepted communication, regardless of whether additional conduct may implicate the prohibitions on use or disclosure.[55]

Once limited to aural acquisitions, ECPA enlarged the definition of "interception" by adding the words "or other acquisition" so that it is no longer limited to interceptions of communications that can be heard.[56] The change complicates the question of whether the wiretap, stored communications, or trap and trace portions of the ECPA govern the legality of various means of capturing information relating to a communication. The analysis might seem to favor wiretap coverage when it begins with an examination of whether an "interception" has occurred. Yet, there is little consensus over when an interception occurs; that is, whether "interception" as used in section 2511 contemplates surreptitious acquisition, either contemporaneous with transmission, or whether such acquisition may occur anytime before the initial cognitive receipt of the contents by the intended recipient, or under some other conditions.[57]

The USA PATRIOT Act resolved some of the statutory uncertainty concerning voice mail when it removed voice mail from the wiretap coverage of Title III (striking the phrase "and such term includes any electronic storage of such communication" from the definition of "wire communications" in Title III (18 U.S.C. 2510(1)) and added stored *wire* communications to the stored communications coverage of 18 U.S.C. 2703.[58]

Content

The interceptions proscribed in Title III are confined to those that capture a communication's "content," that is, "information concerning [its] substance, purport, or meaning."[59] Trap and trace devices and pen registers once captured only information relating to the source and addressee of a communication, not its content. That is no longer the case. The "post-cut-through dialed digit features" of contemporary telephone communications now transmit communications in such a manner that the use of ordinary pen register or trap and trace devices will capture both non-content and content.[60] As a consequence, a few courts have held, either as a matter of statutory construction or constitutional necessity, that the authorities must rely on a Title III wiretap order rather than a pen register/trap and trace order if such information will be captured.[61]

By Electronic, Mechanical, or Other Device

The statute does not cover common law "eavesdropping," but only interceptions "by electronic, mechanical or other device."[62] The term includes computers,[63] but it is defined so as not to include hearing aids or extension telephones in normal use (use in the "ordinary course of business").[64] Whether an extension phone has been installed and is being used in the ordinary course of business or in the ordinary course of law enforcement duties, so that it no longer constitutes an interception device for purposes of Title III and comparable state laws has proven a somewhat vexing question.[65]

Although often intertwined with the consent exception discussed below, the question generally turns on the facts in a given case.[66] When the exemption is claimed as a practice in the ordinary course of business, the interception must be for a legitimate business reason, it must be routinely conducted, and at least in some circuits employees must be notified that their conversations are being monitored.[67] Similarly, "Congress most likely carved out an exception for law enforcement officials to make clear that the routine and almost universal recording of phone lines by police departments and prisons, as well as other law enforcement institutions, is exempt from the statute."[68] The exception contemplates administrative rather than investigative monitoring,[69] which must nevertheless be justified by a lawful, valid law enforcement concern.[70]

Wire, Oral, or Electronic Communications

An interception is only a violation of Title III if the conversation or other form of captured communication is among those kinds which the statute protects, in oversimplified terms—if it is a telephone (wire), face to face (oral), or computer (electronic) communication. Thus, Title III does cover silent video surveillance.[71]

Title III does not cover all wire, oral or electronic communications. "Oral communications," by definition, includes only those face to face conversations for which the speakers have a justifiable expectation of privacy.[72] "Wire communications" are limited to those that are at some point involve voice communications (i.e., only aural transfers).[73] The term "electronic communications" encompasses radio and data transmissions generally, but excludes certain radio transmissions which can be innocently captured without great difficulty.[74] Even when a radio transmission meets the definition, Title III's general exemption may render its capture innocent.[75]

Endeavoring to Intercept

Although the statute condemns attempted wiretapping and electronic eavesdropping ("endeavoring to intercept"),[76] the provisions appear to have escaped use, interest, or comment heretofore, perhaps because the conduct most likely to constitute preparation for an interception—possession of wiretapping equipment—is already a separate crime.[77]

Exemptions: Consent Interceptions

Consent interceptions are common, controversial and have a history all their own. The early bans on divulging telegraph or telephone messages had a consent exception.[78] The Supreme Court upheld consent interceptions against Fourth Amendment challenge both before and after the enactment of Title III.[79] The argument in favor of consent interceptions has always been essentially that a speaker risks the indiscretion of his listeners and holds no superior legal position simply because a listener elects to record or transmit his statements rather than subsequently memorializing or repeating them.[80] Wiretapping or electronic eavesdropping by either the police or anyone else with the consent of at least one party to the conversation is not unlawful under the federal statute.[81] These provisions do no more than shield consent interceptions from the sanctions of federal law; they afford no protection from the sanctions of state law. Many of the states recognize comparable exceptions, but some only permit interception with the consent of *all* parties to a communication.[82]

Under federal law, consent may be either explicitly or implicitly given. For instance, someone, who uses a telephone other than his or her own and has been told by the subscriber that conversations over the instrument are recorded, has been held to have implicitly consented to interception when using the instrument.[83] This is not to say that subscriber consent alone is sufficient, for it is the parties to the conversation whose privacy is protected.[84] Although consent may be given in the hopes of leniency from law enforcement officials or as an election between unpalatable alternatives, it must be freely given and not secured coercively.[85]

Private consent interceptions may not be conducted for a criminal or tortious purpose.[86] Some state wiretap laws do not recognize a one party consent exception. There, interception with the consent of but one party to the conversation is a violation of state law. But the federal exception is available as long as the *purpose* of the interception was neither criminal nor tortious—though the *means* may have been.[87] At one time, the limitation encompassed interceptions for criminal, tortious, *or* otherwise injurious purposes, but ECPA dropped the reference to injurious purposes for fear that First Amendment values might be threatened should the clause be read to outlaw consent interceptions conducted to embarrass.[88]

Exemptions: Publicly Accessible Radio Communications

Radio communications which can be inadvertently heard or are intended to be heard by the public are likewise exempt. These include not only commercial broadcasts, but ship and aircraft distress signals, tone-only pagers, marine radio and citizen band radio transmissions, and interceptions necessary to identify the source of any transmission, radio or otherwise, disrupting communications satellite broadcasts.[89]

Exemptions: Government Officials

Government officials have the benefit of an exemption when executing a Title III eavesdropping order;[90] acting in an emergency situation pending issuance of a court order;[91] acting under the authority of Title III in the case of communications of an intruder in a communications system acting with the approval of the system provider;[92] acting under the authority of the Foreign Intelligence Surveillance Act,[93] or acting pursuant to the authority according them the use of pen registers and trap and trace devices.[94]

Exemptions: Communication Service Providers

A further exemption applies to those who supply communications services: the telephone company, switchboard operators, and the like. The exemption permits interception in the name of improved service; to allow a service provider to itself against fraud;[95] to assist federal and state officials operating under a judicially supervised interception order,[96] and for the regulatory activities of the Federal Communications Commission.[97]

Domestic Exemptions

A few courts recognize a "vicarious consent" exception under which a custodial parent may secretly record the conversations of his or her minor child in the interest of protecting the child.[98] Although rejected by most,[99] a handful of federal courts have held that Title III does not preclude one spouse from wiretapping or electronically eavesdropping upon the other,[100] a result other courts have sometimes reached through the telephone extension exception discussed above.[101]

Illegal Disclosure of Information Obtained by Wiretapping or Electronic Eavesdropping

Title III has three disclosure offenses. The first is a general prohibition focused on the products of an unlawful interception:

- any person [who]
- intentionally
- discloses or endeavors to disclose to another person
- the contents of any wire, oral, or electronic communication
- having reason to know
- that the information was obtained through the interception of a wire, oral, or electronic communication
- in violation of 18 U.S.C. 2511(1)
- is subject to the same sanctions and remedies as the wiretapper or electroniceavesdropper.[102]

This is true of the wiretapper or electronic eavesdropper and of all those who, aware of the information's illicit origins, disclose it. The defendant must be shown to have known that the interception occurred and that the interception was unlawful.[103] There are exceptions. When the illegally secured information relates to a matter of usual public concern, the First Amendment precludes a prosecution for disclosure under §2511(c).[104] Moreover, the legislative history indicates that Congress did not intend to punish the disclosure of intercepted information that is public knowledge. Less clear is whether the limitation is confined to information commonly known at the time of capture, or more likely, information of which the public was generally aware at the time of disclosure.[105] Finally, the results of electronic eavesdropping authorized under Title III may be disclosed and used for law enforcement purposes[106] and for testimonial purposes.[107]

Title III makes it a federal crime to disclose intercepted communications under two other circumstances. It is a federal crime to disclose, with an intent to obstruct criminal justice, any information derived from lawful police wiretapping or electronic eavesdropping, i.e.,:

- any person [who]
- intentionally discloses, or endeavors to disclose, to any other person
- the contents of any wire, oral, or electronic communication
- intercepted by means authorized by sections:
    - 2511(2)(a)(ii) (communication service providers, landlords, etc. who assist police setting up wiretaps or electronic eavesdropping devices)
    - 2511(2)(b) (FCC regulatory activity)
    - 2511(2)(c) (police one party consent)
    - 2511(2)(e) (Foreign Intelligence Surveillance Act)
    - 2516 (court-ordered, police wiretapping or electronic surveillance)
    - 2518 (emergency wiretaps or electronic surveillance)
- knowing or having reason to know that
- the information was obtained through the interception of such a communication
- in connection with a criminal investigation
- having obtained or received the information in connection with a criminal investigation
- with intent to improperly obstruct, impede, or interfere with a duly authorized criminal investigation
- is subject to the same sanctions and remedies as one who illegally wiretaps.[108]

Offenders face the criminal and civil liability as those who wiretap.[109]

This second disclosure proscription applies to efforts to obstruct justice by revealing information gleaned from either federal wiretaps. It may also apply to state wiretaps. It covers information generated from a court-ordered wiretap authorized under §2516. Section 2516 authorizes both federal and state court-ordered wiretaps.[110] On the other hand, strictly speaking, §2516 permits state wiretapping when "authorized" by state law.[111] The courts might conclude that Congress would have spoken more clearly, if it intended to make it a federal crime to obstruct state criminal prosecutions by the disclosing of information derived from a state wiretap.

A third disclosure proscription applies only to electronic communications service providers "who intentionally divulge the contents of the communication while in transmission" to anyone other than sender and intended recipient.[112] The prohibition comes with its own exemptions for divulgence—when one of the parties to the communications consents, when Title III authorizes disclosure of a court approved interception, when necessary for transmission of the communication, or when it involves inadvertent discovery of information relating to the commission of a crime.[113] Although subsection 2511(3) provides no specific sanctions, violators would presumably be exposed to criminal liability under the general disclosure proscription, 18 U.S.C. 2511(1)(c), and to civil liability under 18 U.S.C. 2520.[114]

Illegal Use of Information Obtained by Unlawful Wiretapping or Electronic Eavesdropping

The prohibition on the use of information secured from illegal wiretapping or electronic eavesdropping mirrors its disclosure counterpart:

- any person [who]
- intentionally
- uses or endeavors to use to another person
- the contents of any wire, oral, or electronic communication
- having reason to know
- that the information was obtained through the interception of a wire, oral, orelectronic communication
- in violation of 18 U.S.C. 2511(1)
- is subject to the same sanctions and remedies as the wiretapper or electroniceavesdropper.[115]

The available case law under the use prohibition of paragraph 2511(1)(d) is scant, and the section has rarely been invoked except in conjunction with the disclosure prohibition of paragraph 2511(1)(c).[116] The wording of the two is clearly parallel, the legislative history describes them in the same breath,[117] and they are treated alike for law enforcement purposes.[118]

A few courts had recognized an exception to the disclosure-use bans of subsection 2511(1) when law enforcement officials disclose or use the results of an illegal interception in which they had played no role.[119]

The criminal and civil liability that attend unlawful use of intercepted communications in violation of paragraph 2511(1)(d) are the same as for unlawful disclosure in violation of paragraphs 2511(1)(c) or 2511(1)(e), or for unlawful interception under paragraphs 2511(1)(a) or 2511(1)(b).[120]

Shipping, Manufacturing, Distributing, Possessing or Advertising Wire, Oral, or Electronic Communication Interception Devices

The proscriptions for possession and trafficking in wiretapping and eavesdropping devices are even more demanding than those that apply to the predicate offense itself. There are exemptions for service providers,[121] government officials and those under contract with the government,[122] but there is no exemption for equipment designed to be used by private individuals, lawfully but surreptitiously.[123] Nevertheless, inoperable equipment, though designed to intercept, may not be considered equipment "which can be used to intercept" and consequently may not serve as the basis for a conviction under §2512.[124]

Section 2512's three prohibitions feature several common elements, declaring that:

- any person who
- intentionally
- either

(a)

- sends through the mail or sends or carries in interstate or foreign commerce
- any electronic, mechanical, or other device
- knowing or having reason to know
- that the design of such device renders it primarily useful
- for the purpose of the surreptitious interception of wire, oral, or electronic communications; or

(b)

- manufactures, assembles, possesses, or sells

- any electronic, mechanical, or other device
- knowing or having reason to know
- that the design of such device renders it primarily useful
- for the purpose of the surreptitious interception of wire, oral, or electronic communications, and
- that such device or any component thereof has been or will be sent through the mail or transported in interstate or foreign commerce; or

(c)

- places in any newspaper, magazine, handbill, or other publication or disseminates electronically
- any advertisement of—
    - any electronic, mechanical, or other device
    - knowing or having reason to know
    - that the design of such device renders it primarily useful
    - for the purpose of the surreptitious interception of wire, oral, or electronic communications; or
    - any other electronic, mechanical, or other device
    - where such advertisement promotes the use of such device
    - for the purpose of the surreptitious interception of wire, oral, or electronic communications
- knowing the content of the advertisement and knowing or having reason to know
- that such advertisement will be sent through the mail or transported in interstate or foreign commerce

shall be imprisoned for not more than five years and/or fined not more than $250,000 (not more than $500,000 for organizations).[125]

The legislative history lists among the items Congress considered "primarily useful for the purpose of the surreptitious interception of communications: the martini olive transmitter, the spike mike, the infinity transmitter, and the microphone disguised as a wristwatch, picture frame, cuff link, tie clip, fountain pen, stapler, or cigarette pack."[126]

Questions once raised over whether §2512 covers equipment designed to permit unauthorized reception of scrambled satellite television signals have been resolved.[127] Each of the circuits to consider the question has now concluded that §2512 outlaws such devices,[128] but simple possession does not give rise to a private cause of action.[129]

TITLE III: GOVERNMENT ACCESS

The prohibitions in each of ECPA's three parts—chapter 119 (Title III), chapter 121 (Stored Communications Act), and chapter 206 (pen registers and trap and trace devices)—yield to the need for government access, usually under judicial supervision.

Law Enforcement Wiretapping and Electronic Eavesdropping

Title III exempts federal and state law enforcement officials from its prohibitions on the interception of wire, oral, and electronic communications under three circumstances: (1) pursuant to or in anticipation of a court order,[130] (2) with the consent of one of the parties to the communication;[131] and (3) with respect to the communications of an intruder within an electronic communications system.[132]

To secure a Title III interception order as part of a federal criminal investigation, a senior Justice Department official must approve the application for the court order authorizing the interception of wire or oral communications.[133] The procedure is only available where there is probable cause to believe that the wiretap or electronic eavesdropping will produce evidence of one of a long, but not exhaustive, list of federal crimes,[134] or of the whereabouts of a "fugitive from justice" fleeing from prosecution of one of the offenses on the predicate offense list.[135] Any federal prosecutor may approve an application for a court order under section 2518 authorizing the interception of email or other electronic communications and the authority extends to any federal felony rather than more limited list of federal felonies upon which a wiretap or bug must be predicated.[136]

At the state level, the principal prosecuting attorney of a state or any of its political subdivisions may approve an application for an order authorizing wiretapping or electronic eavesdropping based upon probable cause to believe that it will produce evidence of a felony under the state laws covering murder, kidnaping, gambling, robbery, bribery, extortion, drug trafficking, or any other crime dangerous to life, limb or property. State applications, court orders and other procedures must at a minimum be as demanding as federal requirements.[137]

Applications for a court order authorizing wiretapping and electronic surveillance include:

- the identity of the applicant and the official who authorized the application;
- a full and complete statement of the facts including
  - details of the crime,
  - a particular description of the nature, location and place where the interception is to occur,[138]
  - a particular description of the communications to be intercepted, and
  - the identities (if known) of the person committing the offense and of the persons whose communications are to be intercepted;
- a full and complete statement of the alternative investigative techniques used or an explanation of why they would be futile or dangerous;
- a statement of the period of time for which the interception is to be maintained and if it will not terminate upon seizure of the communications sought, a probable cause demonstration that further similar communications are likely to occur;
- a full and complete history of previous interception applications or efforts involving the same parties or places;
- in the case of an extension, the results to date or explanation for the want of results; and
- any additional information the judge may require.[139]

Before issuing an order authorizing interception, the court must find:

- probable cause to believe that an individual is, has or is about to commit one or more of the predicate offenses;
- probable cause to believe that the particular communications concerning the crime will be seized as a result of the interception requested;
- probable cause to believe that "the facilities from which, or the place where, the wire, oral, or electronic communications are to be intercepted are being used, or are about to be used, in connection with the commission of such offense, or are leased to, listed in the name of, or commonly used by such person";[140] and
- that normal investigative procedures have been or are likely to be futile or toodangerous."[141]

Subsections 2518(4) and (5) demand that any interception order include:

- the identity (if known) of the persons whose conversations are to be intercepted;
- the nature and location of facilities and place covered by the order;
- a particular description of the type of communication to be intercepted and an indication of the crime to which it relates;
- the individual approving the application and the agency executing the order;
- the period of time during which the interception may be conducted and an indication of whether it may continue after the communication sought has been seized;
- an instruction that the order shall be executed
    - as soon as practicable, and
    - so as to minimize the extent of innocent communication seized;[142] and
- upon request, a direction for the cooperation of communications providers and others necessary or useful for the execution of the order.[143]

Compliance with these procedures may be postponed briefly until after the interception effort has begun, upon the approval of senior Justice Department officials in emergency cases involving organized crime or national security threatening conspiracies or involving the risk of death or serious injury.[144]

The court orders remain in effect only as long as required but not more than 30 days. After 30 days, the court may grant 30 day extensions subject to the procedures required for issuance of the original order.[145] During that time the court may require progress reports at such intervals as it considers appropriate.[146] Intercepted communications are to be recorded and the evidence secured and placed under seal (with the possibility of copies for authorized law enforcement disclosure and use) along with the application and the court's order.[147]

Within 90 days of the expiration of the order those whose communications have been intercepted are entitled to notice, and evidence secured through the intercept may be introduced into evidence with 10 days' advance notice to the parties.[148]

Title III also describes conditions under which information derived from a court ordered interception may be disclosed or otherwise used. It permits disclosure and use for official purposes by:

- other law enforcement officials including foreign officials;[149]
- federal intelligence officers to the extent that it involves foreign intelligenceinformation;[150]
- other American or foreign government officials to the extent that it involves the threat of hostile acts by foreign powers, their agents, or international terrorists.[151]

It also allows witnesses testifying in federal or state proceedings to reveal the results of a Title III tap,[152] provided the intercepted conversation or other communication is not privileged.[153]

Without a Title III order and without offending Title III, authorities may intercept the wire, oral, or electronic communications, it they have the consent of one of the parties to the communication.[154] As noted earlier, consent may be either explicitly or implicitly given. For instance, someone who uses a telephone other than his or her own and has been told by the subscriber that conversations over the instrument are recorded has been held to have implicitly consented to interception when using the instrument.[155] This is not to say that subscriber consent alone is sufficient, for it is the parties to the conversation whose privacy is designed to be protected.[156] Although consent may be given in the hopes of leniency from law enforcement officials or as an election between unpalatable alternatives, it must be freely given and not secured coercively.[157]

Little judicial or academic commentary accompanies the narrow "computer trespasser" justification for governmental interception of electronic communications in paragraph 2511(2)(i).[158] The paragraph originated as a temporary provision in the USA PATRIOT Act,[159] and seems designed to enable authorities to track intruders who would surreptitiously use the computer systems of others to cover their trail.[160]

TITLE III: CONSEQUENCES OF A VIOLATION

Criminal Penalties

Interception, use, or disclosure in violation of Title III is generally punishable by imprisonment for not more than five years and/or a fine of not more than $250,000 for individuals and not more than $500,000 for organizations.[161] The same penalties apply to the unlawful capture of cell phone and cordless phone conversations, since the Homeland Security Act[162] repealed the reduced penalty provisions that at one time applied to the unlawful interceptions using radio scanners and the like.[163] There is a reduced penalty, however, for filching satellite communications as long as the interception is not conducted for criminal, tortious, nor mercenary purposes: unauthorized interceptions are broadly proscribed subject to an exception for unscrambled transmissions[164] and are subject to the general five-year penalty, but interceptions for neither criminal, tortious, nor mercenary purposes subject offenders to only civil punishment.[165] Equipment used to wiretap or eavesdrop in violation of Title III is subject to confiscation by the United States, either in a separate civil proceeding or a part of the prosecution of the offender.[166]

In addition to exemptions previously mentioned, Title III provides a defense to criminal liability based on good faith.[167]

Civil Liability

Victims of a violation of Title III may be entitled to equitable relief, damages (equal to the greater of actual damages, $100 per day of violation, or $10,000),[168] punitive damages, reasonable attorney's fees and reasonable litigation costs.[169] A majority of federal courts hold that a court may decline to award damages, attorneys' fees and costs, but a few still consider such awards mandatory.[170] In addition, a majority hold that governmental entities other than the United States may be liable for violations of section 2520[171] and that law enforcement officers enjoy a qualified immunity from suit under section 2520.[172]

The cause of action created in section 2520 is subject to a good faith defense.[173] Efforts to claim the defense by anyone other than government officials or someone working at their direction have been largely unsuccessful.[174] Moreover, as addressed more extensively below, the 2008 Foreign Intelligence Surveillance Amendments Act, under some circumstances, bars any state or federal cause of action against anyone who assists the government with the installation or use of a means of electronic eavesdropping or electronic surveillance.[175]

Civil Liability of the United States

The USA PATRIOT Act authorizes a cause of action against the United States for willful violations of Title III, the Foreign Intelligence Surveillance Act or the provisions governing stored communications in 18 U.S.C. 2701-

2712.[176] Successful plaintiffs are entitled to the greater of $10,000 or actual damages, and reasonable litigation costs.[177]

Administrative Action

Upon a judicial or administrative finding of a Title III violation suggesting possible intentional or willful misconduct on the part of a federal officer or employee, the federal agency or department involved may institute disciplinary action. It is required to explain to its Inspector General's office if it declines to do so.[178]

Attorney Discipline

At one time, the American Bar Association (ABA) considered it ethical misconduct for an attorney to intercept or record a conversation without the consent of all of the parties to the conversation, ABA Formal Op. 337 (1974). The reaction of state regulatory authorities with the power to discipline professional misconduct was mixed. Some agreed with the ABA.[179] Some agreed with the ABA, but expanded the circumstances under which recording could be conducted within ethical bounds.[180] Some disagreed with the ABA view.[181] The ABA has since repudiated its earlier position, ABA Formal Op. 01-422 (2001). Attorneys who engage in *unlawful* wiretapping or electronic eavesdropping will remain subject to professional discipline in every jurisdiction.[182] In light of the ABA's change of position, courts and bar associations have had varied reactions to *lawful* wiretapping or electronic eavesdropping by members of the bar.[183]

Exclusion of Evidence

When the federal wiretap statute prohibits disclosure, the information is inadmissible as evidence before any federal, state, or local tribunal or authority.[184] Individuals whose conversations have been intercepted or against whom the interception was directed[185] have standing to claim the benefits of the section 2515 exclusionary rule through a motion to suppress under 18 U.S.C. 2518(10)(a). Paragraph 2518(10)(a) bars admission as long as the evidence is the product of (1) an unlawful interception, (2) an interception authorized by a facially insufficient court order, or (3) an interception executed in manner substantially contrary to the order authorizing the interception. Mere technical noncompliance is not enough; the defect must be of a nature that substantially undermines the regime of court-supervised interception for law enforcement purposes.[186]

Although the Supreme Court has held that section 2515 may require suppression in instances where the Fourth Amendment exclusionary rule would not,[187] some of the lower courts have recognized the applicability of the good faith exception to the Fourth Amendment exclusionary rule in section 2515 cases.[188] Other courts have held, moreover, that the fruits of an unlawful wiretapping or electronic eavesdropping may be used for impeachment purposes.[189]

The admissibility of tapes or transcripts of tapes of intercepted conversations raise a number of questions quite apart from the legality of the interception. As a consequence of the prerequisites required for admission, privately recorded conversations are more likely to be found inadmissible than those recorded by government officials. Admissibility will require the party moving for admission to show that the tapes or transcripts are accurate, authentic and trustworthy.[190] For some courts this demands a showing that, "(1) the recording device was capable of recording the events offered in evidence; (2) the operator was competent to operate the device; (3) the recording is authentic and correct; (4) changes, additions, or deletions have not been made in the recording; (5) the recording has been preserved in a manner that is shown to the court; (6) the speakers on the tape are identified; and (7) the conversation elicited was made voluntarily and in good faith, without any kind of inducement."[191]

STORED COMMUNICATIONS ACT (SCA)

SCA: Prohibitions

In its original form Title III was ill-suited to ensure the privacy of those varieties of modern communications which are equally vulnerable to intrusion when they are at rest as when they are in transmission. Surreptitious "access" is as least as great a threat as surreptitious "interception" to the patrons of electronic mail (email), electronic bulletin boards, voice mail, pagers, and remote computer storage.

Accordingly, ECPA, in the Stored Communications Act (SCA), bans surreptitious access to communications at rest, although it does so beyond the confines that apply to interception, 18 U.S.C. 2701 - 2711. These separate provisions afford protection for email, voice mail, and other electronic communications only somewhat akin to that available for telephone and face to face conversations under 18 U.S.C. 2510-2522. The SCA has two sets of proscriptions: a general prohibition and a second applicable to only certain communications providers. The general proscription makes it a federal crime to:

- intentionally
- either
  - access without authorization or
  - exceed an authorization to access
- a facility through which an electronic communication service is provided
- and thereby obtain, alter, or prevent authorized access to a wire or electronic communication while it is in electronic storage in such system, 18 U.S.C.2701(a).[192]

The prohibition extends only to "intentional" violations, that is, violations where the defendant had as a conscious objective the forbidden conduct and proscribed result.[193] The offense has three essential components: access, to a facility through which service is supplied, and consequences (obtain, alter, prevent access to a wire or electronic communication). The first requires either unauthorized access or access in excess of authorization. The third requires either acquisition or alteration of an electronic communication or denial of access to it. The courts have encountered little difficulty in determining whether a defendant's conduct constitutes obtaining, altering, or preventing access to a communication. They have divided, however, over cases in which the defendant was granted access to a communication but used access for the purposes other than that for which it was authorized.[194] The question is less divisive when the grant of access is expressly limited[195] or when an individual with authorized access provides an outsider with his user name and password.[196]

The "facility through which an electronic communication service is provided" need not be one made available to the public; but includes as well facilities through which a private employer provides electronic communication services to his employees.[197]

The section only protects communications while "in electronic storage" in a facility through which electronic communications service is provided. "Electronic storage" is defined to encompass temporary, intermediate storage incidental to transmission as well as backup storage.[198] The definition is not always easily applied.[199]

Section 2701's prohibitions yield to several exceptions and defenses. First, the section itself declares that:

> Subsection (a) of this section does not apply with respect to conduct authorized—
>
> (1) by the person or entity providing a wire or electronic communications service;
> (2) by a user of that service with respect to a communication of or intended for that user; or
> (3) in section 2703 [requirements for government access], 2704 [backup preservation] or 2518 [court ordered wiretapping or electronic eavesdropping] of this title.[200]

Second, there are the good faith defenses provided by section 2707:

> A good faith reliance on—
>
> (1) a court warrant or order, a grand jury subpoena, a legislative authorization, or a statutory authorization (including a request of a governmental entity under section 2703(f) of this title) [relating to an official request for a service provider preserve evidence];
> (2) a request of an investigative or law enforcement officer under section 2518(7) of this title [relating to emergency wiretapping and electronic eavesdropping]; or
> (3) a good faith determination that section 2511(3) of this title [relating to the circumstances under which an electronic communications provider may divulge the contents of communication][201] permitted the conduct complained of
>
> is a complete defense to any civil or criminal action brought under this chapter or any other law. 18 U.S.C. 2707(e).

Third, there is the general immunity from civil liability afforded providers under subsection 2703(e):

> [N]o cause of action shall lie in any court against any provider of wire or electronic communication service, its officers, employees, agents, or other specified persons for providing information, facilities, or assistance in accordance with the terms of a court order, warrant, subpoena, statutory authorization, or certification under this chapter.

A second set of prohibitions appears in section 2702 and supplements those in section 2701. Section 2702 bans the disclosure of the content of electronic communications and records relating to them by those who provide the public with electronic communication service or remote computing service. The section forbids providers to disclose the content of certain communications to anyone[202] or to disclose related records to governmental entities.[203]

Public electronic communication service (ECS) providers to the public must keep confidential the content of any "communication while in electronic storage by that service."[204] Public remote computer service (RCS) providers must keep confidential the content of "any communication which is carried or maintained on that service—(A) on behalf of, and received by means of electronic transmission from (or created by means of computer processing of communications received by means of electronic transmission from), a subscriber or customer of such service; (B) solely for the purpose of providing storage or computer processing services to such subscriber or customer, if the provider is not authorized to access the contents of any such communications for purposes of providing any services other than storage or computer processing."[205]

Both sets of providers must keep confidential any "record or other information pertaining to a subscriber to or customer of such service (not including the contents of communications covered by paragraph (1) or (2)) to any government entity."[206]

Section 2702 comes with its own set of exceptions which permit disclosure of the contents of a communication:

> (1) to an addressee or intended recipient of such communication or an agent of such addressee or intended recipient;
> (2) as otherwise authorized in section 2517 [relating to disclosures permitted under Title III], 2511(2)(a)[relating to provider disclosures permitted under Title III for protection of provider property or incidental to service], or 2703 [relating to required provider disclosures pursuant to governmental authority] of this title;

(3) with the lawful consent of the originator or an addressee or intended recipient of such communication, or *the subscriber in the case of remote computing service*;
(4) to a person employed or authorized or whose facilities are used to forward such communication to its destination;
(5) as may be necessarily incident to the rendition of the service or to the protection of the rights or property of the provider of that service;
(6) to the National Center for Missing and Exploited Children, in connection with a report submitted thereto under section 227 of the Victims of Child Abuse Act of 1990;
(7) to a law enforcement agency—(A) if the contents—(i) were inadvertently obtained by the service provider; and (ii) appear to pertain to the commission of a crime;
(8) to a Federal, State, or local government entity, if the provider, in good faith, believes that an emergency involving danger of death or serious physical injury to any person requires disclosure without delay of communications relating to the emergency.[207]

The record disclosure exceptions are similar.[208]

The Ninth Circuit in *Quon* noted that the exception in paragraph 2702(b)(3)(disclosure "with the lawful consent of the originator or an addressee or intended recipient of such communication, or *the subscriber in the case of remote computing service*) permits RCS providers to disclose the contents of otherwise protected communications does not afford ECS providers the same exception.[209] Thus, the service provider violated the SCA when it supplied the Ontario Police Department (the subscriber) with the text of Sergeant Quon's pager messages.[210]

SCA: Government Access

The circumstances and procedural requirements for law enforcement access to stored wire or electronic communications and transactional records are less demanding than those under Title III.[211] They deal with two kinds of information—often in the custody of the communications service provider rather than of any of the parties to the communication—communications records and the content of electronic or wire communications. The Stored Communications Act provides two primary avenues for law enforcement access: permissible provider disclosure (section 2702) and required provided access (section 2703).[212] As noted earlier in the general discussion of section 2702, a public electronic communication service (ECS) provider or a public remote computing service (RCS) provider may disclose the content of a customer's communication without the consent of a communicating party to a law enforcement agency in the case of inadvertent discovery of information relating to commission of a crime,[213] or to any government entity in an emergency situation.[214] ECS and RCS providers may also disclose communications records to any governmental entity in an emergency situation.[215] Federal, state, and local agencies, regardless of the nature of their missions, all qualify as governmental entities for purposes of section 2702.[216]

Section 2702 authorizes voluntary disclosure. Section 2703 speaks to the circumstances under which ECS and RCS providers may be required to disclose communications content and related records. Section 2703 distinguishes between recent communications and those that have been in electronic storage for more than 180 days.[217] The section insists that government entities resort to a search warrant to compel providers to supply the content of wire or electronic communications held in electronic storage for less than 180 days.[218] It permits them to use a warrant, subpoena, or a court order authorized in subsection 2703(d) to force content disclosure with respect to communications held for more than 180 days.[219]

A subsection 2703(d) court order may be issued by a federal magistrate or by a judge qualified to issue an order under Title III.[220] It need not be issued in the district in which the provider is located.[221]

The person whose communication is disclosed is entitled to notice, unless the court authorizes delayed notification because contemporaneous notice might have an adverse impact.[222] Government supervisory officials may certify the need for delayed notification in the case of a subpoena.[223] Traditional exigent circumstances and a final general inconvenience justification form the grounds for delayed notification in either case:

- endangering the life or physical safety of an individual;
- flight from prosecution;
- destruction of or tampering with evidence;
- intimidation of potential witnesses; or
- otherwise seriously jeopardizing an investigation or unduly delaying a trial.[224]

Subsection 2703(d) authorizes issuance of an order when the governmental entity has presented specific and articulable facts sufficient to establish reasonable grounds to believe that the contents are relevant and material to an ongoing criminal investigation.[225] Some courts have held that this "reasonable grounds" standard is a *Terry* standard, a less demanding standard than "probable cause," and that under some circumstances this standard may be constitutionally insufficient to justify government access to provider held email.[226] A Sixth Circuit panel has held that the Fourth Amendment precludes government access to the content of stored communications (email) held by service providers in the absence of a warrant, subscriber consent, or some other indication that the subscriber has waived his or her expectation of privacy.[227] Where the government instead secures access through a subpoena or court order as section 2703 permits, the evidence may be subject to both the Fourth Amendment exclusionary rule and the exceptions to the rule.[228]

The SCA has two provisions which require providers to save customer communications at the government's request. One is found in subsection 2703(f). It requires ECS and RCS providers to preserve "records and other evidence in its possession," at the request of a governmental entity pending receipt of a warrant, court order, or subpoena.[229] Whether providers are bound to preserve emails and other communications that come into their possession both before and after receipt of the request is unclear.[230]

The second preservation provision is more detailed. It permits a governmental entity to insist that providers preserve backup copies of the communications covered by a subpoena or subsection 2703(d) court order. It gives subscribers the right to challenge the relevancy of the information sought.[231] It might also be read to require the preservation of the content of communications received by the provider both before and after receipt of the order, but the requirement that copies be made within two days of receipt of the order seems to preclude such an interpretation.[232]

Section 2703 provides greater protection to communication content than to provider records relating to those communications. Under subsection 2703(c), a governmental entity may require a ECS or RCS provider to disclose records or information pertaining to a customer or subscriber— other than the content of a communication—under a warrant, a court order under subsection 2703(d), or with the consent of the subject of the information.[233] An administrative, grand jury or trial subpoena is sufficient, however, for a limited range of customer or subscriber related information.[234] The customer or subscriber need not be notified of the record disclosure in either case.[235]

The district courts have been divided for some time over the question of what standard applies when the government seeks cell phone location information from a provider, either current or historical.[236] The Third Circuit has held that while issuance of an order under subsection 2703(d) does not require a showing of probable cause as a general rule, the circumstances of a given case may require it.[237]

In *United States v. Jones*,[238] five members of the Supreme Court seemed to suggest that a driver has a reasonable expectation that authorities must comply with the demands of the Fourth Amendment before acquiring access to information that discloses the travel patterns of his car over an extended period of time. There, the Court unanimously agreed that the agents' attachment of a tracking device to Jones' car and long-term capture of the resulting information constituted a Fourth Amendment search.[239] For four Justices, placement of the device constituted a physical intrusion upon a constitutionally protected area.[240] For four others, long-term tracking constituted a breach of Jones' reasonable expectation of privacy.[241] For the ninth Justice, the activity constituted a Fourth Amendment search under either rationale.[242] It remains to be seen whether the Supreme Court's decision in *Jones* will contribute to resolution of the issue.[243]

SCA: Consequences

Breaches of the unauthorized access prohibitions of section 2701 expose offenders to possible criminal, civil, and administrative sanctions. Violations committed for malicious, mercenary, tortious or criminal purposes are punishable by imprisonment for not more than five years (not more than 10 years for a subsequent conviction) and/or a fine of not more than $250,000 (not more than $500,000 for organizations); lesser transgressions, by imprisonment for not more than one year (not more than five years for a subsequent conviction) and/or a fine of not more than $100,000.[244] Victims of a violation of subsection 2701(a) have a cause of action for equitable relief, reasonable attorneys' fees and costs, and damages equal to the amount of any offender profits added to the total of the victim's losses (but not less than $1,000 in any event).[245]

Violations by the United States may give rise to a cause of action and may result in disciplinary action against offending officials or employees under the same provisions that apply to U.S. violations of Title III,[246] Unlike violations of Title III, however, there is no statutory prohibition on disclosure or use of the information through a violation of section 2701;[247] nor is there a statutory rule for the exclusion of evidence as a consequence of a violation.[248] Yet, violations of SCA, which also constitute violations of the Fourth Amendment, will trigger both the Fourth Amendment exclusionary rule and the exceptions to that rule.[249]

No criminal penalties attend a violation of voluntary provider disclosure prohibitions of section 2702. Yet, ECS and RCS providers—unable to claim the benefit of one of the section's exceptions, of the good faith defense under subsection 2707(e), or of the immunity available under subsection 2703(e)—may be liable for civil damages, costs and attorneys' fees under section 2707 for any violation of section 2702.[250]

PEN REGISTERS AND TRAP AND TRACE DEVICES (PR/T&T)

PR/T&T: Prohibitions

A trap and trace device identifies the source of incoming calls, and a pen register indicates the numbers called from a particular instrument.[251] Since they did not allowed the user to overhear the "contents" of the phone conversation or to otherwise capture the content of a communication, they were not considered interceptions within the reach of Title III prior to the enactment of ECPA.[252] Although Congress elected to expand the definition of interception, it chose to regulate these devices beyond the boundaries of Title III for most purposes.[253] Nevertheless, the Title III wiretap provisions apply when, due to the nature of advances in telecommunications technology, pen registers and trap and trace devices are able to capture wire communication "content."[254]

The USA PATRIOT Act enlarged the coverage of sections 3121-3127 to include sender/addressee information relating to email and other forms of electronic communications.[255]

Subsection 3121(a) outlaws installation or use of a pen register or trap and trace device, except under one of seven circumstances:

- pursuant to a court order issued under sections 3121-3127;
- pursuant to a Foreign Intelligence Surveillance Act (FISA) court order;[256]
- with the consent of the user;
- when incidental to service;
- when necessary to protect users from abuse of service;

- when necessary to protect providers from abuse of service;[257] or
- in an emergency situation.[258]

PR/T&T: Government Access

Federal government attorneys and state and local police officers may apply for a court order authorizing the installation and use of a pen register and/or a trap and trace device upon certification that the information that it will provide is relevant to a pending criminal investigation.[259]

An order authorizing installation and use of a pen register or trap and trace device must:

- specify
    - the person (if known) upon whose telephone line the device is to be installed,
    - the person (if known) who is the subject of the criminal investigation,
    - the telephone number, (if known) the location of the line to which the device is to be attached, and geographical range of the device,
    - a description of the crime to which the investigation relates;
- upon request, direct carrier assistance pursuant to section 3124;
- terminate within 60 days, unless extended;
- involve a report of particulars of the order's execution in Internet cases; and
- impose necessary nondisclosure requirements.[260]

The order may be issued by a judge of "competent jurisdiction" over the offense under investigation, including a federal magistrate judge.[261] Senior Justice Department or state prosecutors may approve the installation and use of a pen register or trap and trace device prior to the issuance of court authorization in emergency cases that involve either an organized crime conspiracy, an immediate danger of death or serious injury, a threat to national security, or a serious attack on a "protected computer."[262] Emergency use must end within 48 hours, or sooner if an application for court approval is denied.[263]

Federal authorities have applied for court orders, under the Stored Communications Act (18 U.S.C. 2701-2712) and the trap and trace authority of 18 U.S.C. 3121-3127, seeking to direct communications providers to supply them with the information necessary to track cell phone users in conjunction with an ongoing criminal investigation. Thus far, their efforts have met with mixed success.[264]

PRT&T: Consequences

The use or installation of pen registers or trap and trace devices by anyone other than the telephone company, service provider, or those acting under judicial authority is a federal crime, punishable by imprisonment for not more than a year and/or a fine of not more than $100,000 ($200,000 for an organization).[265] Subsection 3124(e) creates a good faith defense for reliance upon a court order under subsection 3123(b), an emergency request under subsection 3125(a), "a legislative authorization, or a statutory authorization."[266] There is no accompanying exclusionary rule, and consequently a violation of section 3121 will not serve as a basis to suppress any resulting evidence.[267]

Moreover, unlike violations of Title III, there is no requirement that the target of an order be notified upon the expiration of the order; nor is there a separate federal private cause of action for victims of a pen register or trap and trace device violation.[268] One court, in order to avoid First Amendment concerns, has held that the statute precludes imposing permanent gag orders upon providers.[269] Nevertheless permitting providers to disclose the existence of an order to a target does not require them to do so. Some of the states have established a separate criminal offense for unlawful use of a pen register or trap and trace device,[270] yet most of these seem to follow the federal lead and have not established a separate private cause of action for unlawful installation or use of the devices.[271]

ELECTRONIC COMMUNICATIONS PRIVACY ACT (TEXT)

Chapter 119 ("Title III")

18 U.S.C. 2510. Definitions

As used in this chapter—

(1) "wire communication" means any aural transfer made in whole or in part through the use of facilities for the transmission of communications by the aid of wire, cable, or other like connection

between the point of origin and the point of reception (including the use of such connection in a switching station) furnished or operated by any person engaged in providing or operating such facilities for the transmission of interstate or foreign communications or communications affecting interstate or foreign commerce;

(2) "oral communication" means any oral communication uttered by a person exhibiting an expectation that such communication is not subject to interception under circumstances justifying such expectation, but such term does not include any electronic communication;

(3) "State" means any State of the United States, the District of Columbia, the Commonwealth of Puerto Rico, and any territory or possession of the United States;

(4) "intercept" means the aural or other acquisition of the contents of any wire, electronic, or oral communication through the use of any electronic, mechanical, or other device;

(5) "electronic, mechanical, or other device" means any device or apparatus which can be used to intercept a wire, oral, or electronic communication other than—

 (a) any telephone or telegraph instrument, equipment or facility, or any component thereof, (i) furnished to the subscriber or user by a provider of wire or electronic communication service in the ordinary course of its business and being used by the subscriber or user in the ordinary course of its business or furnished by such subscriber or user for connection to the facilities of such service and used in the ordinary course of its business; or (ii) being used by a provider of wire or electronic communication service in the ordinary course of its business, or by an investigative or law enforcement officer in the ordinary course of his duties;

 (b) a hearing aid or similar device being used to correct subnormal hearing to not better than normal;

(6) "person" means any employee, or agent of the United States or any State or political subdivision thereof, and any individual, partnership, association, joint stock company, trust, or corporation;

(7) "Investigative or law enforcement officer" means any officer of the United States or of a State or political subdivision thereof, who is empowered by law to conduct investigations of or to make arrests for offenses enumerated in this chapter, and any attorney authorized by law to prosecute or participate in the prosecution of such offenses;

(8) "contents," when used with respect to any wire, oral, or electronic communication, includes any information concerning the substance, purport, or meaning of that communication;

(9) "Judge of competent jurisdiction" means—

(a) a judge of a United States district court or a United States court of appeals; and

(b) a judge of any court of general criminal jurisdiction of a State who is authorized by a statute of that State to enter orders authorizing interceptions of wire, oral, or electronic communications;

(10) "communication common carrier" has the meaning given the term in section 3 of the Communications Act of 1934;

(11) "aggrieved person" means a person who was a party to any intercepted wire, oral, or electronic communication or a person against whom the interception was directed;

(12) "electronic communication" means any transfer of signs, signals, writing, images, sounds, data, or intelligence of any nature transmitted in whole or in part by a wire, radio, electromagnetic, photoelectronic or photo optical system that affects interstate or foreign commerce, but does not include—

(A) any wire or oral communication;

(B) any communication made through a tone-only paging device;

(C) any communication from a tracking device (as defined in section 3117 of this title); or

(D) electronic funds transfer information stored by a financial institution in a communications system used for the electronic storage and transfer of funds;

(13) "user" means any person or entity who—

(A) uses an electronic communication service; and

(B) is duly authorized by the provider of such service to engage in such use;

(14) "electronic communications system" means any wire, radio, electromagnetic, photo optical or photo electronic facilities for the transmission of wire or electronic communications, and any computer facilities or related electronic equipment for the electronic storage of such communications;

(15) "electronic communication service" means any service which provides to users thereof the ability to send or receive wire or electronic communications;

(16)"readily accessible to the general public" means, with respect to a radio communication, that such communication is not—

(A) scrambled or encrypted;

(B) transmitted using modulation techniques whose essential parameters have been withheld from the public with the intention of preserving the privacy of such communication;

(C) carried on a subcarrier or other signal subsidiary to a radio transmission;

(D) transmitted over a communication system provided by a common carrier, unless the communication is a tone only paging system communication; or

(E) transmitted on frequencies allocated under part 25, subpart D, E, or F of part 74, or part 94 of the Rules of the Federal Communications Commission, unless, in the case of a communication transmitted on a frequency allocated under part 74 that is not exclusively allocated to broadcast auxiliary services, the communication is a two-way voice communication by radio;

(17)"electronic storage" means—

(A) any temporary, intermediate storage of a wire or electronic communication incidental to the electronic transmission thereof; and

(B) any storage of such communication by an electronic communication service for purposes of backup protection of such communication;

(18)"aural transfer" means a transfer containing the human voice at any point between and including the point of origin and the point of reception.

(19)"foreign intelligence information", for purposes of section 2517(6) of this title, means—

(A) information, whether or not concerning a United States person, that relates to the ability of the United States to protect against—

(i) actual or potential attack or other grave hostile acts of a foreign power or an agent of a foreign power;

(ii) sabotage or intentional terrorism by a foreign power or an agent of a foreign power; or

(iii) clandestine intelligence activities by and intelligence service or network of a foreign power or by an agent of a foreign power; or

(B) information, whether or not concerning a United States person, with respect to a foreign power or foreign territory that relates to—
   (i) the national defense or the security of the United States; or
   (ii) the conduct of the foreign affairs of the United States.

(20)“protected computer” has the meaning set forth in section 1030; and

(21)“computer trespasser”—
   (A) means a person who accesses a protected computer without authorization and thus has no reasonable expectation of privacy in any communication transmitted to, through, or from the protected computer; and
   (B) does not include a person known by the owner or operator of the protected computer to have an existing contractual relationship with the owner or operator of the protected computer for access to all or part of the protected computer.

18 U.S.C. 2511. Interception and disclosure of wire, oral, or electronic communications prohibited

(1) Except as otherwise specifically provided in this chapter any person who—
   (a) intentionally intercepts, endeavors to intercept, or procures any other person to intercept or endeavor to intercept, any wire, oral, or electronic communication;
   (b) intentionally uses, endeavors to use, or procures any other person to use or endeavor to use any electronic, mechanical, or other device to intercept any oral communication when—
      (i) such device is affixed to, or otherwise transmits a signal through, a wire, cable, or other like connection used in wire communication; or
      (ii) such device transmits communications by radio, or interferes with the transmission of such communication; or
      (iii) such person knows, or has reason to know, that such device or any component thereof has been sent through the mail or transported in interstate or foreign commerce; or
      (iv) such use or endeavor to use (A) takes place on the premises of any business or other commercial establishment the operations of which affect interstate or foreign commerce; or (B) obtains or is for the purpose of obtaining information relating to the operations of any business or other commercial

establishment the operations of which affect interstate or foreign commerce; or

(v) such person acts in the District of Columbia, the Commonwealth of Puerto Rico, or any territory or possession of the United States;

(c) intentionally discloses, or endeavors to disclose, to any other person the contents of any wire, oral, or electronic communication, knowing or having reason to know that the information was obtained through the interception of a wire, oral, or electronic communication in violation of this subsection;

(d) intentionally uses, or endeavors to use, the contents of any wire, oral, or electronic communication, knowing or having reason to know that the information was obtained through the interception of a wire, oral, or electronic communication in violation of this subsection; or

(e) (i) intentionally discloses, or endeavors to disclose, to any other person the contents of any wire, oral, or electronic communication, intercepted by means authorized by sections 2511(2)(a)(ii), 2511(2)(b)-(c), 2511(2)(e), 2516, and 2518 of this chapter, (ii) knowing or having reason to know that the information was obtained through the interception of such a communication in connection with a criminal investigation, (iii) having obtained or received the information in connection with a criminal investigation, and (iv) with intent to improperly obstruct, impede, or interfere with a duly authorized criminal investigation, shall be punished as provided in subsection (4) or shall be subject to suit as provided in subsection (5).

(2)

(a)

(i) It shall not be unlawful under this chapter for an operator of a switchboard, or an officer, employee, or agent of a provider of wire or electronic communication service, whose facilities are used in the transmission of a wire or electronic communication, to intercept, disclose, or use that communication in the normal course of his employment while engaged in any activity which is a necessary incident to the rendition of his service or to the protection of the rights or property of the provider of that service, except that a provider of wire communication service to the public shall not utilize service observing or random monitoring except for mechanical or service quality control checks.

(ii) Notwithstanding any other law, providers of wire or electronic communication service, their officers, employees, and agents, landlords, custodians, or other persons, are authorized to provide information, facilities, or technical assistance to persons authorized by law to intercept wire, oral, or electronic communications or to conduct electronic surveillance, as defined in section 101 of the Foreign Intelligence Surveillance Act of 1978, if such provider, its officers, employees, or agents, landlord, custodian, or other specified person, has been provided with—

[P.L. 110-261, Sec. 101(c)(1)] (A) a court order directing such assistance *or a court order pursuant to section 704 of the Foreign Intelligence Surveillance Act of 1978* signed by the authorizing judge,

[P.L. 110-261, Sec. 403(b)(2)(C)] *Effective December 31, 2012 ... (C) except as provided in section 404, section 2511(2) (A)(ii)(A) of title 18, United States Code, is amended by striking "or a court order pursuant to section 704 of the Foreign Intelligence Surveillance Act of 1978."*

[P.L. 110-261, Sec. 404(b)(3)] *Challenge of directives; protection from liability; use of information— Notwithstanding any other provision of this Act or of the Foreign Intelligence Surveillance Act of 1978 (50 U.S.C. 1801 et seq.) ... (E) section 2511(2)(a)(ii)(A) of title 18, United States Code, as amended by section 101(c)(1), shall continue to apply to an order issued pursuant to section 704 of the Foreign Intelligence Surveillance Act of 1978, as added by section 101(a)[50 U.S.C. 1881c];* or

(B) a certification in writing by a person specified in section 2518(7) of this title or the Attorney General of the United States that no warrant or court order is required by law, that all statutory requirements have been met, and that the specified assistance is required, setting forth the period of time during which the provision of the information, facilities, or technical assistance is authorized and specifying the information, facilities, or technical assistance required. No provider of wire or electronic communication service, officer, employee, or agent thereof, or landlord, custodian, or other specified person shall disclose the existence of any interception or surveillance or the device used to accomplish the interception or surveillance with respect to which the person has been furnished a court order or certification under this chapter, except as may otherwise be required by legal process and then only after prior notification to the Attorney General or to the principal prosecuting attorney of a State or any political subdivision of a State, as may be appropriate. Any such disclosure, shall render such person liable for the civil damages provided for in section 2520. No cause of action shall lie in any court against any provider of wire or electronic communication service, its officers, employees, or agents, landlord, custodian, or other specified person for providing information, facilities, or assistance in accordance with the terms of a court order, statutory authorization, or certification under this chapter.

(iii)If a certification under subparagraph (ii)(B) for assistance to obtain foreign intelligence information is based on statutory authority, the certification shall identify the specific statutory provision and shall certify that the statutory requirements have been met.

(b) It shall not be unlawful under this chapter for an officer, employee, or agent of the Federal Communications Commission, in the normal course of his employment and in discharge of the monitoring responsibilities exercised by the Commission in the enforcement of chapter 5 of title 47 of the United States Code, to intercept a wire or electronic communication, or oral communication transmitted by radio, or to disclose or use the information thereby obtained.

(c) It shall not be unlawful under this chapter for a person acting under color of law to intercept a wire, oral, or electronic communication, where such person is a party to the communication or one of the parties to the communication has given prior consent to such interception.

(d) It shall not be unlawful under this chapter for a person not acting under color of law to intercept a wire, oral, or electronic communication where such person is a party to the communication or where one of the parties to the communication has given prior consent to such interception unless such communication is intercepted for the purpose of committing any criminal or tortious act in violation of the Constitution or laws of the United States or of any State.

(e) Notwithstanding any other provision of this title or section 705 or 706 of the Communications Act of 1934, it shall not be unlawful for an officer, employee, or agent of the United States in the normal course of his official duty to conduct electronic surveillance, as defined in section 101 of the Foreign Intelligence Surveillance Act of 1978, as authorized by that Act.

(f) Nothing contained in this chapter or chapter 121 or 206 of this title, or section 705 of the Communications Act of 1934, shall be deemed to affect the acquisition by the United States Government of foreign intelligence information from international or foreign communications, or foreign intelligence activities conducted in accordance with otherwise applicable Federal law involving a foreign electronic communications system, utilizing a means other than electronic surveillance as defined in section 101 of the Foreign Intelligence Surveillance Act of 1978, and procedures in this chapter or chapter 121 and the Foreign Intelligence Surveillance Act of 1978 shall be the exclusive means by which electronic surveillance, as defined in section 101 of such Act, and the interception of domestic wire, oral, and electronic communications may be conducted.

(g) It shall not be unlawful under this chapter or chapter 121 of this title for any person—

- (i) to intercept or access an electronic communication made through an electronic communication system that is configured so that such electronic communication is readily accessible to the general public;
- (ii) to intercept any radio communication which is transmitted—
  - (I) by any station for the use of the general public, or that relates to ships, aircraft, vehicles, or persons in distress;
  - (II) by any governmental, law enforcement, civil defense, private land mobile, or public safety communications system, including police and fire, readily accessible to the general public;

(III) by a station operating on an authorized frequency within the bands allocated to the amateur, citizens band, or general mobile radio services; or

(IV) by any marine or aeronautical communications system;

(iii) to engage in any conduct which—

(I) is prohibited by section 633 of the Communications Act of 1934; or

(II) is excepted from the application of section 705(a) of the Communications Act of 1934 by section 705(b) of that Act;

(iv) to intercept any wire or electronic communication the transmission of which is causing harmful interference to any lawfully operating station or consumer electronic equipment, to the extent necessary to identify the source of such interference; or

(v) for other users of the same frequency to intercept any radio communication made through a system that utilizes frequencies monitored by individuals engaged in the provision or the use of such system, if such communication is not scrambled or encrypted.

(h) It shall not be unlawful under this chapter—

(i) to use a pen register or a trap and trace device (as those terms are defined for the purposes of chapter 206 (relating to pen registers and trap and trace devices) of this title); or

(ii) for a provider of electronic communication service to record the fact that a wire or electronic communication was initiated or completed in order to protect such provider, another provider furnishing service toward the completion of the wire or electronic communication, or a user of that service, from fraudulent, unlawful or abusive use of such service.

(i) It shall not be unlawful under this chapter for a person acting under color of law to intercept the wire or electronic communications of a computer trespasser transmitted to, through, or from the protected computer, if—

(I) the owner or operator of the protected computer authorizes the interception of the computer trespasser's communications on the protected computer;

(II) the person acting under color of law is lawfully engaged in an investigation;

(III) the person acting under color of law has reasonable grounds to believe that the contents of the computer trespasser's communications will be relevant to the investigation; and

(IV) such interception does not acquire communications other than those transmitted to or from the computer trespasser.

(3)

(a) Except as provided in paragraph (b) of this subsection, a person or entity providing an electronic communication service to the public shall not intentionally divulge the contents of any communication (other than one to such person or entity, or an agent thereof) while in transmission on that service to any person or entity other than an addressee or intended recipient of such communication or an agent of such addressee or intended recipient.

(b) A person or entity providing electronic communication service to the public may divulge the contents of any such communication—

(i) as otherwise authorized in section 2511(2) (a) or 2517 of this title;

(ii) with the lawful consent of the originator or any addressee or intended recipient of such communication;

(iii) to a person employed or authorized, or whose facilities are used, to forward such communication to its destination; or

(iv) which were inadvertently obtained by the service provider and which appear to pertain to the commission of a crime, if such divulgence is made to a law enforcement agency.

(4)

(a) Except as provided in paragraph (b) of this subsection or in subsection (5), whoever violates subsection (1) of this section shall be fined under this title or imprisoned not more than five years, or both.

(b) Conduct otherwise an offense under this subsection that consists of or relates to the interception of a satellite transmission that is not encrypted or scrambled and that is transmitted—

(i) to a broadcasting station for purposes of retransmission to the general public; or

(ii) as an audio subcarrier intended for redistribution to facilities open to the public, but not including data transmissions or telephone calls, is not an offense under this subsection unless the conduct is for the purposes of direct or indirect commercial advantage or private financial gain.

(c) [Redesignated (b)]

(5)

(a)

(i) If the communication is—

(A) a private satellite video communication that is not scrambled or encrypted and the conduct in violation of this chapter is the private viewing of that communication and is not for a tortious or illegal purpose or for purposes of direct or indirect commercial advantage or private commercial gain; or

(B) a radio communication that is transmitted on frequencies allocated under subpart D of part 74 of the rules of the Federal Communications Commission that is not scrambled or encrypted and the conduct in violation of this chapter is not for a tortious or illegal purpose or for purposes of direct or indirect commercial advantage or private commercial gain, then the person who engages in such conduct shall be subject to suit by the Federal Government in a court of competent jurisdiction.

(ii) In an action under this subsection—

(A) if the violation of this chapter is a first offense for the person under paragraph (a) of subsection (4) and such person has not been found liable in a civil action under section 2520 of this title, the Federal Government shall be entitled to appropriate injunctive relief; and

(B) if the violation of this chapter is a second or subsequent offense under paragraph (a) of subsection (4) or such person has been found liable in any prior civil action under section 2520, the person shall be subject to a mandatory $500 civil fine.

(b) The court may use any means within its authority to enforce an injunction issued under paragraph (ii)(A), and shall impose a civil fine of not less than $500 for each violation of such an injunction.

18 U.S.C. 2512. Manufacture, distribution, possession, and advertising of wire, oral, or electronic communication intercepting devices prohibited

(1) Except as otherwise specifically provided in this chapter, any person who intentionally—

(a) sends through the mail, or sends or carries in interstate or foreign commerce, any electronic, mechanical, or other device, knowing or having reason to know that the design of such device renders it primarily useful for the purpose of the surreptitious interception of wire, oral, or electronic communications;

(b) manufactures, assembles, possesses, or sells any electronic, mechanical, or other device, knowing or having reason to know that the design of such device renders it primarily useful for the purpose of the surreptitious interception of wire, oral, or electronic communications, and that such device or any component thereof has been or will be sent through the mail or transported in interstate or foreign commerce; or

(c) places in any newspaper, magazine, handbill, or other publication or disseminates by electronic means any advertisement of—

(i) any electronic, mechanical, or other device knowing or having reason to know that the design of such device renders it primarily useful for the purpose of the surreptitious interception of wire, oral, or electronic communications; or

(ii) any other electronic, mechanical, or other device, where such advertisement promotes the use of such device for the purpose of the surreptitious interception of wire, oral, or electronic communications,

knowing the content of the advertisement and knowing or having reason to know that such advertisement will be sent through the mail or transported in interstate or foreign commerce, shall be fined under this title or imprisoned not more than five years, or both.

(2) It shall not be unlawful under this section for—

(a) a provider of wire or electronic communication service or an officer, agent, or employee of, or a person under contract with, such a provider, in the normal course of the business of providing that wire or electronic communication service, or

(b) an officer, agent, or employee of, or a person under contract with, the United States, a State, or a political subdivision thereof, in the normal course of the activities of the United States, a State, or a political subdivision thereof, to send through the mail, send or carry in interstate or foreign commerce, or manufacture, assemble, possess, or sell any electronic, mechanical, or other device knowing or having reason to know that the design of such device renders it primarily useful for the purpose of the surreptitious interception of wire, oral, or electronic communications.

(3) It shall not be unlawful under this section to advertise for sale a device described in subsection (1) of this section if the advertisement is mailed, sent, or carried in interstate or foreign commerce solely to a domestic provider of wire or electronic communication service or to an agency of the United States, a State, or a political subdivision thereof which is duly authorized to use such device.

18 U.S.C. 2513. Confiscation of wire, oral, or electronic communication interception devices

Any electronic, mechanical, or other device used, sent, carried, manufactured, assembled, possessed, sold, or advertised in violation of section 2511 or section 2512 of this chapter may be seized and forfeited to the United States. All provisions of law relating to (1) the seizure, summary and judicial forfeiture, and condemnation of vessels, vehicles, merchandise, and baggage for violations of the customs laws contained in title 19 of the United States Code, (2) the disposition of such vessels, vehicles, merchandise, and baggage or the proceeds from the sale thereof, (3) the remission or mitigation of such forfeiture, (4) the compromise of claims, and (5) the award of compensation to informers in respect of such forfeitures, shall apply to seizures and forfeitures incurred, or alleged to have been incurred, under the provisions of this section, insofar as applicable and not inconsistent with the provisions of this section; except that such duties as are imposed upon the collector of customs or any other person with respect to the seizure and forfeiture of vessels, vehicles, merchandise, and baggage under the provisions of the customs laws contained in title 19 of the United States Code shall be performed with respect to seizure and forfeiture of electronic, mechanical, or other intercepting devices under this section by such officers, agents, or other persons as may be authorized or designated for that purpose by the Attorney General.

18 U.S.C. 2515. Prohibition of use as evidence of intercepted wire or oral communications

Whenever any wire or oral communication has been intercepted, no part of the contents of such communication and no evidence derived therefrom may be received in evidence in any trial, hearing, or other proceeding in or before any court, grand jury, department, officer, agency, regulatory body, legislative committee, or other authority of the United States, a State, or a political subdivision thereof if the disclosure of that information would be in violation of this chapter.

18 U.S.C. 2516. Authorization for interception of wire, oral, or electronic communications

(1) The Attorney General, Deputy Attorney General, Associate Attorney General, or any Assistant Attorney General, any acting Assistant Attorney General, or any Deputy Assistant Attorney General or acting Deputy Assistant Attorney General in the Criminal Division or National Security Division specially designated by the Attorney General, may authorize an application to a Federal judge of competent jurisdiction for, and such judge may grant in conformity with section 2518 of this chapter an order authorizing or approving the interception of wire or oral communications by the Federal Bureau of Investigation, or a Federal agency having responsibility for the investigation of the offense as to which the application is made, when such interception may provide or has provided evidence of—

(a) any offense punishable by death or by imprisonment for more than one year under sections 2122 and 2274 through 2277 of title 42 of the United States Code (relating to the enforcement of the Atomic Energy Act of 1954), section 2284 of title 42 of the United States Code (relating to sabotage of nuclear facilities or fuel), or under the following chapters of this title: chapter 10 (relating to biological weapons) chapter 37 (relating to espionage), chapter 55 (relating to kidnapping), chapter 90 (relating to protection of trade secrets), chapter 105 (relating to sabotage), chapter 115 (relating to treason), chapter 102 (relating to riots), chapter 65 (relating to malicious mischief), chapter 111 (relating to destruction of vessels), or chapter 81 (relating to piracy);

(b) a violation of section 186 or section 501(c) of title 29, United States Code (dealing with restrictions on payments and loans to labor organizations), or any offense which involves murder, kidnapping, robbery, or extortion, and which is punishable under this title;

(c) any offense which is punishable under the following sections of this title: section 37 (relating to violence at international airports), section 43 (relating to animal enterprise terrorism), section 81 (arson within special maritime and territorial jurisdiction), section 201 (bribery of public officials and witnesses), section 215 (relating to bribery of bank officials), section 224 (bribery in sporting contests), subsection (d), (e), (f), (g), (h), or (i) of section 844 (unlawful use of explosives), section 1032 (relating to concealment of assets), section 1084 (transmission of wagering information), section 751 (relating to escape), section 832 (relating to nuclear and weapons of mass destruction threats), section 842 (relating to explosive materials), section 930 (relating to possession of weapons in Federal facilities), section 1014 (relating to loans and credit applications generally; renewals and discounts), section 1114 (relating to officers and employees of the United States), section 1116 (relating to protection of foreign officials), sections 1503, 1512, and 1513 (influencing or injuring an officer, juror, or witness generally), section 1510 (obstruction of criminal investigations), section 1511 (obstruction of State or local law enforcement), section 1591 (sex trafficking of children by force, fraud, or coercion), section 1751 (Presidential and Presidential staff assassination, kidnapping, and assault), section 1951 (interference with commerce by threats or violence), section 1952 (interstate and foreign travel or transportation in aid of racketeering enterprises), section 1958 (relating to use of interstate commerce facilities in the commission of murder for hire), section 1959 (relating to violent crimes in aid of racketeering activity), section 1954 (offer, acceptance, or solicitation to influence operations of employee benefit plan), section 1955 (prohibition of business enterprises of gambling), section 1956 (laundering of monetary instruments), section 1957 (relating to engaging in monetary transactions in property derived from specified unlawful activity), section 659 (theft from interstate shipment), section 664 (embezzlement from pension and welfare funds), section 1343 (fraud by wire, radio, or television), section 1344 (relating to bank fraud), section 1992 (relating to terrorist attacks against mass transportation), sections 2251 and 2252 (sexual exploitation of children), section 2251A (selling or buying of children), section 2252A (relating to material constituting or containing child pornography), section 1466A (relating to child obscenity), section 2260 (production of sexually explicit depictions of a minor for importation into the United States), sections 2421, 2422, 2423, and 2425 (relating to transportation for illegal sexual activity and related crimes), sections 2312, 2313, 2314, and 2315 (interstate transportation of stolen property), section 2321 (relating to trafficking in certain motor vehicles or motor vehicle parts), section 2340A (relating to torture), section 1203 (relating to hostage taking), section 1029 (relating to fraud and related activity in connection with access devices), section 3146 (relating to penalty for failure to appear), section 3521(b)(3) (relating to witness relocation and assistance), section 32 (relating to destruction of aircraft or aircraft facilities), section 38 (relating to aircraft parts fraud), section 1963 (violations with respect to racketeer influenced and corrupt organizations), section 115 (relating to threatening or retaliating against a Federal official), section 1341 (relating to mail fraud), a felony violation of section 1030 (relating to computer fraud and abuse), section 351 (violations with respect to congressional, Cabinet, or Supreme Court assassinations, kidnapping, and assault), section 831 (relating to prohibited transactions involving nuclear materials), section 33 (relating to destruction of motor vehicles or motor vehicle facilities), section 175 (relating to biological weapons), section 175c (relating to variola virus), section 956 (conspiracy to harm persons or property overseas), section a felony violation of section 1028 (relating to production of false identification documentation), section 1425 (relating to the procurement of citizenship or nationalization unlawfully), section 1426 (relating to the reproduction of naturalization or citizenship papers), section 1427 (relating to the sale of naturalization or citizenship papers), section 1541 (relating to passport issuance without authority), section 1542 (relating to false statements in passport applications), section 1543 (relating to forgery or false use of passports), section 1544 (relating to misuse of passports), or section 1546 (relating to fraud and misuse of visas, permits, and other documents); section 555 (relating to construction or use of international border tunnels);

(d) any offense involving counterfeiting punishable under section 471, 472, or 473 of this title;
(e) any offense involving fraud connected with a case under title 11 or the manufacture, importation, receiving, concealment, buying, selling, or otherwise dealing in narcotic drugs, marihuana, or other dangerous drugs, punishable under any law of the United States;
(f) any offense including extortionate credit transactions under sections 892, 893, or 894 of this title;
(g) a violation of section 5322 of title 31, United States Code (dealing with the reporting of currency transactions), or section 5324 of title 31, United States Code (relating to structuring transactions to evade reporting requirement prohibited);
(h) any felony violation of sections 2511 and 2512 (relating to interception and disclosure of certain communications and to certain intercepting devices) of this title;
(i) any felony violation of chapter 71 (relating to obscenity) of this title;
(j) any violation of section 60123(b) (relating to destruction of a natural gas pipeline), section 46502 (relating to aircraft piracy), the second sentence of section 46504 (relating to assault on a flight crew with dangerous weapon), or section 46505(b)(3) or (c) (relating to explosive or incendiary devices, or endangerment of human life, by means of weapons on aircraft) of title 49;
(k) any criminal violation of section 2778 of title 22 (relating to the Arms Export Control Act);
(l) the location of any fugitive from justice from an offense described in this section;
(m) a violation of section 274, 277, or 278 of the Immigration and Nationality Act (8 U.S.C. 1324, 1327, or 1328) (relating to the smuggling of aliens);
(n) any felony violation of sections 922 and 924 of title 18, United States Code (relating to firearms);
(o) any violation of section 5861 of the Internal Revenue Code of 1986 (relating to firearms);
(p) a felony violation of section 1028 (relating to production of false identification documents), section 1542 (relating to false statements in passport applications), section 1546 (relating to fraud and misuse of visas, permits, and other documents, section

1028A (relating to aggravated identity theft)) of this title or a violation of section 274, 277, or 278 of the Immigration and Nationality Act (relating to the smuggling of aliens); or

(q) any criminal violation of section 229 (relating to chemical weapons): or sections 2332, 2332a, 2332b, 2332d, 2332f, 2332g, 2332h 2339, 2339A, 2339B, 2339C, or 2339D of this title (relating to terrorism);

(r) any criminal violation of section 1 (relating to illegal restraints of trade or commerce), 2 (relating to illegal monopolizing of trade or commerce), or 3 (relating to illegal restraints of trade or commerce in territories or the District of Columbia) of the Sherman Act (15 U.S.C. 1, 2, 3); or

(s) any conspiracy to commit any offense described in any subparagraph of this paragraph.

(2) The principal prosecuting attorney of any State, or the principal prosecuting attorney of any political subdivision thereof, if such attorney is authorized by a statute of that State to make application to a State court judge of competent jurisdiction for an order authorizing or approving the interception of wire, oral, or electronic communications, may apply to such judge for, and such judge may grant in conformity with section 2518 of this chapter and with the applicable State statute an order authorizing, or approving the interception of wire, oral, or electronic communications by investigative or law enforcement officers having responsibility for the investigation of the offense as to which the application is made, when such interception may provide or has provided evidence of the commission of the offense of murder, kidnapping, gambling, robbery, bribery, extortion, or dealing in narcotic drugs, marihuana or other dangerous drugs, or other crime dangerous to life, limb, or property, and punishable by imprisonment for more than one year, designated in any applicable State statute authorizing such interception, or any conspiracy to commit any of the foregoing offenses.

(3) Any attorney for the Government (as such term is defined for the purposes of the Federal Rules of Criminal Procedure) may authorize an application to a Federal judge of competent jurisdiction for, and such judge may grant, in conformity with section 2518 of this title, an order authorizing or approving the interception of electronic communications by an investigative or law enforcement officer having responsibility for the investigation of the offense as to which

the application is made, when such interception may provide or has provided evidence of any Federal felony.

18 U.S.C. 2517. Authorization for disclosure and use of intercepted wire, oral, or electronic communications

(1) Any investigative or law enforcement officer who, by any means authorized by this chapter, has obtained knowledge of the contents of any wire, oral, or electronic communication, or evidence derived therefrom, may disclose such contents to another investigative or law enforcement officer to the extent that such disclosure is appropriate to the proper performance of the official duties of the officer making or receiving the disclosure.

(2) Any investigative or law enforcement officer who, by any means authorized by this chapter, has obtained knowledge of the contents of any wire, oral, or electronic communication or evidence derived therefrom may use such contents to the extent such use is appropriate to the proper performance of his official duties.

(3) Any person who has received, by any means authorized by this chapter, any information concerning a wire, oral, or electronic communication, or evidence derived therefrom intercepted in accordance with the provisions of this chapter may disclose the contents of that communication or such derivative evidence while giving testimony under oath or affirmation in any proceeding held under the authority of the United States or of any State or political subdivision thereof.

(4) No otherwise privileged wire, oral, or electronic communication intercepted in accordance with, or in violation of, the provisions of this chapter shall lose its privileged character.

(5) When an investigative or law enforcement officer, while engaged in intercepting wire, oral, or electronic communications in the manner authorized herein, intercepts wire, oral, or electronic communications relating to offenses other than those specified in the order of authorization or approval, the contents thereof, and evidence derived therefrom, may be disclosed or used as provided in subsections (1) and (2) of this section. Such contents and any evidence derived therefrom may be used under subsection (3) of this section when authorized or approved by a judge of competent jurisdiction where such judge finds on subsequent application that the contents were

otherwise intercepted in accordance with the provisions of this chapter. Such application shall be made as soon as practicable.

(6) Any investigative or law enforcement officer, or attorney for the Government, who by any means authorized by this chapter, has obtained knowledge of the contents of any wire, oral, or electronic communication, or evidence derived therefrom, may disclose such contents to any Federal law enforcement, intelligence, protective, immigration, national defense, or national security official to the extent that such contents include foreign intelligence or counterintelligence (as defined in section 3 of the National Security act of 1947 (50 U.S.C. 401a), or foreign intelligence information (as defined in subsection (19) of section 2510 of this title), to assist the official who is to receive that information in the performance of his official duties. Any Federal official who receives information pursuant to this provision may use that information only as necessary in the conduct of that person's official duties subject to any limitations on the unauthorized disclosure of such information.

(7) Any investigative or law enforcement officer, or other Federal official in carrying out official duties as such Federal official, who by any means authorized by this chapter, has obtained knowledge of the contents of any wire, oral, or electronic communication, or evidence derived therefrom, may disclose such contents or derivative evidence to a foreign investigative or law enforcement officer to the extent that such disclosure is appropriate to the proper performance of the official duties of the officer making or receiving the disclosure, and foreign investigative or law enforcement officers may use or disclose such contents or derivative evidence to the extent such use or disclosure is appropriate to the proper performance of their official duties.

(8) Any investigative or law enforcement officer, or other Federal official in carrying out official duties as such Federal official, who by any means authorized by this chapter, has obtained knowledge of the contents of any wire, oral, or electronic communication, or evidence derived therefrom, may disclose such contents or derivative evidence to any appropriate Federal, State, local, or foreign government official to the extent that such contents or derivative evidence reveals a threat of actual or potential attack or other grave hostile acts of a foreign power of an agent of as foreign power, domestic or international sabotage, domestic or international terrorism, or clandestine intelligence gathering activities by an intelligence service or network

of a foreign power or by an agent of a foreign power, within the United States or elsewhere, for the purpose of preventing or responding to such a threat. Any official who receives information pursuant to this provision may use that information only as necessary in the conduct of that person's official duties subject to any limitations on the unauthorized disclosure of such information, and any State, local, or foreign official who receives information pursuant to this provision may use that information only consistent with such guidelines as the Attorney General and Director of Central Intelligence shall jointly issue.

18 U.S.C. 2518. Procedure for interception of wire, oral, or electronic communications

(1) Each application for an order authorizing or approving the interception of a wire, oral, or electronic communication under this chapter shall be made in writing upon oath or affirmation to a judge of competent jurisdiction and shall state the applicant's authority to make such application. Each application shall include the following information:

(a) the identity of the investigative or law enforcement officer making the application, and the officer authorizing the application;

(b) a full and complete statement of the facts and circumstances relied upon by the applicant, to justify his belief that an order should be issued, including (i) details as to the particular offense that has been, is being, or is about to be committed, (ii) except as provided in subsection (11), a particular description of the nature and location of the facilities from which or the place where the communication is to be intercepted, (iii) a particular description of the type of communications sought to be intercepted, (iv) the identity of the person, if known, committing the offense and whose communications are to be intercepted;

(c) a full and complete statement as to whether or not other investigative procedures have been tried and failed or why they reasonably appear to be unlikely to succeed if tried or to be too dangerous;

(d) a statement of the period of time for which the interception is required to be maintained. If the nature of the investigation is such that the authorization for interception should not automatically terminate when the described type of communication has been first obtained, a particular description of facts establishing probable cause to believe that additional communications of the same type will occur thereafter;

(e) a full and complete statement of the facts concerning all previous applications known to the individual authorizing and making the application, made to any judge for authorization to intercept, or for approval of interceptions of, wire, oral, or electronic communications involving any of the same persons, facilities or places specified in the application, and the action taken by the judge on each such application; and

(f) where the application is for the extension of an order, a statement setting forth the results thus far obtained from the interception, or a reasonable explanation of the failure to obtain such results.

(2) The judge may require the applicant to furnish additional testimony or documentary evidence in support of the application.

(3) Upon such application the judge may enter an ex parte order, as requested or as modified, authorizing or approving interception of wire, oral, or electronic communications within the territorial jurisdiction of the court in which the judge is sitting (and outside that jurisdiction but within the United States in the case of a mobile interception device authorized by a Federal court within such jurisdiction), if the judge determines on the basis of the facts submitted by the applicant that—

(a) there is probable cause for belief that an individual is committing, has committed, or is about to commit a particular offense enumerated in section 2516 of this chapter;

(b) there is probable cause for belief that particular communications concerning that offense will be obtained through such interception;

(c) normal investigative procedures have been tried and have failed or reasonably appear to be unlikely to succeed if tried or to be too dangerous;

(d) except as provided in subsection (11), there is probable cause for belief that the facilities from which, or the place where, the wire, oral, or electronic communications are to be intercepted are being used, or are about to be used, in connection with the commission of such offense, or are leased to, listed in the name of, or commonly used by such person.

(4) Each order authorizing or approving the interception of any wire, oral, or electronic communication under this chapter shall specify—

(a) the identity of the person, if known, whose communications are to be intercepted;

(b) the nature and location of the communications facilities as to which, or the place where, authority to intercept is granted;

(c) a particular description of the type of communication sought to be intercepted, and a statement of the particular offense to which it relates;

(d) the identity of the agency authorized to intercept the communications, and of the person authorizing the application; and

(e) the period of time during which such interception is authorized, including a statement as to whether or not the interception shall automatically terminate when the described communication has been first obtained. An order authorizing the interception of a wire, oral, or electronic communication under this chapter shall, upon request of the applicant, direct that a provider of wire or electronic communication service, landlord, custodian or other person shall furnish the applicant forthwith all information, facilities, and technical assistance necessary to accomplish the interception unobtrusively and with a minimum of interference with the services that such service provider, landlord, custodian, or person is according the person whose communications are to be intercepted. Any provider of wire or electronic communication service, landlord, custodian or other person furnishing such facilities or technical assistance shall be compensated therefor by the applicant for reasonable expenses incurred in providing such facilities or assistance. Pursuant to section 2522 of this chapter, an order may also be issued to enforce the assistance capability and capacity requirements under the Communications Assistance for Law Enforcement Act.

(5) No order entered under this section may authorize or approve the interception of any wire, oral, or electronic communication for any period longer than is necessary to achieve the objective of the authorization, nor in any event longer than thirty days. Such thirty-day period begins on the earlier of the day on which the investigative or law enforcement officer first begins to conduct an interception under the order or ten days after the order is entered. Extensions of an order

may be granted, but only upon application for an extension made in accordance with subsection (1) of this section and the court making the findings required by subsection (3) of this section. The period of extension shall be no longer than the authorizing judge deems necessary to achieve the purposes for which it was granted and in no event for longer than thirty days. Every order and extension thereof shall contain a provision that the authorization to intercept shall be executed as soon as practicable, shall be conducted in such a way as to minimize the interception of communications not otherwise subject to interception under this chapter, and must terminate upon attainment of the authorized objective, or in any event in thirty days. In the event the intercepted communication is in a code or foreign language, and an expert in that foreign language or code is not reasonably available during the interception period, minimization may be accomplished as soon as practicable after such interception. An interception under this chapter may be conducted in whole or in part by Government personnel, or by an individual operating under a contract with the Government, acting under the supervision of an investigative or law enforcement officer authorized to conduct the interception.

(6) Whenever an order authorizing interception is entered pursuant to this chapter, the order may require reports to be made to the judge who issued the order showing what progress has been made toward achievement of the authorized objective and the need for continued interception. Such reports shall be made at such intervals as the judge may require.

(7) Notwithstanding any other provision of this chapter, any investigative or law enforcement officer, specially designated by the Attorney General, the Deputy Attorney General, the Associate Attorney General, or by the principal prosecuting attorney of any State or subdivision thereof acting pursuant to a statute of that State, who reasonably determines that—

(a) an emergency situation exists that involves—

(i) immediate danger of death or serious physical injury to any person,

(ii) conspiratorial activities threatening the national security interest, or

(iii) conspiratorial activities characteristic of organized crime, that requires a wire, oral, or electronic communication to be intercepted before an order authorizing such interception can, with due diligence, be obtained, and

(b) there are grounds upon which an order could be entered under this chapter to authorize such interception, may intercept such wire, oral, or electronic communication if an application for an order approving the interception is made in accordance with this section within forty-eight hours after the interception has occurred, or begins to occur. In the absence of an order, such interception shall immediately terminate when the communication sought is obtained or when the application for the order is denied, whichever is earlier. In the event such application for approval is denied, or in any other case where the interception is terminated without an order having been issued, the contents of any wire, oral, or electronic communication intercepted shall be treated as having been obtained in violation of this chapter, and an inventory shall be served as provided for in subsection (d) of this section on the person named in the application.

(8)

(a) The contents of any wire, oral, or electronic communication intercepted by any means authorized by this chapter shall, if possible, be recorded on tape or wire or other comparable device. The recording of the contents of any wire, oral, or electronic communication under this subsection shall be done in such way as will protect the recording from editing or other alterations. Immediately upon the expiration of the period of the order, or extensions thereof, such recordings shall be made available to the judge issuing such order and sealed under his directions. Custody of the recordings shall be wherever the judge orders. They shall not be destroyed except upon an order of the issuing or denying judge and in any event shall be kept for ten years. Duplicate recordings may be made for use or disclosure pursuant to the provisions of subsections (1) and (2) of section 2517 of this chapter for investigations. The presence of the seal provided for by this subsection, or a satisfactory explanation for the absence thereof, shall be a prerequisite for the use or disclosure of the contents of any wire, oral, or electronic communication or evidence derived therefrom under subsection (3) of section 2517.

(b) Applications made and orders granted under this chapter shall be sealed by the judge. Custody of the applications and orders shall be wherever the judge directs. Such applications and orders shall be disclosed only upon a showing of good cause before a judge of competent jurisdiction and shall not be destroyed except on order of the issuing or denying judge, and in any event shall be kept for ten years.

(c) Any violation of the provisions of this subsection may be punished as contempt of the issuing or denying judge.

(d) Within a reasonable time but not later than ninety days after the filing of an application for an order of approval under section 2518(7)(b) which is denied or the termination of the period of an order or extensions thereof, the issuing or denying judge shall cause to be served, on the persons named in the order or the application, and such other parties to intercepted communications as the judge may determine in his discretion that is in the interest of justice, an inventory which shall include notice of—

(1) the fact of the entry of the order or the application;

(2) the date of the entry and the period of authorized, approved or disapproved interception, or the denial of the application; and

(3) the fact that during the period wire, oral, or electronic communications were or were not intercepted.

The judge, upon the filing of a motion, may in his discretion make available to such person or his counsel for inspection such portions of the intercepted communications, applications and orders as the judge determines to be in the interest of justice. On an ex parte showing of good cause to a judge of competent jurisdiction the serving of the inventory required by this subsection may be postponed.

(9) The contents of any wire, oral, or electronic communication intercepted pursuant to this chapter or evidence derived therefrom shall not be received in evidence or otherwise disclosed in any trial, hearing, or other proceeding in a Federal or State court unless each party, not less than ten days before the trial, hearing, or proceeding, has been furnished with a copy of the court order, and accompanying application, under which the interception was authorized or approved. This ten-day period may be waived by the judge if he finds that it was not possible to furnish the party with the above information ten days before the trial, hearing, or proceeding and that the party will not be prejudiced by the delay in receiving such information.

(10)

(a) Any aggrieved person in any trial, hearing, or proceeding in or before any court, department, officer, agency, regulatory body, or other authority of the United States, a State, or a political subdivision thereof, may move to suppress the contents of any wire or oral communication intercepted pursuant to this chapter, or evidence derived therefrom, on the grounds that

(i) the communication was unlawfully intercepted;

(ii) the order of authorization or approval under which it was intercepted is insufficient on its face; or

(iii) the interception was not made in conformity with the order of authorization or approval. Such motion shall be made before the trial, hearing, or proceeding unless there was no opportunity to make such motion or the person was not aware of the grounds of the motion. If the motion is granted, the contents of the intercepted wire or oral communication, or evidence derived therefrom, shall be treated as having been obtained in violation of this chapter. The judge, upon the filing of such motion by the aggrieved person, may in his discretion make available to the aggrieved person or his counsel for inspection such portions of the intercepted communication or evidence derived therefrom as the judge determines to be in the interests of justice.

(b) In addition to any other right to appeal, the United States shall have the right to appeal from an order granting a motion to suppress made under paragraph (a) of this subsection, or the denial of an application for an order of approval, if the United States attorney shall certify to the judge or other official granting such motion or denying such application that the appeal is not taken for purposes of delay. Such appeal shall be taken within thirty days after the date the order was entered and shall be diligently prosecuted.

(c) The remedies and sanctions described in this chapter with respect to the interception of electronic communications are the only judicial remedies and sanctions for nonconstitutional violations of this chapter involving such communications.

(11) The requirements of subsections (1) (b)(ii) and (3) (d) of this section relating to the specification of the facilities from which, or the place where, the communication is to be intercepted do not apply if—

(a) in the case of an application with respect to the interception of an oral communication—
   (i) the application is by a Federal investigative or law enforcement officer and is approved by the Attorney General, the Deputy Attorney General, the Associate Attorney General, an Assistant Attorney General, or an acting Assistant Attorney General;
   (ii) the application contains a full and complete statement as to why such specification is not practical and identifies the person committing the offense and whose communications are to be intercepted; and
   (iii) the judge finds that such specification is not practical; and
(b) in the case of an application with respect to a wire or electronic communication—
   (i) the application is by a Federal investigative or law enforcement officer and is approved by the Attorney General, the Deputy Attorney General, the Associate Attorney General, an Assistant Attorney General, or an acting Assistant Attorney General;
   (ii) the application identifies the person believed to be committing the offense and whose communications are to be intercepted and the applicant makes a showing that there is probable cause to believe that the person's actions could have the effect of thwarting interception from a specified facility;
   (iii) the judge finds that such showing has been adequately made; and
   (iv) the order authorizing or approving the interception is limited to interception only for such time as it is reasonable to presume that the person identified in the application is or was reasonably proximate to the instrument through which such communication will be or was transmitted.

(12) An interception of a communication under an order with respect to which the requirements of subsections (1) (b)(ii) and (3) (d) of this section do not apply by reason of subsection (11)(a) shall not begin until the place where the communication is to be intercepted is ascertained by the person implementing the interception order. A provider of wire or electronic communications service that has received an order as provided for in subsection (11)(b) may move the court to modify or quash the order on the ground that its assistance

with respect to the interception cannot be performed in a timely or reasonable fashion. The court, upon notice to the government, shall decide such a motion expeditiously.

18 U.S.C. 2519. Reports concerning intercepted wire, oral, or electronic communications

(1) In January of each year, any judge who has issued an order (or an extension thereof) under section 2518 that expired during the preceding year, or who has denied approval of an interception during that year, shall report to the Administrative Office of the United States Courts—

(a) the fact that an order or extension was applied for;

(b) the kind of order or extension applied for (including whether or not the order was an order with respect to which the requirements of sections 2518(1) (b)(ii) and 2518(3) (d) of this title did not apply by reason of section 2518(11) of this title);

(c) the fact that the order or extension was granted as applied for, was modified, or was denied;

(d) the period of interceptions authorized by the order, and the number and duration of any extensions of the order;

(e) the offense specified in the order or application, or extension of an order;

(f) the identity of the applying investigative or law enforcement officer and agency making the application and the person authorizing the application; and

(g) the nature of the facilities from which or the place where communications were to be intercepted.

(2) In March of each year the Attorney General, an Assistant Attorney General specially designated by the Attorney General, or the principal prosecuting attorney of a State, or the principal prosecuting attorney for any political subdivision of a State, shall report to the Administrative Office of the United States Courts—

(a) the information required by paragraphs (a) through (g) of subsection (1) of this section with respect to each application for an order or extension made during the preceding calendar year;

(b) a general description of the interceptions made under such order or extension, including (i) the approximate nature and frequency of incriminating communications intercepted, (ii) the approximate nature and frequency of other communications intercepted, (iii) the approximate number of persons whose communications were intercepted, (iv) the number of orders in which encryption was encountered and whether such encryption prevented law enforcement from obtaining the plain text of communications intercepted pursuant to such order, and (v) the approximate nature, amount, and cost of the manpower and other resources used in the interceptions;

(c) the number of arrests resulting from interceptions made under such order or extension, and the offenses for which arrests were made;

(d) the number of trials resulting from such interceptions;

(e) the number of motions to suppress made with respect to such interceptions, and the number granted or denied;

(f) the number of convictions resulting from such interceptions and the offenses for which the convictions were obtained and a general assessment of the importance of the interceptions; and

(g) the information required by paragraphs (b) through (f) of this subsection with respect to orders or extensions obtained in a preceding calendar year.

(3) In June of each year the Director of the Administrative Office of the United States Courts shall transmit to the Congress a full and complete report concerning the number of applications for orders authorizing or approving the interception of wire, oral, or electronic communications pursuant to this chapter and the number of orders and extensions granted or denied pursuant to this chapter during the preceding calendar year. Such report shall include a summary and analysis of the data required to be filed with the Administrative Office by subsections (1) and (2) of this section. The Director of the Administrative Office of the United States Courts is authorized to issue binding regulations dealing with the content and form of the reports required to be filed by subsections (1) and (2) of this section.

18 U.S.C. 2520. Recovery of civil damages authorized

(a) In general.—Except as provided in section 2511(2) (a)(ii), any person whose wire, oral, or electronic communication is intercepted, disclosed, or intentionally used in violation of this chapter may in a civil action recover from the person or entity other than the United States which engaged in that violation such relief as may be appropriate.

(b) Relief.—In an action under this section, appropriate relief includes—

(1) such preliminary and other equitable or declaratory relief as may be appropriate;
(2) damages under subsection (c) and punitive damages in appropriate cases; and
(3) a reasonable attorney's fee and other litigation costs reasonably incurred.

(c) Computation of damages.—(1) In an action under this section, if the conduct in violation of this chapter is the private viewing of a private satellite video communication that is not scrambled or encrypted or if the communication is a radio communication that is transmitted on frequencies allocated under subpart D of part 74 of the rules of the Federal Communications Commission that is not scrambled or encrypted and the conduct is not for a tortious or illegal purpose or for purposes of direct or indirect commercial advantage or private commercial gain, then the court shall assess damages as follows:

(A) If the person who engaged in that conduct has not previously been enjoined under section 2511(5) and has not been found liable in a prior civil action under this section, the court shall assess the greater of the sum of actual damages suffered by the plaintiff, or statutory damages of not less than $50 and not more than $500.

(B) If, on one prior occasion, the person who engaged in that conduct has been enjoined under section 2511(5) or has been found liable in a civil action under this section, the court shall assess the greater of the sum of actual damages suffered by the plaintiff, or statutory damages of not less than $100 and not more than $1000.

(2) In any other action under this section, the court may assess as damages whichever is the greater of—

(A) the sum of the actual damages suffered by the plaintiff and any profits made by the violator as a result of the violation; or
(B) statutory damages of whichever is the greater of $100 a day for each day of violation or $10,000.

(d) Defense.—A good faith reliance on—

(1) a court warrant or order, a grand jury subpoena, a legislative authorization, or a statutory authorization;
(2) a request of an investigative or law enforcement officer under section 2518(7) of this title; or

(3) a good faith determination that section 2511(3) or 2511(2)(i) of this title permitted the conduct complained of; is a complete defense against any civil or criminal action brought under this chapter or any other law.

(e) Limitation.—A civil action under this section may not be commenced later than two years after the date upon which the claimant first has a reasonable opportunity to discover the violation.

(f) Administrative Discipline.—If a court or appropriate department or agency determines that the United States or any of its departments or agencies has violated any provision of this chapter, and the court finds that the circumstances surrounding the violation raise serious questions about whether or not an officer or employee of the United States acted willfully or intentionally with respect to the possible violation, the department or agency shall, upon receipt of a true and correct copy of the decision and findings of the court or appropriate department or agency promptly initiate a proceeding to determine whether disciplinary action against the officer or employee is warranted. If the head of the department or agency involved determines that disciplinary action is not warranted, he or she shall notify the Inspector General with jurisdiction over the department or agency concerned and shall provide the Inspector General with the reasons for such determination.

(g) Improper Disclosure Is Violation.—Any willful disclosure or use by an investigative or law enforcement officer or governmental entity of information beyond the extent permitted by section 2517 is a violation of this chapter for purposes of section 2510(a).

18 U.S.C. 2521. Injunction against illegal interception

Whenever it shall appear that any person is engaged or is about to engage in any act which constitutes or will constitute a felony violation of this chapter, the Attorney General may initiate a civil action in a district court of the United States to enjoin such violation. The court shall proceed as soon as practicable to the hearing and determination of such an action, and may, at any time before final determination, enter such a restraining order or prohibition, or take such other action, as is warranted to prevent a continuing and substantial injury to the United States or to any person or class of persons for whose protection the action is brought. A proceeding under this section is governed by the Federal Rules of Civil Procedure, except that, if an indictment has been returned against the respondent, discovery is governed by the Federal Rules of Criminal Procedure.

18 U.S.C. 2522. Enforcement of the Communications Assistance for Law Enforcement Act

(a) Enforcement by court issuing surveillance order.—If a court authorizing an interception under this chapter, a State statute, or the Foreign Intelligence Surveillance Act of 1978 (50 U.S.C. 1801 et seq.) or authorizing use of a pen register or a trap and trace device under chapter 206 or a State statute finds that a telecommunications carrier has failed to comply with the requirements of the Communications Assistance for Law Enforcement Act, the court may, in accordance with section 108 of such Act, direct that the carrier comply forthwith and may direct that a provider of support services to the carrier or the manufacturer of the carrier's transmission or switching equipment furnish forthwith modifications necessary for the carrier to comply.

(b) Enforcement upon application by Attorney General.—The Attorney General may, in a civil action in the appropriate United States district court, obtain an order, in accordance with section 108 of the Communications Assistance for Law Enforcement Act, directing that a telecommunications carrier, a manufacturer of telecommunications transmission or switching equipment, or a provider of telecommunications support services comply with such Act.

(c) Civil penalty.—

(1) In general.—A court issuing an order under this section against a telecommunications carrier, a manufacturer of telecommunications transmission or switching equipment, or a provider of telecommunications support services may impose a civil penalty of up to $10,000 per day for each day in violation after the issuance of the order or after such future date as the court may specify.

(2) Considerations.—In determining whether to impose a civil penalty and in determining its amount, the court shall take into account—

(A) the nature, circumstances, and extent of the violation;

(B) the violator's ability to pay, the violator's good faith efforts to comply in a timely manner, any effect on the violator's ability to continue to do business, the degree of culpability, and the length of any delay in undertaking efforts to comply; and

(c) such other matters as justice may require.

(d) Definitions.—As used in this section, the terms defined in section 102 of the Communications Assistance for Law Enforcement Act have the meanings provided, respectively, in such section.

Chapter 121 ("Stored Communications Act")

18 U.S.C. 2701. Unlawful access to stored communications

(a) Offense.—Except as provided in subsection (c) of this section whoever—
- (1) intentionally accesses without authorization a facility through which an electronic communication service is provided; or
- (2) intentionally exceeds an authorization to access that facility; and thereby obtains, alters, or prevents authorized access to a wire or electronic communication while it is in electronic storage in such system shall be punished as provided in subsection (b) of this section.

(b) Punishment.—The punishment for an offense under subsection (a) of this section is—
- (1) if the offense is committed for purposes of commercial advantage, malicious destruction or damage, or private commercial gain, or in furtherance of any criminal or tortious act in violation of the constitution and laws of the United States or any state—
  - (A) a fine under this title or imprisonment for not more than 5 years, or both, in the case of a first offense under this subparagraph; and
  - (B) a fine under this title or imprisonment for not more than 10 years, or both, for any subsequent offense under this subparagraph; and
- (2)
  - (A) a fine under this title or imprisonment for not more than 1 year or both, in the case of a first offense under this paragraph; and
  - (B) a fine under this title or imprisonment for not more than 5 years, or both, in the case of an offense under this subparagraph that occurs after a conviction of another offense under this section.

(c) Exceptions.—Subsection (a) of this section does not apply with respect to conduct authorized—

(1) by the person or entity providing a wire or electronic communications service;

(2) by a user of that service with respect to a communication of or intended for that user; or

(3) in section 2703, 2704 or 2518 of this title.

18 U.S.C. 2702. Voluntary disclosure of customer communications or records

(a) Prohibitions.—Except as provided in subsection (b) or (c)—

(1) a person or entity providing an electronic communication service to the public shall not knowingly divulge to any person or entity the contents of a communication while in electronic storage by that service; and

(2) a person or entity providing remote computing service to the public shall not knowingly divulge to any person or entity the contents of any communication which is carried or maintained on that service—

(A) on behalf of, and received by means of electronic transmission from (or created by means of computer processing of communications received by means of electronic transmission from), a subscriber or customer of such service;

(B) solely for the purpose of providing storage or computer processing services to such subscriber or customer, if the provider is not authorized to access the contents of any such communications for purposes of providing any services other than storage or computer processing; and

(3) a provider of remote computing service or electronic communication service to the public shall not knowingly divulge a record or other information pertaining to a subscriber to or customer of such service (not including the contents of communications covered by paragraph (1) or (2)) to any governmental entity.

(b) Exceptions for disclosure of communications.—A provider described in subsection (a) may divulge the contents of a communication—

(1) to an addressee or intended recipient of such communication or an agent of such addressee or intended recipient;

(2) as otherwise authorized in section 2517, 2511(2) (a), or 2703 of this title;
(3) with the lawful consent of the originator or an addressee or intended recipient of such communication, or the subscriber in the case of remote computing service;
(4) to a person employed or authorized or whose facilities are used to forward such communication to its destination;
(5) as may be necessarily incident to the rendition of the service or to the protection of the rights or property of the provider of that service;
(6) to the National Center for Missing and Exploited Children, in connection with a report submitted thereto under section 2258A;
(7) to a law enforcement agency—
 (A) if the contents—
  (i) were inadvertently obtained by the service provider; and
  (ii) appear to pertain to the commission of a crime; or
 [(B) Repealed. P.L. 108-21, Title V, §508(b)(1) (A), April 30, 2003, 117 Stat. 684]
 [(C) Repealed. P.L. 107-296, Title II, §225(d)(1)(C), November 25, 2002, 116 Stat. 2157]
(8) to a governmental entity, if the provider, in good faith, believes that an emergency involving danger of death or serious physical injury to any person requires disclosure without delay of communications relating to the emergency.

(c) Exceptions for disclosure of customer records.—A provider described in subsection (a) may divulge a record or other information pertaining to a subscriber to or customer of such service (not including the contents of communications covered by subsection (a)(1) or (a)(2))—
(1) as otherwise authorized in section 2703;
(2) with the lawful consent of the customer or subscriber;
(3) as may be necessarily incident to the rendition of the service or to the protection of the rights or property of the provider of that service;
(4) to a governmental entity, if the provider, in good faith, believes that an emergency involving danger of death or serious physical injury to any person requires disclosure without delay of information relating to the emergency;

(5) to the National Center for Missing and Exploited Children, in connection with a report submitted thereto under section 2258A7; or

(6) to any person other than a governmental entity.

(d) Reporting of emergency disclosures.—On an annual basis, the Attorney General shall submit to the Committee on the Judiciary of the House of Representatives and the Committee on the Judiciary of the Senate a report containing—

(1) the number of accounts from which the Department of Justice has received voluntary disclosures under subsection (b)(8); and

(2) a summary of the basis for disclosure in those instances where—

(A) voluntary disclosures under subsection (b)(8) were made to the Department of Justice; and

(B) the investigation pertaining to those disclosures was closed without the filing of criminal charges.

18 U.S.C. 2703. Required disclosure of customer communications or records

(a) Contents of wire or electronic communications in electronic storage.—A governmental entity may require the disclosure by a provider of electronic communication service of the contents of a wire or electronic communication, that is in electronic storage in a wire or electronic communications system for one hundred and eighty days or less, only pursuant to a warrant issued using the procedures described in the Federal Rules of Criminal Procedure (or, in the case of a State court, issued using State warrant procedures) by a court of competent jurisdiction. A governmental entity may require the disclosure by a provider of electronic communications services of the contents of a wire or electronic communication that has been in electronic storage in an electronic communications system for more than one hundred and eighty days by the means available under subsection (b) of this section.

(b)

(1) Contents of electronic communications in a remote computing service.—(1) A governmental entity may require a provider of remote computing service to disclose the contents of any wire or electronic communication to which this paragraph is made applicable by paragraph (2) of this subsection—

(A) without required notice to the subscriber or customer, if the governmental entity obtains a warrant issued using the procedures described in the Federal Rules of Criminal Procedure (or, in the case of a State court, issued using State warrant procedures) by a court of competent jurisdiction by a court with jurisdiction; or

(B) with prior notice from the governmental entity to the subscriber or customer if the governmental entity—

(i) uses an administrative subpoena authorized by a Federal or State statute or a Federal or State grand jury or trial subpoena; or

(ii) obtains a court order for such disclosure under subsection (d) of this section; except that delayed notice may be given pursuant to section 2705 of this title.

(2) Paragraph (1) is applicable with respect to any wire or electronic communication that is held or maintained on that service—

(A) on behalf of, and received by means of electronic transmission from (or created by means of computer processing of communications received by means of electronic transmission from), a subscriber or customer of such remote computing service; and

(B) solely for the purpose of providing storage or computer processing services to such subscriber or customer, if the provider is not authorized to access the contents of any such communications for purposes of providing any services other than storage or computer processing.

(c) Records concerning electronic communication service or remote computing service.—

(1)

(A) A government entity may require a provider of electronic communication service or remote computing service to disclose a record or other information pertaining to a subscriber to or customer of such service (not including the contents of communications).

(B) A provider of electronic communication service or remote computing service shall disclose a record or other information pertaining to a subscriber to or customer of such service (not including the contents of communications covered by subsection (a) or (b) of this section) to a governmental entity only when the governmental entity—

(A) obtains a warrant issued using the procedures described in the Federal Rules of Criminal Procedure (or, in the case of a State court, issued using State warrant procedures) by a court of competent jurisdiction by a court with jurisdiction;

(B) obtains a court order for such disclosure under subsection (d) of this section;

(C) has the consent of the subscriber or customer to such disclosure; or

(D) submits a formal written request relevant to a law enforcement investigation concerning telemarketing fraud for the name, address, and place of business of a subscriber or customer of such provider, which subscriber or customer is engaged in telemarketing (as such term is defined in section 2325 of this title); or

(E) seeks information under paragraph (2).

(2) A provider of electronic communication service or remote computing service shall disclose to a governmental entity the (A) name; (B) address; (C) local and long distance telephone connection records, or records of session times and durations; (D) length of service (including start date) and types of service utilized; (E) telephone or instrument number or other subscriber number or identity, including any temporarily assigned network address; and (F) means and source of payment (including any credit card or bank account number), of a subscriber to or customer of such service, when the governmental entity uses an administrative subpoena authorized by a Federal or State statute or a Federal or State grand jury or trial subpoena or any means available under paragraph (1) .

(3) A governmental entity receiving records or information under this subsection is not required to provide notice to a subscriber or customer.

(d) Requirements for court order.—A court order for disclosure under subsection (b) or (c) may be issued by any court that is a court of competent jurisdiction and shall issue only if the governmental entity offers specific and articulable facts showing that there are reasonable grounds to believe that the contents of a wire or electronic communication, or the records or other information sought, are relevant and material to an ongoing criminal investigation. In the case of a State governmental authority, such a court order shall not issue if prohibited by the law of such State. A court issuing an order pursuant to this section, on a motion made promptly by the service provider, may quash or modify such order, if the information or records requested are unusually voluminous in nature or compliance with such order otherwise would cause an undue burden on such provider.

(e) No cause of action against a provider disclosing information under this chapter.—No cause of action shall lie in any court against any provider of wire or electronic communication service, its officers, employees, agents, or other specified persons for providing information, facilities, or assistance in accordance with the terms of a court order, warrant, subpoena, statutory authorization, or certification under this chapter.

(f) Requirement to preserve evidence.—

(1) In general.—A provider of wire or electronic communication services or a remote computing service, upon the request of a governmental entity, shall take all necessary steps to preserve records and other evidence in its possession pending the issuance of a court order or other process.

(2) Period of retention.—Records referred to in paragraph (1) shall be retained for a period of 90 days, which shall be extended for an additional 90-day period upon a renewed request by the governmental entity.

(g) Presence of Officer not Required.—Notwithstanding section 3105 of this title, the presence of an officer shall not be required for service or execution of a search warrant issued in accordance with this chapter requiring disclosure by a provider of electronic communications service or remote computing service of the contents of communications or records or other information pertaining to a subscriber to or customer of such service.

18 U.S.C. 2704. Backup preservation

(a) Backup preservation.—

(1) A governmental entity acting under section 2703(b)(2) may include in its subpoena or court order a requirement that the service provider to whom the request is directed create a backup copy of the contents of the electronic communications sought in

order to preserve those communications. Without notifying the subscriber or customer of such subpoena or court order, such service provider shall create such backup copy as soon as practicable consistent with its regular business practices and shall confirm to the governmental entity that such backup copy has been made. Such backup copy shall be created within two business days after receipt by the service provider of the subpoena or court order.

(2) Notice to the subscriber or customer shall be made by the governmental entity within three days after receipt of such confirmation, unless such notice is delayed pursuant to section 2705(a).

(3) The service provider shall not destroy such backup copy until the later of—

(A) the delivery of the information; or

(B) the resolution of any proceedings (including appeals of any proceeding) concerning the government's subpoena or court order.

(4) The service provider shall release such backup copy to the requesting governmental entity no sooner than fourteen days after the governmental entity's notice to the subscriber or customer if such service provider—

(A) has not received notice from the subscriber or customer that the subscriber or customer has challenged the governmental entity's request; and

(B) has not initiated proceedings to challenge the request of the governmental entity.

(5) A governmental entity may seek to require the creation of a backup copy under subsection (a)(1) of this section if in its sole discretion such entity determines that there is reason to believe that notification under section 2703 of this title of the existence of the subpoena or court order may result in destruction of or tampering with evidence. This determination is not subject to challenge by the subscriber or customer or service provider.

(b) Customer challenges. —

(1) Within fourteen days after notice by the governmental entity to the subscriber or customer under subsection (a)

(2) of this section, such subscriber or customer may file a motion to quash such subpoena or vacate such court order, with copies

served upon the governmental entity and with written notice of such challenge to the service provider. A motion to vacate a court order shall be filed in the court which issued such order. A motion to quash a subpoena shall be filed in the appropriate United States district court or State court. Such motion or application shall contain an affidavit or sworn statement—

(A) stating that the applicant is a customer or subscriber to the service from which the contents of electronic communications maintained for him have been sought; and

(B) stating the applicant's reasons for believing that the records sought are not relevant to a legitimate law enforcement inquiry or that there has not been substantial compliance with the provisions of this chapter in some other respect.

(2) Service shall be made under this section upon a governmental entity by delivering or mailing by registered or certified mail a copy of the papers to the person, office, or department specified in the notice which the customer has received pursuant to this chapter. For the purposes of this section, the term "delivery" has the meaning given that term in the Federal Rules of Civil Procedure.

(3) If the court finds that the customer has complied with paragraphs (1) and (2) of this subsection, the court shall order the governmental entity to file a sworn response, which may be filed in camera if the governmental entity includes in its response the reasons which make in camera review appropriate. If the court is unable to determine the motion or application on the basis of the parties' initial allegations and response, the court may conduct such additional proceedings as it deems appropriate. All such proceedings shall be completed and the motion or application decided as soon as practicable after the filing of the governmental entity's response.

(4) If the court finds that the applicant is not the subscriber or customer for whom the communications sought by the governmental entity are maintained, or that there is a reason to believe that the law enforcement inquiry is legitimate and that the communications sought are relevant to that inquiry, it shall deny the motion or application and order such process enforced. If the court finds that the applicant is the subscriber or customer for whom the communications sought by the governmental entity are maintained, and that there is not a reason to believe that the communications sought are relevant to a legitimate law enforcement inquiry, or that there has not been substantial

compliance with the provisions of this chapter, it shall order the process quashed.

(5) A court order denying a motion or application under this section shall not be deemed a final order and no interlocutory appeal may be taken therefrom by the customer.

18 U.S.C. 2705. Delayed notice

(a) Delay of notification.—

(1) A governmental entity acting under section 2703(b) of this title may—

(A) where a court order is sought, include in the application a request, which the court shall grant, for an order delaying the notification required under section 2703(b) of this title for a period not to exceed ninety days, if the court determines that there is reason to believe that notification of the existence of the court order may have an adverse result described in paragraph (2) of this subsection; or

(B) where an administrative subpoena authorized by a Federal or State statute or a Federal or State grand jury subpoena is obtained, delay the notification required under section 2703(b) of this title for a period not to exceed ninety days upon the execution of a written certification of a supervisory official that there is reason to believe that notification of the existence of the subpoena may have an adverse result described in paragraph (2) of this subsection.

(2) An adverse result for the purposes of paragraph (1) of this subsection is—

(A) endangering the life or physical safety of an individual;

(B) flight from prosecution;

(C) destruction of or tampering with evidence;

(D) intimidation of potential witnesses; or

(E) otherwise seriously jeopardizing an investigation or unduly delaying a trial.

(3) The governmental entity shall maintain a true copy of certification under paragraph (1)(B).

(4) Extensions of the delay of notification provided in section 2703 of up to ninety days each may be granted by the court upon application, or by certification by a governmental entity, but only in accordance with subsection (b) of this section.

(5) Upon expiration of the period of delay of notification under paragraph (1) or (4) of this subsection, the governmental entity shall serve upon, or deliver by registered or first-class mail to, the customer or subscriber a copy of the process or request together with notice that—

(A) states with reasonable specificity the nature of the law enforcement inquiry; and

(B) informs such customer or subscriber—

(i) that information maintained for such customer or subscriber by the service provider named in such process or request was supplied to or requested by that governmental authority and the date on which the supplying or request took place;

(ii) that notification of such customer or subscriber was delayed;

(iii) what governmental entity or court made the certification or determination pursuant to which that delay was made; and

(iv) which provision of this chapter allowed such delay.

(6) As used in this subsection, the term "supervisory official" means the investigative agent in charge or assistant investigative agent in charge or an equivalent of an investigating agency's headquarters or regional office, or the chief prosecuting attorney or the first assistant prosecuting attorney or an equivalent of a prosecuting attorney's headquarters or regional office.

(b) Preclusion of notice to subject of governmental access.—A governmental entity acting under section 2703, when it is not required to notify the subscriber or customer under section 2703(b)(1) , or to the extent that it may delay such notice pursuant to subsection (a) of this section, may apply to a court for an order commanding a provider of electronic communications service or remote computing service to whom a warrant, subpoena, or court order is directed, for such period as the court deems appropriate, not to notify any other person of the existence of the warrant, subpoena, or court order. The court shall enter such an order if it determines that there is reason to believe that notification of the existence of the warrant, subpoena, or court order will result in—

(1) endangering the life or physical safety of an individual;

(2) flight from prosecution;

(3) destruction of or tampering with evidence;
(4) intimidation of potential witnesses; or
(5) otherwise seriously jeopardizing an investigation or unduly delaying a trial.

18 U.S.C. 2706. Cost reimbursement

(a) Payment.—Except as otherwise provided in subsection (c), a governmental entity obtaining the contents of communications, records, or other information under section 2702, 2703, or 2704 of this title shall pay to the person or entity assembling or providing such information a fee for reimbursement for such costs as are reasonably necessary and which have been directly incurred in searching for, assembling, reproducing, or otherwise providing such information. Such reimbursable costs shall include any costs due to necessary disruption of normal operations of any electronic communication service or remote computing service in which such information may be stored.

(b) Amount.—The amount of the fee provided by subsection (a) shall be as mutually agreed by the governmental entity and the person or entity providing the information, or, in the absence of agreement, shall be as determined by the court which issued the order for production of such information (or the court before which a criminal prosecution relating to such information would be brought, if no court order was issued for production of the information).

(c) Exception.—The requirement of subsection (a) of this section does not apply with respect to records or other information maintained by a communications common carrier that relate to telephone toll records and telephone listings obtained under section 2703 of this title. The court may, however, order a payment as described in subsection (a) if the court determines the information required is unusually voluminous in nature or otherwise caused an undue burden on the provider.

18 U.S.C. 2707. Civil action

(a) Cause of action.—Except as provided in section 2703(e), any provider of electronic communication service, subscriber, or other person aggrieved by any violation of this chapter in which the conduct constituting the violation is engaged in with a knowing or intentional state of mind may, in a civil action, recover from the person or entity other than the United States which engaged in that violation such relief as may be appropriate.

(b) Relief.—In a civil action under this section, appropriate relief includes—
   (1) such preliminary and other equitable or declaratory relief as may be appropriate;
   (2) damages under subsection (c); and
   (3) a reasonable attorney's fee and other litigation costs reasonably incurred.

(c) Damages.—The court may assess as damages in a civil action under this section the sum of the actual damages suffered by the plaintiff and any profits made by the violator as a result of the violation, but in no case shall a person entitled to recover receive less than the sum of $1,000. If the violation is willful or intentional, the court may assess punitive damages. In the case of a successful action to enforce liability under this section, the court may assess the costs of the action, together with reasonable attorney fees determined by the court.

(d) Administrative Discipline.—If a court or appropriate department or agency determines that the United States or any of its departments or agencies has violated any provision of this chapter, and the court or appropriate department or agency finds that the circumstances surrounding the violation raise serious questions about whether or not an officer or employee of the United States acted willfully or intentionally with respect to the possible violation, the department or agency shall, upon receipt of a true and correct copy of the decision and findings of the court or appropriate department or agency promptly initiate a proceeding to determine whether disciplinary action against the officer or employee is warranted. If the head of the department or agency involved determines that disciplinary action is not warranted, he or she shall notify the Inspector General with jurisdiction over the department or agency concerned and shall provide the Inspector General with the reasons for such determination.

(e) Defense.—A good faith reliance on—
   (1) a court warrant or order, a grand jury subpoena, a legislative authorization, or a statutory authorization (including a request of a governmental entity under section 2703(f) of this title);
   (2) a request of an investigative or law enforcement officer under section 2518(7) of this title; or

(3) a good faith determination that section 2511(3) of this title permitted the conduct complained of; is a complete defense to any civil or criminal action brought under this chapter or any other law.

(f) Limitation.—A civil action under this section may not be commenced later than two years after the date upon which the claimant first discovered or had a reasonable opportunity to discover the violation.

(g) Improper Disclosure Is Violation.—Any willful disclosure of a "record", as that term is defined in section 552a(a) of title 5, United States Code, obtained by an investigative or law enforcement officer, or governmental entity, pursuant to section 2703 of this title, or from a device installed pursuant to section 3123 or 3125 of this title, that is not a disclosure made in the proper performance of the official duties of the officer or governmental entity making the disclosure, is a violation of this chapter. This provision shall not apply to information previously lawfully disclosed (prior to the commencement of any civil or administrative proceeding under this chapter) to the public by a Federal, State, or local governmental entity or by the plaintiff in a civil action under this chapter.

18 U.S.C. 2708. Exclusivity of remedies.

The remedies and sanctions described in this chapter are the only judicial remedies and sanctions for nonconstitutional violations of this chapter.

18 U.S.C. 2709. Counterintelligence access to telephone toll and transactional records

(a) Duty to provide—A wire or electronic communication service provider shall comply with a request for subscriber information and toll billing records information, or electronic communication transactional records in its custody or possession made by the Director of the Federal Bureau of Investigation under subsection (b) of this section.

(b) Required certification—The Director of the Federal Bureau of Investigation, or his designee in a position not lower than Deputy Assistant Director at Bureau headquarters or a Special Agent in Charge in a Bureau field office designated by the Director, may—

(1) request the name, address, length of service, and local and long distance toll billing records of a person or entity if the Director (or his designee) certifies in writing to the wire or electronic

communication service provider to which the request is made that the name, address, length of service, and toll billing records sought are relevant to an authorized investigation to protect against international terrorism or clandestine intelligence activities, provided that such an investigation of a United States person is not conducted solely on the basis of activities protected by the first amendment to the Constitution of the United States; and

(2) request the name, address, and length of service of a person or entity if the Director (or his designee) certifies in writing to the wire or electronic communication service provider to which the request is made that the information sought is relevant to an authorized investigation to protect against international terrorism or clandestine intelligence activities, provided that such an investigation of a United States person is not conducted solely upon the basis of activities protected by the first amendment to the Constitution of the United States.

(c) Prohibition of certain disclosure—(1) If the Director of the Federal Bureau of Investigation, or his designee in a position not lower than Deputy Assistant Director at Bureau headquarters or a Special Agent in Charge in a Bureau field office designated by the Director, certifies that otherwise there may result a danger to the national security of the United States, interference with a criminal, counter terrorism, or counterintelligence investigation, interference with diplomatic relations, or danger to the life or physical safety of any person, no wire or electronic communications service provider, or officer, employee, or agent thereof, shall disclose to any person (other than those to whom such disclosure is necessary to comply with the request or an attorney to obtain legal advice or legal assistance with respect to the request) that the Federal Bureau of Investigation has sought or obtained access to information or records under this section.

(2) The request shall notify the person or entity to whom the request is directed of the nondisclosure requirement under paragraph (1).

(3) Any recipient disclosing to those persons necessary to comply with the request or to an attorney to obtain legal advice or legal assistance with respect to the request shall inform such person of any applicable nondisclosure requirement. Any person who receives a disclosure under this subsection shall be subject to the same prohibitions on disclosure under paragraph (1).

(4) At the request of the Director of the Federal Bureau of Investigation or the designee of the Director, any person making or intending to make a disclosure under this section shall identify to the Director or such designee the person to whom such disclosure will be made or to whom such disclosure was made prior to the request, except that nothing in this section shall require a person to inform the Director or such designee of the identity of an attorney to whom disclosure was made or will be made to obtain legal advice or legal assistance with respect to the request under subsection (a).

(d) Dissemination by bureau—The Federal Bureau of Investigation may disseminate information and records obtained under this section only as provided in guidelines approved by the Attorney General for foreign intelligence collection and foreign counterintelligence investigations conducted by the Federal Bureau of Investigation, and, with respect to dissemination to an agency of the United States, only if such information is clearly relevant to the authorized responsibilities of such agency.

(e) Requirement that certain congressional bodies be informed—On a semiannual basis the Director of the Federal Bureau of Investigation shall fully inform the Permanent Select Committee on Intelligence of the House of Representatives and the Select Committee on Intelligence of the Senate, and the Committee on the Judiciary of the House of Representatives and the Committee on the Judiciary of the Senate, concerning all requests made under subsection (b) of this section.

(f) Libraries—A library (as that term is defined in section 213(1) of the Library Services and Technology Act (20 U.S.C. 9122(1)), the services of which include access to the Internet, books, journals, magazines, newspapers, or other similar forms of communication in print or digitally by patrons for their use, review, examination, or circulation, is not a wire or electronic communication service provider for purposes of this section, unless the library is providing the services defined in section 2510(15) ("electronic communication service") of this title.

18 U.S.C. 2711. Definitions for chapter

As used in this chapter—

(1) the terms defined in section 2510 of this title have, respectively, the definitions given such terms in that section;
(2) the term "remote computing service" means the provision to the public of computer storage or processing services by means of an electronic communications system;
(3) the term "court of competent jurisdiction" includes
  (A) any district court of the United States (including a magistrate judge of such a court) or any United States court of appeals that -
    (i) has jurisdiction over the offense being investigated;
    (ii) is in or for a district in which the provider of a wire or electronic communication service is located or in which the wire or electronic communications, records, or other information are stored; or
    (iii) is acting on a request for foreign assistance pursuant to section 3512 of this title; or
  (B) a court of general criminal jurisdiction of a State authorized by the law of that State to issue search warrants; and
(4) the term "governmental entity" means a department or agency of the United States or State or political subdivision thereof.

18 U.S.C. 2712. Civil Action against the United States

(a) In General.— Any person who is aggrieved by any willful violation of this chapter or of chapter 119 of this title or of sections 106(a), 305(a), or 405(a) of the Foreign Intelligence Surveillance Act (50 U.S.C. 1801 et seq.) may commence an action in United States District Court against the United States to recover money damages. In any such action, if a person who is aggrieved successfully establishes a violation of this chapter or of chapter 119 of this title or of the above special provisions of title 50, the Court may assess as damages—
  (1) actual damages, but not less than $10,000, whichever amount is greater; and
  (2) litigation costs, reasonably incurred.
(b) Procedures.—
  (1) Any action against the United States under this section may be commenced only after a claim is presented to the appropriate department or agency under the procedures of the Federal Tort Claims Act, as set forth in title 28, United States Code.
  (2) Any action against the United States under this section shall be forever barred unless it is presented in writing to the appropriate

Federal agency within 2 years after such claim accrues or unless action is begun within 6 months after the date of mailing, by certified or registered mail, of notice of final denial of the claim by the agency to which it was presented. The claim shall accrue on the date upon which the claimant first has a reasonable opportunity to discover the violation.

(3) Any action under this section shall be tried in the court without a jury.

(4) Notwithstanding any other provision of law, the procedures set forth in section 106(f), 305(g), or 405(f) of the Foreign Intelligence Surveillance Act of 1978 (50 U.S.C. 1801 et seq.) shall be the exclusive means by which materials governed by those sections may be reviewed.

(5) An amount equal to any award against the United States under this section shall be reimbursed by the department or agency concerned to the fund described in section 1304 of title 31, United States Code, out of any appropriation, fund, or other account (excluding any part of such appropriation, fund, or account that is available for the enforcement of any Federal law) that is available for the operating expenses of the department or agency concerned.

(c) Administrative Discipline.—If a court or appropriate department or agency determines that the United States or any of the departments or agencies has violated any provision of this chapter, and the court or appropriate department or agency finds that the circumstances surrounding the violation raise serious questions about whether or not an officer or employee of the United States acted willfully or intentionally with respect to the possible violation, the department or agency shall, upon receipt of a true and correct copy of the decision and findings of the court or appropriate department or agency promptly initiate a proceeding to determine whether disciplinary action against the officer or employee is warranted. If the head of the department or agency involved determines that disciplinary action is not warranted, he or she shall notify the Inspector General with jurisdiction over the department or agency concerned and shall provide the Inspector General with the reasons for such determination.

(d) Exclusive Remedy.—Any action against the United States under this subsection shall be the exclusive remedy against the United States for any claims within the purview of this section.

(e) Stay of Proceedings.—

(1) Upon the motion of the united States, the curt shall stay any action commenced under this section f the court determines that civil discovery will adversely affect the ability of the Government to conduct a related investigation or the prosecution of a related criminal case. Such a stay shall toll the limitations periods of paragraph (2) of subsection (b).

(2) In this subsection, the terms "related criminal case" and "related investigation" means an actual prosecution or investigation in progress at the time at which the request for the stay or any subsequent motion to lift the stay is made. In determining whether any investigation or a criminal case is related to an action commenced under this section, the court shall consider the degree of similarity between the parties, witnesses, facts, and circumstances involved in the 2 proceedings, without requiring that nay one or more factors be identical.

(3) In requesting a stay under paragraph (1), the Government may, in appropriate cases submit evidence ex parte in order to avoid disclosing any matter that may adversely affect a related investigation or a related criminal case. If the Government makes such an ex parte submission, the plaintiff shall be given an opportunity to make a submission to the court, not ex parte, and the court may, in its discretion, request further information from either party.

Chapter 206 ("Pen Register and Trap and Trace Devices")

18 U.S.C. 3121. General prohibition on pen register and tape and trace device use; exception

(a) In general—Except as provided in this section, no person may install or use a pen register or a trap and trace device without first obtaining a court order under section 3123 of this title or under the Foreign Intelligence Surveillance Act of 1978 (50 U.S.C. 1801 et seq.).

(b) Exception—The prohibition of subsection (a) does not apply with respect to the use of a pen register or a trap and trace device by a provider of electronic or wire communication service—

(1) relating to the operation, maintenance, and testing of a wire or electronic communication service or to the protection of the rights

or property of such provider, or to the protection of users of that service from abuse of service or unlawful use of service; or

(2) to record the fact that a wire or electronic communication was initiated or completed in order to protect such provider, another provider furnishing service toward the completion of the wire communication, or a user of that service, from fraudulent, unlawful or abusive use of service; or

(3) where the consent of the user of that service has been obtained.

(c) Limitation—A government agency authorized to install and use a pen register or trap and trace device under this chapter or under State law shall use technology reasonably available to it that restricts the recording or decoding of electronic or other impulses to the dialing, routing, addressing, and signaling information utilized in identifying the origination or destination of wire or electronic communications.

(d) Penalty—Whoever knowingly violates subsection (a) shall be fined under this title or imprisoned not more than one year, or both.

18 U.S.C. 3122. Application for an order for a pen register or a trap and trace device

(a) Application.

(1) An attorney for the Government may make application for an order or an extension of an order under section 3123 of this title authorizing or approving the installation and use of a pen register or a trap and trace device under this chapter, in writing under oath or equivalent affirmation, to a court of competent jurisdiction.

(2) Unless prohibited by State law, a State investigative or law enforcement officer may make application for an order or an extension of an order under section 3123 of this title authorizing or approving the installation and use of a pen register or a trap and trace device under this chapter, in writing under oath or equivalent affirmation, to a court of competent jurisdiction of such State.

(b) Contents of application—An application under subsection (a) of this section shall include—

(1) the identity of the attorney for the Government or the State law enforcement or investigative officer making the application and the identity of the law enforcement agency conducting the investigation; and

(2) a certification by the applicant that the information likely to be obtained is relevant to an ongoing criminal investigation being conducted by that agency.

18 U.S.C. 3123. Issuance of an order for a pen register or a trap and trace device

(a) In general.

(1) Upon an application made under section 3122(a)(1) of this title, the court shall enter an ex parte order authorizing the installation and use of a pen register or a trap and trace device if the court finds, based on facts contained in the application, that the information likely to be obtained by such installation and use is relevant to an ongoing criminal investigation. Such order shall, upon service of such order, apply to any entity providing wire or electronic communication service in the United States whose assistance may facilitate the execution of the order.

(2) Upon an application made under section 3122(a)(2) of this title, the court shall enter an ex parte order authorizing the installation and use of a pen register or a trap and trace device within the jurisdiction of the court if the court finds, based on facts contained in the application, that the information likely to be obtained by such installation and use is relevant to an ongoing criminal investigation.

(3)

(A) Where the law enforcement agency implementing an ex part order under this subsection seeks to do so by installing and using its own pen register or trap and trace device on a packet-switched data network of a provider of electronic communication service to the public the agency shall ensure that a record will be maintained which will identify—

(i) any officer or officers who installed the device and any officer or officers who accessed the device to obtain information from the network;

(ii) the date and time the device was installed, the date and time the device was uninstalled, and the date, time, and duration of each time the device is accessed to obtain information;

(iii) the configuration of the device at the time of its installation and any subsequent modification thereof; and

(iv) any information which has been collected by the device.

To the extent that the pen register or trap and trace device can be set automatically to record this information electronically, the record shall be maintained electronically throughout the installation and use of the such device.

(B) The record maintained under subparagraph (A) shall be provided ex parte and under seal to the court which entered the ex parte order authorizing the installation and use of the device within 30 days after termination of the order (including any extensions thereof).

(b) Contents of order—An order issued under this section—

(1) shall specify—

(A) the identity, if known, of the person to whom is leased or in whose name is listed the telephone line or other facility to which the pen register or trap and trace device is to be attached or applied;

(B) the identity, if known, of the person who is the subject of the criminal investigation;

(C) the attributes of the communications to which the order applies, including the number or other identifier and, if known, the location of the telephone line or other facility to which the pen register or trap and trace device is to be attached or applied, and, in the case of an order authorizing installation and use of a trap and trace device under subsection (a)(2), the geographic limits of the order; and

(D) a statement of the offense to which the information likely to be obtained by the pen register or trap and trace device relates; and

(2) shall direct, upon the request of the applicant, the furnishing of information, facilities, and technical assistance necessary to accomplish the installation of the pen register or trap and trace device under section 3124 of this title.

(c) Time period and extensions—

(1) An order issued under this section shall authorize the installation and use of a pen register or a trap and trace device for a period not to exceed sixty days.

(2) Extensions of such an order may be granted, but only upon an application for an order under section 3122 of this title and upon

the judicial finding required by subsection (a) of this section. The period of extension shall be for a period not to exceed sixty days.

(d) Nondisclosure of existence of pen register or a trap and trace device—An order authorizing or approving the installation and use of a pen register or a trap and trace device shall direct that—
  (1) the order be sealed until otherwise ordered by the court; and
  (2) the person owning or leasing the line or other facility to which the pen register or a trap and trace device is attached, or applied, or who is obligated by the order to provide assistance to the applicant, not disclose the existence of the pen register or trap and trace device or the existence of the investigation to the listed subscriber, or to any other person, unless or until otherwise ordered by the court.

18 U.S.C. 3124. Assistance in installation and use of a pen register or a trap and trace device

(a) Pen registers—Upon the request of an attorney for the Government or an officer of a law enforcement agency authorized to install and use a pen register under this chapter, a provider of wire or electronic communication service, landlord, custodian, or other person shall furnish such investigative or law enforcement officer forthwith all information, facilities, and technical assistance necessary to accomplish the installation of the pen register unobtrusively and with a minimum of interference with the services that the person so ordered by the court accords the party with respect to whom the installation and use is to take place, if such assistance is directed by a court order as provided in section 3123(b)(2) of this title.

(b) Trap and trace device—Upon the request of an attorney for the Government or an officer of a law enforcement agency authorized to receive the results of a trap and trace device under this chapter, a provider of a wire or electronic communication service, landlord, custodian, or other person shall install such device forthwith on the appropriate line or other facility and shall furnish such investigative or law enforcement officer all additional information, facilities and technical assistance including installation and operation of the device unobtrusively and with a minimum of interference with the services that the person so ordered by the court accords the party with respect to whom the installation and use is to take place, if such installation and assistance is directed by a court order as provided in section

3123(b)(2) of this title. Unless otherwise ordered by the court, the results of the trap and trace device shall be furnished, pursuant to section 3123(b) or section 3125 of this title, to the officer of a law enforcement agency, designated in the court order, at reasonable intervals during regular business hours for the duration of the order.

(c) Compensation—A provider of a wire or electronic communication service, landlord, custodian, or other person who furnishes facilities or technical assistance pursuant to this section shall be reasonably compensated for such reasonable expenses incurred in providing such facilities and assistance.

(d) No cause of action against a provider disclosing information under this chapter—No cause of action shall lie in any court against any provider of a wire or electronic communication service, its officers, employees, agents, or other specified persons for providing information, facilities, or assistance in accordance with a court order under this chapter or request pursuant to section 3125 of this title.

(e) Defense—A good faith reliance on a court order under this chapter, a request pursuant to section 3125 of this title, a legislative authorization, or a statutory authorization is a complete defense against any civil or criminal action brought under this chapter or any other law.

(f) Communications assistance enforcement orders—Pursuant to section 2522, an order may be issued to enforce the assistance capability and capacity requirements under the Communications Assistance for Law Enforcement Act.

18 U.S.C. 3125. Emergency pen register and trap and trace device installation

(a) Notwithstanding any other provision of this chapter, any investigative or law enforcement officer, specially designated by the Attorney General, the Deputy Attorney General, the Associate Attorney General, any Assistant Attorney General, any acting Assistant Attorney General, or any Deputy Assistant Attorney General, or by the principal prosecuting attorney of any State or subdivision thereof acting pursuant to a statute of that State, who reasonably determines that—

(1) an emergency situation exists that involves—

(A) immediate danger of death or serious bodily injury to any person; or

(B) conspiratorial activities characteristic of organized crime;
(C) an immediate threat to a national security interest; or
(D) an ongoing attack on a protected computer (as defined in section 1030) that constitutes a crime

punishable by a term of imprisonment greater than one year; that requires the installation and use of a pen register or a trap and trace device before an order authorizing such installation and use can, with due diligence, be obtained, and

(2) there are grounds upon which an order could be entered under this chapter to authorize such installation and use; may have installed and use a pen register or trap and trace device if, within forty-eight hours after the installation has occurred, or begins to occur, an order approving the installation or use is issued in accordance with section 3123 of this title.

(b) In the absence of an authorizing order, such use shall immediately terminate when the information sought is obtained, when the application for the order is denied or when forty-eight hours have lapsed since the installation of the pen register or trap and trace device, whichever is earlier.

(c) The knowing installation or use by any investigative or law enforcement officer of a pen register or trap and trace device pursuant to subsection (a) without application for the authorizing order within forty-eight hours of the installation shall constitute a violation of this chapter.

(d) A provider of a wire or electronic service, landlord, custodian, or other person who furnished facilities or technical assistance pursuant to this section shall be reasonably compensated for such reasonable expenses incurred in providing such facilities and assistance.

18 U.S.C. 3126. Reports concerning pen registers and trap and trace devices

The Attorney General shall annually report to Congress on the number of pen register orders and orders for trap and trace devices applied for by law enforcement agencies of the Department of Justice, which report shall include information concerning—

(1) the period of interceptions authorized by the order, and the number and duration of any extensions of the order;

(2) the offense specified in the order or application, or extension of an order;
(3) the number of investigations involved;
(4) the number and nature of the facilities affected; and
(5) the identity, including district, of the applying investigative or law enforcement agency making the application and the person authorizing the order.

18 U.S.C. 3127. Definitions for chapter

As used in this chapter—

(1) the terms "wire communication", "electronic communication", "electronic communication service" and "contents" have the meanings set forth for such terms in section 2510 of this title;
(2) the term "court of competent jurisdiction" means—
  (A) any district court of the United States (including a magistrate judge of such a court) or any United States court of appeals that
    (i) has jurisdiction over the offense being investigated;
    (ii) is in or for a district in which the provider of a wire or electronic communication service is located;
    (iii) is in or for a district in which a landlord, custodian, or other person subject to subsections (a) or (b) of section 3124 of this title is located; or
    (iv) is acting on a request for foreign assistance pursuant to section 3512 of this title; or
  (B) a court of general criminal jurisdiction of a State authorized by the law of that State to enter orders authorizing the use of a pen register or a trap and trace device;
(3) the term "pen register" means a device or process which records or decodes or other dialing, routing, addressing, and signaling information reasonably likely to identify the source of a wire or electronic communication, provided, however, that such information shall not include the contents of any communication, but such term does not include any device or process used by a provider or customer of a wire or electronic communication service for billing, or recording as an incident to billing, for communications services provided by such provider or any device or process used by a provider or customer of a wire communication service for cost accounting or other like purposes in the ordinary course of its business;

(4) the term "trap and trace device" means a device or process which captures the incoming electronic or other impulses which identify the originating number or other dialing, routing, addressing, and signaling information reasonably likely to identify the source of a wire or electronic communication, provided, however, that such information shall not include the contents of any communication;
(5) the term "attorney for the Government" has the meaning given such term for the purposes of the Federal Rules of Criminal Procedure; and
(6) the term "State" means a State, the District of Columbia, Puerto Rico, and any other possession or territory of the United States.

APPENDIX A. STATE STATUTES OUTLAWING THE INTERCEPTION OF WIRE(W), ORAL(O) AND ELECTRONIC COMMUNICATIONS(E)

Alabama: Ala.Code §§13A-11-30 to 13A-11-37(w/o);
Alaska: Alaska Stat. §§42.20.300 to 42.20.390 (w/o/e);
Arizona: Ariz.Rev.Stat.Ann. §§13-3001 to 13-3009 (w/o/e);
Arkansas: Ark.Code §§5-60-120, 23-17-107(w/o/e);
California: Cal.Penal Code §§631(w), 632(o), 632.7(e);
Colorado: Colo.Rev.Stat. §§18-9-301 to 18-9-305(w/o/e);
Connecticut: Conn.Gen.Stat.Ann. §§53a-187 to 53a-189, 54-41t (w/o);
Delaware: Del.Code tit.11 §§2401, 2402(w/o/e);
Florida: Fla.Stat.Ann. §§934.02, 934.03(w/o/e);
Georgia: Ga.Code §16-11-62 (w/o/e);
Hawaii: Hawaii Rev.Stat. §§711-1111, 803-41, 803-42(w/o/e);
Idaho: Idaho Code §§18-6701, 18-6702(w/o/e);
New Jersey: N.J.Stat.Ann. §§2A:156A-2, 2A:156A-3(w/o/e);
New Mexico: N.M.Stat.Ann. §30-12-1(w);
New York: N.Y.Penal Law §§250.00, 250.05(w/o/e);
North Carolina: N.C.Gen.Stat. §§15A-286, 15A-287(w/o/e);
North Dakota: N.D.Cent.Code §§12.1-15-02, 12.1-15-04(w/o);
Ohio: Ohio Rev.Code §§2933.51, 2933.52 (w/o/e);
Oklahoma: Okla.Stat.Ann. tit.13 §§176.2, 176.3 (w/o/e);
Oregon: Ore.Rev.Stat. §§165.535 to 165.545 (w/o/e);
Pennsylvania: Pa.Stat.Ann. tit.18 §§5702, 5703 (w/o/e);
Rhode Island: R.I.Gen.Laws §§11-35-21(w/o/e);
South Carolina: S.C. Code Ann. §§16-17-470, 17-30-10 to 17-30-20 (w/o/e);

Illinois: Ill.Comp.Stat.Ann. ch.720 §§5/14-1 to 5/14-3(w/o/e);
Indiana: Ind.Code Ann. §§35-33.5-2-1, 35-33.5-5-6(w/o/e);
Iowa: Iowa Code Ann. §§272.8, 808B.2(w/o/e);
Kansas: Kan.Stat.Ann. §21-6101(w/o);
Kentucky: Ky.Rev.Stat. §§526.010, 526.020(w/o);
Louisiana: La.Rev.Stat.Ann. §§15:1302, 15:1303 (w/o/e);
Maine: Me.Rev.Stat.Ann. tit. 15 §§709, 710(w/o);
Maryland: Md.Cts. & Jud.Pro.Code Ann. §§10-401, 10-402(w/o/e);
Massachusetts: Mass.Gen.Laws Ann. ch.272 §99 (w/o);
Michigan: Mich.Comp.Laws Ann. §§750.539a, to 750.540(w/o/e);
Minnesota: Minn.Stat.Ann. §§626A.01, 626A.02 (w/o/e);
Missouri: Mo.Ann.Stat. §§542.400 to 542.402 (w/o/e);

Montana: Mont.Code Ann. §45-8-213(w/o/e);
Nebraska: Neb.Rev.Stat. §§86-271 to 86-290 (w/o/e);
Nevada: Nev.Rev.Stat. §§200.610, 200.620(w), 200.650(o);
New Hampshire: N.H.Rev.Stat.Ann. §§570-A:1, 570-A:2 (w/o);
South Dakota: S.D.Cod.Laws §§23A-35A-1, 23A-35A-20 (w/o);
Tennessee: Tenn.Code Ann. §39-13-601(w/o/e);
Texas: Tex.Penal Code. §16.02; Tex. Crim. Pro. Code art. 18.20 (w/o/e);
Utah: Utah Code Ann. §§76-9-405, 77-23a-3, 77-23a-4 (w/o/e);

Virginia: Va.Code §§19.2-61, 19.2-62(w/o/e);
Washington: Wash.Rev.Code Ann.§9.73.030 (w/o);
West Virginia: W.Va.Code §§62-1D-2, 62-1D-3(w/o/e);
Wisconsin: Wis.Stat.Ann. §§968.27, 968.31(w/o/e);
Wyoming: Wyo.Stat. §§7-3-701, 7-3-702(w/o/e);
District of Columbia: D.C.Code §§23-541, 23-542(w/o).

Appendix B. Consent Interceptions under State Law

Alabama: Ala.Code §13A-11-30 (one partyconsent);
Alaska: Alaska Stat. §§42.20.300to 42.20.320 (one party consent);
Arizona: Ariz.Rev.Stat.Ann. §13-3005 (one party consent);
Arkansas: Ark.Code §5-60-120(one party consent);
California: Cal. Penal Code §§631, 632 (one party consent for police; all party consent otherwise), 632.7 (all partyconsent);
Colorado: Colo.Rev.Stat. §§18-9-303, 18-9-304 (one party consent);
Connecticut: Conn.Gen.Stat.Ann. §§53a-187, 53a-188 (criminal proscription: one party consent); §52-570d (civil liability: all party consent except for police);
Delaware: Del. Code tit.11 §2402 (one party consent);
Florida: Fla.Stat.Ann. §934.03 (one party consent for the police; all party consent for others);
Georgia: Ga.Code §16-11-66 (one party consent);
Hawaii: Hawaii Rev.Stat. §§711-1111, 803-42 (one party consent);
Idaho: Idaho Code §18-6702 (one party consent);
Illinois: Ill.Comp.Stat.Ann. ch.720 §§5/14-2,5/14-3 (all party consent with law enforcement exceptions);
Indiana: Ind.Code Ann. §35-33.5-5-5 (one party consent), *Parker v.*

New Jersey: N.J.Stat.Ann. §§2A:156A-4 (one party consent);
New Mexico: N.M.Stat.Ann. §§30-12-1 (one party consent);
New York: N.Y.Penal Law §250.00 (one party consent);
North Carolina: N.C. Gen.Stat. §15A-287 (one party consent);
North Dakota: N.D.Cent.Code §§12.1-15-02 (one party consent);
Ohio: Ohio Rev.Code §2933.52 (one party consent);

Oklahoma: Okla.Stat.Ann. tit.13 §176.4 (one party consent);
Oregon: Ore.Rev.Stat. §165.540 (one party consent for wiretapping and all parties must consent for other forms of electronic eavesdropping);
Pennsylvania: Pa.Stat.Ann. tit.18 §5704 (one party consent for the police; all parties consent otherwise);
Rhode Island: R.I.Gen.Laws §§11-35-21 (oneparty consent);

State, 800 N.E.2d 574 (Ind.App. 2003);
Iowa: Iowa Code Ann. §808B.2 (one party consent);
Kansas: Kan.Stat.Ann. §§21-6101 (one party consent);
Kentucky: Ky.Rev.Stat. §526.010 (one party consent);
Louisiana: La.Rev.Stat.Ann. §15:1303 (one party consent);
Maine: Me.Rev.Stat.Ann. tit. 15 §709 (one party consent);
Maryland: Md.Cts. & Jud.Pro.Code Ann. §10-402 (one party consent);
Massachusetts: Mass.Gen. Laws Ann. ch.272 §99 (all parties must consent, except in some law enforcement cases);
Michigan: Mich.Comp.Laws Ann. §750.539c (proscription regarding eavesdropping on oral conversation: all party consent, except that the proscription does not apply to otherwise lawful activities of police officers);
Minnesota: Minn.Stat.Ann. §626A.02 (one party consent);
Missouri: Mo.Ann.Stat. §542.402 (one party consent);
Montana: Mont.Code Ann. §§45-8-213 (all party consent with an exception for the performance of official duties);
Nebraska: Neb.Rev.Stat. §86-290 (one party consent);
Nevada: Nev.Rev.Stat. §§200.620, 200.650 (onep arty consent);
South Carolina: S.C. Code Ann. §17-30-30 (one party consent);
South Dakota: S.D.Comp.Laws §§23A-35A-20 (one party consent);
Tennessee: Tenn.Code Ann. §39-13-601 (one party consent)
Texas: Tex.Penal Code §16.02 (one party consent);
Utah: Utah Code Ann. §§77-23a-4 (one party consent);
Virginia: Va.Code §19.2-62 (one party consent);
Washington: Wash.Rev.Code Ann. §9.73.030 (all parties must consent, except that one party consent is sufficient in certain law enforcement cases);
West Virginia: W.Va. Code §62-1D-3 (one party consent);
Wisconsin: Wis.Stat.Ann. §968.31 (one party consent);
Wyoming: Wyo.Stat. §7-3-702 (one party consent);
District of Columbia: D.C.Code §23-542 (one party consent).

APPENDIX C. STATUTORY CIVIL LIABILITY FOR INTERCEPTIONS UNDER STATE LAW

Arizona: Ariz.Rev.Stat.Ann. §12-731;
California: Cal. Penal Code §§637.2;
Colorado: Colo.Rev.Stat. §18-9-309.5;
Connecticut: Conn.Gen.Stat. Ann. §§54-41r,52-570d;
Delaware: Del.Code tit.11 §2409;

Florida: Fla.Stat.Ann. §§934.10, 934.27;
Hawaii: Hawaii Rev.Stat. §803-48;
Idaho: Idaho Code §18-6709;
Illinois: Ill.Comp.Stat. Ann. ch.720 §5/14-6;
Indiana: Ind.Code Ann. §35-33.5-5-4;
Iowa: Iowa Code Ann. §808B.8;
Kansas: Kan.Stat.Ann. §22-2518
Louisiana: La.Rev.Stat.Ann. §15:1312;
Maine: Me.Rev.Stat.Ann. ch.15 §711;
Maryland: Md.Cts. & Jud.Pro.Code Ann. §§10-410, 10-4A-08;

Massachusetts: Mass.Gen. LawsAnn. ch.272 §99;
Michigan: Mich.Comp. Laws Ann. §750.539h;
Minnesota: Minn.Stat.Ann. §§626A.02, 626A.13;
Nebraska: Neb.Rev.Stat. §86-297;
Nevada: Nev.Rev.Stat. §200.690;
New Hampshire: N.H.Rev.Stat. Ann. §570-A:11;
New Jersey: N.J.Stat.Ann. §§2A: 156A-24;
New Mexico: N.M.Stat.Ann. §§30 - 12-11;
North Carolina: N.C.Gen.Stat. §15A -296;
Ohio: Ohio Rev.Code §2933.65;
Oregon: Ore.Rev.Stat. §133.739;
Pennsylvania: Pa.Stat. Ann. tit.18 §§5725, 5747;
Rhode Island: R.I.Gen.Laws §12-5.1-13;
South Carolina: S.C. Code Ann. §17-30-135;
Tennessee: Tenn.Code Ann. §39-13-603;
Texas: Tex.Code Crim.Pro. art. 18.20;
Utah: Utah Code Ann. §§77-23a-11; 77-23b-8;
Virginia: Va.Code §19.2-69;
Washington: Wash.Rev.Code Ann. §9.73.060;
West Virginia: W.Va.Code §62-1D-12;
Wisconsin: Wis.Stat.Ann. §968.31;
Wyoming: Wyo.Stat. §7-3-710;
District of Columbia: D.C.Code §23-554.

Appendix D. Court Authorized Interception under State Law

Alaska: Alaska Stats. §§12.37.010 to 12.37.900;
Arizona: Ariz.Rev.Stat.Ann. §§13-3010 to 13-3019;
California: Cal.Penal Code §629.50 to 629.98;
Colorado: Colo.Rev.Stat. §§16-15-101 to 16-15-104;
Connecticut: Conn.Gen.Stat.Ann. §§54-41a to54-41u;
Delaware: Del.Code tit.11 §§2401 to 2412;
Florida: Fla.Stat.Ann. §§934.02 to 934.43;
Georgia: Ga.Code §16-11-64 to 16-11-69;
Hawaii: Hawaii Rev.Stat. §§803-41 to 803-49;
Idaho: Idaho Code §§18-6701 to 18-6709; 6719 to 6725;
Illinois: Ill.Stat.Ann. ch.725 §§5/108A-1 to108B-14;
Indiana:Ind.Code §§35-33.5-2-1to 35-33.5-5-6;
Iowa: Iowa Code Ann. §§808B.3to 808B.7;
Kansas: Kan.Stat.Ann. §§22-2514 to 22-2519;
Louisiana: La.Rev.Stat.Ann. §§15:1301 to 15:1316;
Maryland: Md.Cts. & Jud.Pro.Code Ann. §§10-401 to10-410;
Massachusetts: Mass.Gen.LawsAnn. ch.272 §99;
Minnesota: Minn.Stat.Ann.

North Carolina: N.C.Gen.Stat. §§15A-286 to 15A-298;
North Dakota: N.D.Cent.Code §§29-29.2-01 to 29-29.2-05;
Ohio: Ohio Rev.Code §§2933.51 to 2933.66;
Oklahoma: Okla.Stat.Ann. tit.13 §§176.1 to 176.14
Oregon: Ore.Rev.Stat. §§133.721 to 133.739;
Pennsylvania: Pa.Stat.Ann. tit.18 §§5701 to 5728
Rhode Island: R.I.Gen.Laws §§12-5.1-1 to12-5.1-16;
South Carolina: S.C. Code Ann. §§17-30-10 to 17-30-145;
South Dakota: S.D.Cod.Laws §§23A-35A-1 to 23A-35A-34;
Tennessee: Tenn.Code Ann. §§40-6-301 to 40-6-311;
Texas: Tex.Crim.Pro. Code. art. 18.20;
Utah: Utah Code Ann. §§77-23a-1 to 77-23a-16;
Virginia: Va.Code §§19.2-61 to19.2-70.3;
Washington: Wash.Rev.Code Ann. §§9.73.040 to 9.73.250;
West Virginia: W.Va.Code §§62-

§§626A.01 to 626.41;
Missouri: Mo.Ann.Stat. §§542.400 to 542.422;
Nebraska: Neb.Rev.Stat. §§86-271 to 86-2,115;

Nevada: Nev.Rev.Stat. §§179.410 to 179.515;
New Hampshire: N.H.Rev.Stat.Ann. §§570-A:1 to570-A:9;
New Jersey: N.J.Stat.Ann. §§2A:156A-8 to 2A:156A-26;
New Mexico: N.M.Stat.Ann. §§30-12-1 to 30-12-11;
New York: N.Y.Crim.Pro. Law §§700.05 to700.70;

1D-1 to 62-1D-16;
Wisconsin: Wis.Stat.Ann. §§968.27 to 968.33;
Wyoming: Wyo.Stat. §§7-3-701 to 7-3-712;
District of Columbia: D.C.Code §§23-541 to 23-556.

End Notes

[1] Portions of this report draw upon a series of earlier reports, no longer available, entitled: *Wiretapping and Electronic Surveillance: A Brief Discussion of Pertinent Supreme Court Cases, A Summary and Compilation of Federal State Statutes, and a Selected Legal Bibliography* (1970); *Wiretapping and Electronic Surveillance: A Brief Discussion of Pertinent Supreme Court Cases, A Summary and Compilation of Federal State Statutes, and a Selected Legal Bibliography* (1971); *Wiretapping and Electronic Surveillance: Federal and State Statutes* (1974); *Taps and Bugs: A Compilation of Federal and State Statutes Governing the Interception of Wire and Oral Communications* (1981); *The Interception of Communications: A Legal Overview of Bugs and Taps* (1988); *Wiretapping & Electronic Surveillance: The Electronic Communications Privacy Act and Related Matters* (1992); *Taps, Bugs & Telephony: An Overview of Federal Statutes Governing Wiretapping and Electronic Eavesdropping* (1998); *Privacy: An Overview of Federal Statutes Governing Wiretapping and Electronic Eavesdropping* (2001); *id.* (2003); *id.* (2006); *id.* (2009). It constitutes the ECPA portion of a separate report that includes a discussion of the Foreign Intelligence Surveillance Act (FISA), CRS Report 98-326, *Privacy: An Overview of Federal Statutes Governing Wiretapping and Electronic Eavesdropping*.
As used in this report "electronic eavesdropping" refers to the use of hidden microphones, recorders and any other mechanical or electronic means of capturing ongoing communications, other than wiretapping (tapping into telephone conversations). In previous versions of this report and other earlier writings, it was common to use a more neutral, and consequently preferred, term—electronic surveillance—at least when referring to law enforcement use. Unfortunately, continued use of the term "electronic surveillance" rather than "electronic eavesdropping" risks confusion with forms of surveillance that either have individualistic definitions (*e.g.*, "electronic surveillance" under the Foreign Intelligence

Surveillance Act, 50 U.S.C. 1801(f)), involve surveillance that does not capture conversation (*e.g.*, thermal imaging or electronic tracking devices), or may or may not capture conversation (*e.g.*, the coverage of video surveillance depends upon the circumstances and the statutory provision question).

Related developments are discussed in CRS Report R42725, *Reauthorization of the FISA Amendments Act*; CRS Report R40138, *Amendments to the Foreign Intelligence Surveillance Act (FISA) Extended Until June 1, 2015*; CRS Report R40980, *Government Collection of Private Information: Background and Issues Related to the USA PATRIOT Act Reauthorization*; CRS Report 97-1025, *Cybercrime: An Overview of the Federal Computer Fraud and Abuse Statute and Related Federal Criminal Laws*, by Charles Doyle; CRS Report RL33424, *Government Access to Phone Calling Activity and Related Records: Legal Authorities*; CRS Report RL30677, *The Communications Assistance for Law Enforcement Act*, by Patricia Moloney Figliola; and CRS Report RL34693, *Online Data Collection and Disclosure to Private Entities: Selected Federal Laws and Self-Regulatory Regimes*, by Kathleen Ann Ruane.

[2] 18 U.S.C. 2510-2522. This part of ECPA was originally enacted as Title III of the Omnibus Crime Control and Safe Streets Act of 1968, 18 U.S.C. 2510-2520 (1964 ed,)(Supp. IV).

[3] *Id.*

[4] 18 U.S.C. 27-1-2712.

[5] 18 U.S.C. 3121-3127.

[6] 18 U.S.C. 3121.

[7] 4 BLACKSTONE,COMMENTARIES ON THE LAWS OF ENGLAND, 169 (1769).

[8] "Eavesdropping is indictable at the common law, not only in England but in our states. It is seldom brought to the attention of the courts, and our books contain too few decisions upon it to enable an author to define it with confidence.... It never occupied much space in the law, and it has nearly faded from the legal horizon." 1 BISHOP, COMMENTARIES ON THE CRIMINAL LAW, 670 (1882).

[9] 40 Stat.1017-18 (1918)("whoever during the period of governmental operation of the telephone and telegraph systems of the United States ... shall, without authority and without the knowledge and consent of the other users thereof, except as may be necessary for operation of the service, tap any telegraph or telephone line ... or whoever being employed in any such telephone or telegraph service shall divulge the contents of any such telephone or telegraph message to any person not duly authorized or entitled the receive the same, shall be fined not exceeding $1,000 or imprisoned for not more than one year or both"); 56 *Cong. Rec.* 10761-765 (1918).

[10] 44 Stat. 1172 (1927)(" ... no person not being authorized by the sender shall intercept any message and divulge or publish the contents, substance, purpose, effect, or meaning of such intercepted message to any person ... ").

[11] *Olmstead v. United States*, 277 U.S. 438, 479-80 n.13 (1928)(Brandeis, J., dissenting). *Olmstead* is remembered most today for the dissents of Holmes and Brandeis, but for four decades it stood for the view that the Fourth Amendment's search and seizure commands did not apply to government wiretapping accomplished without a trespass onto private property.

[12] Curtilage originally meant the land and buildings enclosed by the walls of a castle; in later usage it referred to the barns, stables, garden plots and the like immediately proximate to a dwelling; it is understood in Fourth Amendment parlance to describe that area which "harbors those intimate activities associated with domestic life and the privacies of the home," *United States v. Dunn*, 480 U.S. 294, 301 n.4 (1987).

[13] 277 U.S. at 466. Olmstead had not been compelled to use his phone and so the Court rejected his Fifth Amendment challenge. 277 U.S.C. at 462. Any violation of the Washington state wiretap statute was thought insufficient to warrant the exclusion of evidence, 277 U.S. at 466-68. Justice Holmes in his dissent tersely characterized the conduct of federal wiretappers as "dirty business," 277 U.S. at 470. The dissent of Justice Brandeis observed

that the drafters of the Constitution "conferred as against the Government, the right to be let alone—the most comprehensive of rights and the right most valued by civilized men. To protect that right, every unjustifiable intrusion by the Government against privacy of the individual whatever the means employed, must be deemed in violation of the Fourth Amendment," 277 U.S. at 478-79.

[14] "Congress may of course protect the secrecy of telephone messages by making them, when intercepted inadmissible in evidence in federal criminal trials, by direct legislation," 277 U.S. at 465.

[15] 48 Stat. 1103-104 (1934), 47 U.S.C. 605 (1940 ed.). The Act neither expressly condemned law enforcement interceptions nor called for the exclusion of wiretap evidence, but it was read to encompass both, *Nardone v. United States*, 302 U.S. 379 (1937); *Nardone v. United States*, 308 U.S. 321 (1939).

[16] Section 605 did ban the interception and divulgence of radio broadcasts but it did not reach the radio transmission of conversations that were broadcast unbeknownst to all of the parties to the conversation. Late in the game, the FCC supplied a partial solution when it banned the use of licensed radio equipment to overhear or record private conversation without the consent of all the parties involved in the conversation, 31 *Fed. Reg.* 3400 (March 4, 1966), amending then 47 C.F.R. §§2.701, 15.11. The FCC excluded "operations of any law enforcement offices conducted under lawful authority," *id.*

[17] The volume of all Fourth Amendment cases calling for Supreme Court review increased dramatically after *Mapp v. Ohio*, 367 U.S. 643 (1961), acknowledged the application of the Fourth Amendment exclusionary rule to the states.

[18] *Goldman v. United States*, 316 U.S. 129 (1942).

[19] *On Lee v. United States*, 343 U.S. 747 (1952).

[20] *Silverman v. United States*, 365 U.S. 505 (1961).

[21] "The absence of a physical invasion of the petitioner's premises was also a vital factor in the Court's decision in *Olmstead v. United States*.... In holding that the wiretapping there did not violate the Fourth Amendment, the Court noted that the insertions were made without trespass upon any property of the defendants. They were made in the basement of the large office building. The taps from house lines were made in the streets near the houses. 277 U.S. at 457. There was no entry of the houses or offices of the defendants. 277 U.S. at 464. Relying upon these circumstances, the Court reasoned that the intervening wires are not part of (the defendant's) house or office any more than are the highways along which they are stretched. 277 U.S. at 465.

"Here, by contrast, the officers overheard the petitioners' conversations only by usurping part of the petitioners' house or office—a heating system which was an integral part of the premises occupied by the petitioners, a usurpation that was effected without their knowledge and without their consent. In these circumstances we need not pause to consider whether or not there was a technical trespass under the local property law relating to party walls. Inherent Fourth Amendment rights are not inevitably measurable in terms of ancient niceties of tort or real property law . . . .

"The Fourth Amendment, and the personal rights which it secures, have a long history. At the very core stands the right of a man to retreat into his own home and there be free from unreasonable governmental intrusion ... This Court has never held that a federal officer may without warrant and without consent physically entrench into a man's office or home, there secretly observe or listen, and relate at the man's subsequent criminal trial what was seen or heard.

"A distinction between the dictaphone employed in Goldman and the spike mike utilized here seemed to the Court of Appeals too fine a one to draw. The court was unwilling to believe that the respective rights are to be measured in fractions of inches. But decision here does not turn upon the technicality of a trespass upon a party wall as a matter of local law. It is based upon the reality of an actual intrusion into a constitutionally protected area. What the Court said long ago bears repeating now: It may be that it is the obnoxious thing in its mildest and least repulsive form; but illegitimate and unconstitutional practices get their first footing in that way, namely, by silent approaches and slight deviations from legal modes of procedure. *Boyd v. United States*, 116 U.S. 616, 635. We find no occasion to re-examine Goldman here, but we decline to go beyond it, by even a fraction of an inch," 365 U.S. at 510-12 (internal quotation marks omitted).

[22] *Wong Sun v. United States*, 371 U.S. 471, 485 (1963).

[23] 389 U.S. 347 (1967).

[24] "We conclude that the underpinnings of *Olmstead* and *Goldman* have been so eroded by our subsequent decisions that the trespass doctrine there enunciated can no longer be regarded as controlling. The Government's activities in electronically listening to and recording the petitioner's words violated the privacy upon which he justifiably relied while using the telephone booth and thus constituted a search and seizure within the meaning of the Fourth Amendment. The fact that the electronic device employed to achieve that end did not happen to penetrate the wall of the booth can have no constitutional significance." Later courts seem to prefer the "expectation of privacy" language found in Justice Harlan's concurrence: "My understanding of the rule that has emerged from prior decisions is that there is a twofold requirement, first that a person have exhibited an actual (subjective) expectation of privacy and, second, that the expectation be one that society is prepared to recognize as reasonable," 389 U.S. at 361.

[25] 388 U.S. 41 (1967).

[26] 388 U.S. at 58-60.

[27] 87 Stat. 197, 18 U.S.C. 2510 -2520 (1970 ed.).

[28] 18 U.S.C. 2511(3)(1970 ed.)("Nothing contained in this chapter or in section 605 of the Communications Act ... shall limit the constitutional power of the President to take such measures as he deems necessary to protect the Nation against actual or potential attack or other hostile acts of a foreign power, to obtain foreign intelligence information deemed essential to the security of the United States, or to protect national security information against foreign intelligence activities ... ").

[29] *United States v. United States District Court*, 407 U.S. 297 (1972).

[30] 92 Stat. 1783, 50 U.S.C. 1801-1862.

[31] 425 U.S. 435, 441-43 (1976).

[32] *Id.* at 44-45.

[33] 442 U.S. 735, 741-46 (1979).

[34] *Id.* In *United States v. New York Telephone Co.*, the Court held that the Title III did not apply to the use of pen registers and that federal courts had the power to authorize their installation for law enforcement purposes, 434 U.S.157, 168 (1977).

[35] 100 Stat. 1848 (1986).

[36] 18 U.S.C. 2510-2522.

[37] 18 U.S.C. 2701-2712.

[38] 18 U.S.C. 3121-3126.

[39] P.L. 107-56, 115 Stat. 272 (2001).

[40] P.L. 107-108, 115 Stat. 1394 (2001).

[41] P.L. 107-273, 116 Stat. 1758 (2002).

[42] P.L. 107-296, 116 Stat. 2135 (2002).

[43] P.L. 109-177, 120 Stat. 192 (2006).

[44] P.L. 110-261, 122 Stat. 2436 (2008).

[45] 18 U.S.C. 2511. Elsewhere, federal law proscribes: unlawful access to stored communications, 18 U.S.C. 2701; unlawful use of a pen register or a trap and trace device, 18 U.S.C. 3121; and abuse of eavesdropping and search authority or unlawful disclosures under the Foreign Intelligence Surveillance Act, 50 U.S.C. 1809, 1827.

[46] 18 U.S.C. 2511(1).

[47] 18 U.S.C. 2510(6). Although the governmental entities are not subject to criminal liability, as noted *infra*, some courts believe them subject to civil liability under 18 U.S.C. 2520; *Smoot v. United Transportation Union*, 246 F.3d633, 640-41 (6th Cir. 2001).

[48] "In order to underscore that the inadvertent reception of a protected communication is not a crime, the subcommittee changed the state of mind requirement under Title III of the Omnibus Crime Control and Safe Streets Act of 1968 from 'willful' to 'intentional,'" S.Rept. 541, at 23 (1986); "This provision makes clear that the inadvertent interception of a protected communication is not unlawful under this Act," H.Rept. 99-647, at 48-9 (1986). *See, e.g., In re Pharmatrak, Inc*., 329 F.3d 9, 23 (1st Cir. 2003); *Sanders v. Robert Bosch Corp*., 38 F.3d 736, 742-43 (4th Cir. 1994); *Lonegan v. Hasty*, 436 F.Supp.2d 419, 429 (E.D.N.Y. 2006); *Lewton v. Divingnzzo*, 772 F.Supp.2d 1046, 1059 (D. Nev. 2011)."But the plaintiffs need not produce direct evidence of the intentional interception; for often the only way to prove that a stealthy interception occurred is through circumstantial evidence," *McCann v. Iroquois Memorial Hospital*, 622 F.3d745, 752 (7th Cir. 2010), citing, *DirecTV v. Webb*, 545 F.3d 837, 844 (9th Cir. 2008).

[49] *Narducci v. Village of Bellwood*, 444 F. Supp. 924, 935 (N.D. Ill. 2006).

[50] "(1) Except as otherwise specifically provided in this chapter any person who—(a) intentionally intercepts, endeavors to intercept, or procures any other person to intercept or endeavor to intercept, any wire, oral, or electronic communication;

"(b) intentionally uses, endeavors to use, or procures any other person to use or endeavor to use any electronic, mechanical, or other device to intercept any oral communication when—(I) such device is affixed to, or otherwise transmits a signal through, a wire, cable, or other like connection used in wire communication; or (ii) such device transmits communications by radio, or interferes with the transmission of such communication; or (iii) such person knows, or has reason to know, that such device or any component thereof has been sent through the mail or transported in interstate or foreign commerce; or (iv) such use or endeavor to use (A) takes place on the premises of any business or other commercial establishment the operations of which affect interstate or foreign commerce; or (B) obtains or is for the purpose of obtaining information relating to the operations of any business or other commercial establishment the operations of which affect interstate or foreign commerce; or (v) such person acts in the District of Columbia, the Commonwealth of Puerto Rico, or any territory or possession of the United States," 18 U.S.C. 2511(1)(a),(b).

[51] "Subparagraph (a) establishes a blanket prohibition against the interception of wire communication. Since the facilities used to transmit wire communications form part of the interstate or foreign communications network, Congress has plenary power under the commerce clause to prohibit all interception of such communications whether by wiretapping or otherwise.

"The broad prohibition of subparagraph (a) is also applicable to the interception of oral communications. The interception of such communications, however, does not necessarily interfere with the interstate or foreign commerce network, and the extent of the constitutional power of Congress to prohibit such interception is less clear than in the case of interception of wire communications. . . .

"Therefore, in addition to the broad prohibitions of subparagraph (a), the committee has included subparagraph (b),which relies on accepted jurisdictional bases under the commerce clause, and other provisions of the Constitution toprohibit the interception of oral communications," S.Rept. 90-1097, at 91-2 (1968).

[52] DEPARTMENT OF JUSTICE CRIMINAL RESOURCE MANUAL §9-60.200 at 1050, available at http://www.justice.gov/usao/eousa/foia_reading_room/usam/title9/60mcrm.htm#9-60.400. As will be noted in a moment, the statutory definitions of wire and electronic communications contain specific commerce clause elements, but the definition of oral communications does not. Subsequent Supreme Court jurisprudence relating to the breadth of Congress's commerce clause powers indicates that the precautions may have been well

advised, *United States v. Lopez*, 514 U.S. 549 (1995) and *United States v. Morrison*, 529 U.S. 598 (2000).

[53] 18 U.S.C. 2510(4). The dictionary definition of "aural" is "of or relating to the ear or to the sense of hearing," MERRIAM-WEBSTER'S COLLEGIATE DICTIONARY 76 (10th ed. 1996).

[54] *United States v. Luong*, 471 F.3d 1107, 1109 (9th Cir. 2006)("an interception occurs where the tapped phone is located and where the law enforcement officers first overheard the call ... *United States v. Rodriguez*, 968 F.2d 130, 136 (2d Cir. 1992); *accord, United States v. Ramirez*, 112 F.3d 849, 852 (7th Cir. 1997)(concluding that an interception occurs in the jurisdiction where the tapped phone is located, where the second phone in the conversation is located, and where the scanner used to overhear the call is located); *United States v. Denman*, 100 F.3d 399, 403 (5th Cir. 1996)").

[55] *Noel v. Hall*, 568 F.3d 743, 749 (9th Cir. 2009)("In reaching this conclusion, we join a number of other circuits that have held that replaying of tapes containing recorded phone conversations does not amount to a new interception in violation of the Wiretap Act"), *citing inter alia, United States v. Hammond*, 286 F.3d 189, 193 (4th Cir. 2002); *Reynolds v. Spears*, 93 F.3d 428, 432-33 (8th Cir. 1996); *United States v. Shields*, 675 F.2d 1152, 1156 (11th Cir. 1982).

[56] S.Rept. 99-541, at 13 (1986)(the "amendment clarifies that it is illegal to intercept the non-voice portion of a wire communication. For example, it is illegal to intercept the data or digitized portion of a voice communication"); *see also*, H.Rept. 99-647, at 34 (1986).

[57] *See, United States v. Szymuszkiewicz*, 622 F.3d 701, 705-706 (7th Cir. 2010)(an employee's surreptitiously programming his supervisor's computer, so that the server forwards duplicates to the employee of all emails sent to the supervisor, constitutes an interception in violation of Title III); *United States v. Councilman*, 418 F.3d 67, 79-80(1st Cir. 2005)(en banc)(service provider's access to email "during transient storage" constitutes "interception"; without deciding whether "interception is limited to acquisition contemporaneous with transmission"); *Konop v. Hawaiian Airlines, Inc.*, 302 F.3d 868, 878 (9th Cir. 2002)(fraudulent access to stored communication does not constitute an "interception"; interception requires access contemporaneous with transmission); *United States v. Smith*, 155 F.3d 1051, 1058 (9th Cir. 1998)(unauthorized retrieval and recording of another's voice mail messages constitutes an "interception"); *United States v. Jones*, 451 F.Supp.2d 71, 75 (D.D.C. 2006)(government's acquisition from the phone company of text messages was no interception because there was no contemporaneous access); *Fraser v. National Mutual Insurance Co.*, 135 F.Supp.2d 623, 634-37 (E.D.Pa. 2001)("interception" of email occurs with its unauthorized acquisition prior to initial receipt by its addressee); *Steve Jackson Games, Inc. v. United States Secret Service*, 36 F.3d 457, 461-62 n.7 (5th Cir. 1994)(Congress did not intend for "interception" to apply to email stored on an electronic bulletin board; stored wire communications (voice mail), however, is protected from "interception"); *United States v. Meriwether*, 917 F.2d 955, 959-60 (6th Cir. 1990)(access to stored information through the use of another's pager does not constitute an "interception"); *United States v. Reyes*, 922 F. Supp. 818, 836-37 (S.D.N.Y. 1996)(same); *Wesley College v. Pitts*, 947 F. Supp. 375, 385 (D. Del. 1997)(no "interception" occurs when the contents of electronic communications are acquired unless contemporaneous with their transmission); *Cardinal Health 414, Inc. v. Adams*, 582 F.Supp.2d 967, 979-81 (M.D. Tenn. 2008)(same); *see also, Adams v. Battle Creek*, 250 F.3d 980, 982 (6th Cir. 2001)(use of a "clone" or duplicate pager to simultaneously receive the same message as a target pager is an "interception"); *Brown v. Waddell*, 50 F.3d 285, 294 (4th Cir. 1995)(same).

[58] 115 Stat. 283 (2001). Such recourse to the procedures of the Stored Communications Act must still comply with the demands of the Fourth Amendment, *see, United States v. Warshak*, 631 F.3d 266, 288 (6th Cir. 2010)("Accordingly, we hold that a subscriber enjoys a reasonable expectation of privacy in the contents of emails that are stored with, or sent or received through, a commercial ISP. The government may not compel a commercial ISP to turn over the contents of a subscriber's emails without first obtaining a warrant based on

probable cause. Therefore, because they did not obtain a warrant, the government agents violated the Fourth Amendment when they obtained the contents of Warshak's emails. Moreover, to the extent that the SCA purports to permit the government to obtain such emails warrantlessly, the SCA is unconstitutional").

[59] 18 U.S.C. 2510(8). *In re iPhone Application Litigation*, 844 F.Supp.2d 1040, 1061 (2012)("In *United States v. Reed*, 575 F.3d 900 (9th Cir. 2009), the Ninth Circuit held that data automatically generated about a telephone call, such as the call's time of origination and its duration, do not constitute 'content' for purposes of the Wiretap Act's sealing provisions because such data 'contains no "information concerning the substance, purport, or meaning of [the] communication."' *Id.* at 916 (quoting 18 U.S.C. 2510[(8)]). Rather, 'content' is limited to information the user intended to communicate, such as the words spoken in a phone call. *Id.* Here, the allegedly intercepted electronic communications are simply users' geolocation data. This data is generated automatically, rather than through the intent of the user, and therefore does not constitute 'content' susceptible to interception").

[60] "'Post-cut-through dialed digits' are any numbers dialed from a telephone after the call is initially setup or 'cut-through.' Sometimes these digits are other telephone numbers, as when a party places a credit card call by first dialing the long distance carrier access number and then the phone number of the intended party. Sometimes these digits transmit real information, such as bank account numbers, Social Security numbers, prescription numbers, and the like. In the latter case, the digits represent communications content; in the former, they are non-content call processing numbers," *In re United States*, 441 F.Supp.2d 816, 818 (S.D. Tex. 2006).

[61] *In re United States for Orders (1) Authorizing Use of Pen Registers and Trap and Trace Devices*, 515 F.Supp.2d 325, 328-38 (E.D.N.Y. 2007); *In re United States*, 441 F.Supp.2d 816, 818-27 (S.D. Tex. 2006).

[62] 18 U.S.C. 2510(4). *United States v. Jones*, 451 F.Supp.2d 71, 75 (D.D.C. 2006)(government's acquisition from the phone company of text messages was not an interception because it did not involve contemporaneous access and because no electronic, mechanical, or other devices were used).

[63] *United States v. Szymuszkiewicz*, 622 F.3d 701, 707 (7th Cir. 2010)("Thus Szymuszkiewicz acquired the emails by using at least three devices: Infusino's computer (where the rule [directing surreptitious duplication of incoming emails] was set up), the Kansas City server (where the rule caused each message to be duplicated and sent his way),and his own computer (where the messages were received, read, and sometimes stored").

[64] "'[E]lectronic, mechanical, or other device' means any device or apparatus which can be used to intercept a wire, oral, or electronic communication other than—(a) any telephone or telegraph instrument, equipment or facility, or any component thereof, (i) furnished to the subscriber or user by a provider of wire or electronic communication service in the ordinary course of its business and being used by the subscriber or user in the ordinary course of its business or furnished by such subscriber or user for connection to the facilities of such service and used in the ordinary course of its business; or (ii) being used by a provider of wire or electronic communication service in the ordinary course of its business, or by an investigative or law enforcement officer in the ordinary course of his duties; (b) a hearing aid or similar device being used to correct subnormal hearing to not better than normal," 18 U.S.C. 2510(5).

[65] See the cases cited and commentary in Barnett & Makar, *"In the Ordinary Course of Business": The Legal Limits of Workplace Wiretapping*, 10 HASTINGS JOURNAL OF COMMUNICATIONS AND ENTERTAINMENT LAW 715 (1988); *Application to Extension Telephones of Title III of the Omnibus Crime Control and Safe Streets Act of 1968 (18 U.S.C. §§2510 et seq.), Pertaining to Interceptions of Wire Communications*, 58 ALR Fed. 594; *Eavesdropping on Extension Telephone as Invasion of Privacy*, 49 ALR 4th 430.

[66] *E.g., Deal v. Spears*, 780 F. Supp. 618, 623 (W.D. Ark. 1991), *aff'd*, 980 F.2d 1153 (8th Cir. 1992)(employer regularly taped employee calls by means of a device attached to an

extension phone; most of the calls were personal and recording and disclosing them served no business purpose).

67 *Adams v. Battle Creek*, 250 F.3d 980, 983 (6th Cir. 2001); *Arias v. Mutual Central Alarm Service*, 202 F.3d 553, 558 (2d Cir. 2000); *Berry v. Funk*, 146 F.3d 1003, 1008 (D.C. Cir. 1998); *Sanders v. Robert Bosch Corp.*, 38 F.3d 736, 741 (4th Cir. 1994). *See also, Hall v. Earthlink Network Inc.*, 396 F.3d 500, 503-04 (2d Cir. 2005) (Internet service provider's receipt and storage of former customer's email after termination of the customer's account was done in ordinary course of business and consequently did not constitute an interception).

Some courts include surreptitious, extension phone interceptions conducted within the family home as part of the "business extension" exception, *Anonymous v. Anonymous*, 558 F.2d 677, 678-79 (2d Cir. 1977); *Scheib v. Grant*, 22 F.3d 149, 154 (7th Cir. 1994); *Newcomb v. Ingle*, 944 F.2d 1534, 1536 (10th Cir. 1991); *contra, United States v. Murdock*, 63 F.3d 1391, 1400 (6th Cir. 1995).

68 *Adams v. Battle Creek*, 250 F.3d at 984; *see also, United States v. Lewis*, 406 F.3d 11, 18 (1st Cir. 2005); *United States v. Hammond*, 286 F.3d 189, 192 (4th Cir. 2002); *Smith v. U.S. Dept. of Justice*, 251 F.3d 1047, 1049-50 (D.C. Cir. 2001); *United States v. Poyck*, 77 F.3d 285, 292 (9th Cir. 1996); *United States v. Daniels*, 902 F.2d 1238, 1245 (7th Cir. 1990); *United States v. Paul*, 614 F.2d 115, 117 (6th Cir. 1980).

69 *Amati v. Woodstock*, 176 F.3d 952, 955 (7th Cir. 1999)("Investigation is within the ordinary course of law enforcement, so if 'ordinary' were read literally warrants would rarely if ever be required for electronic eavesdropping, which was surely not Congress's intent. Since the purpose of the statute was primarily to regulate the use of wiretapping and other electronic surveillance for investigatory purposes, gordinary' should not be read so broadly; it is more reasonably interpreted to refer to routine non investigative recording of telephone conversations"); *accord, United States v. Lewis*, 416 F.3d at 11; *Colandrea v. Orangetown*, 411 F.Supp.2d 342, 347-48 (S.D.N.Y. 2007).

70 The exception, however, does not permit a county to record all calls in and out of the offices of county judges merely because a detention center and the judges share a common facility, *Abraham v. Greenville*, 237 F.3d 386, 390 (4th Cir. 2001), nor does it permit jailhouse telephone monitoring of an inmate's confession to a clergyman, *Mockaitis v. Harcleroad*, 104 F.3d 1522, 1530 (9th Cir. 1997). The courts are divided over whether private corrections officials are covered by the law enforcement exception. *Compare, United States v. Faulkner*, 323 F. Supp.2d 1111, 1113-17 (D. Kan. 2004), *aff'd on other grounds*, 439 F.3d 1221 (10th Cir. 2006) (not covered) *with, United States v. Rivera*, 292 F. Supp.2d 838, 842-43 (E.D.Va. 2003) (covered).

71 *United States v. Larios*, 593 F.3d 82, 90-91 (1st Cir. 2010); *United States v. Falls*, 34 F.3d 674, 679-80 (8th Cir. 1994); *United States v. Koyomejian*, 970 F.2d 536, 538 (9th Cir. 1992); *United States v. Biasucci*, 786 F.2d 505, 508-509 (2d Cir. 1986); *United States v. Torres*, 751 F.2d 875, 880-81 (7th Cir. 1984).

72 "'[O]ral communication' means any oral communication uttered by a person exhibiting an expectation that such communication is not subject to interception under circumstances justifying such expectation, but such term does not include any electronic communication," 18 U.S.C. 2510(2). *United States v. Larios*, 593 F.3d 82, 92 (1st Cir. 2010)(emphasis in the original but most internal quotation marks and citations omitted)(The "legislative history of this statutory provision shows that Congress intended this definition to parallel the 'reasonable expectation of privacy test' articulated by the Supreme Court in *Katz*. Thus, for Title III to apply, the court must conclude: (1) the defendant had an actual, subjective expectation of privacy—*i.e.*, that his communications were not subject to interception; and (2) the defendant's expectation is one society would objectively consider reasonable.... We conclude that the most reasonable reading of the statute is that the meaning of 'oral communication' was intended to parallel *evolving* Fourth Amendment jurisprudence on

reasonable expectations of privacy in one's communications"); *Pattee v. Georgia Ports Authority*, 512 F.Supp.2d 1372, 1376-377 (S.D.Ga. 2007).

[73] "'[W]ire communication' means any aural transfer made in whole or in part through the use of facilities for the transmission of communications by the aid of wire, cable, or other like connection between the point of origin and the point of reception (including the use of such connection in a switching station) furnished or operated by any person engaged in providing or operating such facilities for the transmission of interstate or foreign communications or communications affecting interstate or foreign commerce," 18 U.S.C. 2510(1).

[74] "'[E]lectronic communication' means any transfer of signs, signals, writing, images, sounds, data, or intelligence of any nature transmitted in whole or in part by a wire, radio, electromagnetic, photoelectronic or photooptical system that affects interstate or foreign commerce, but does not include—(A) the radio portion of a cordless telephone communication that is transmitted between the cordless handset and the base unit; (B) any wire or oral communication; (C) any communication made through a tone-only paging device; or (D) any communication from a tracking device (as defined in section 3117 of this title)," 18 U.S.C. 2510(12).

[75] 18 U.S.C. 2511(2)(g).

[76] 18 U.S.C. 2511(1).

[77] 18 U.S.C. 2512, discussed, *infra*.

[78] *E.g.*, 47 U.S.C. 605 (1940 ed.).

[79] *On Lee v. United States*, 343 U.S. 747 (1952); *Lopez v. United States*, 373 U.S. 427 (1963); *United States v. White*, 401 U.S. 745 (1971).

[80] *United States v. White*, 401 U.S. at 751 (1971)("Concededly a police agent who conceals his police connections may write down for official use his conversations with a defendant and testify concerning them, without a warrant authorizing his encounters with the defendant and without otherwise violating the latter's Fourth Amendment rights.... For constitutional purposes, no different result is required if the agent instead of immediately reporting and transcribing his conversations with defendant, either (1) simultaneously records them with electronic equipment which he is carrying on his person, *Lopez v. United States, supra*; (2) or carries radio equipment which simultaneously transmits the conversations either to recording equipment located elsewhere or to other agents monitoring the transmitting frequency. *On Lee v. United States, supra*. If the conduct and revelations of an agent operating without electronic equipment do not invade the defendant's constitutionally justifiable expectations of privacy, neither does a simultaneous recording of the same conversations made by the agent or by others from transmissions received from the agent to whom the defendant is talking and whose trustworthiness the defendant necessarily risks"); *Lopez v. United States* 373 U.S. 427, 439 (1963)("Stripped to its essentials, petitioner's argument amounts to saying that he has a constitutional right to rely on possible flaws in the agent's memory, or to challenge the agent's credibility without being beset by corroborating evidence that is not susceptible of impeachment. For no other argument can justify excluding an accurate version of a conversation that the agent could testify to from memory. We think the risk that petitioner took in offering a bribe to Davis fairly included the risk that the offer would be accurately reproduced in court, whether by faultless memory or mechanical recording").

[81] "(c) It shall not be unlawful under this chapter for a person acting under color of law to intercept a wire, oral, or electronic communication, where such person is a party to the communication or one of the parties to the communication has given prior consent to such interception.

"(d) It shall not be unlawful under this chapter for a person not acting under color of law to intercept a wire, oral, or electronic communication where such person is a party to the communication or where one of the parties to the communication has given prior consent to such interception unless such communication is intercepted for the purpose of committing any criminal or tortious act in violation of the Constitution or laws of the United States or of any State," 18 U.S.C. 2511(2)(c), (d).

[82] For citations to state law, *see*, **Appendix B.**

[83] *United States v. Verdin-Garcia*, 516 F.3d 884, 894-95 (10th Cir. 2008) (inmate use of prison phone); *United States v. Friedman*, 300 F.3d 111, 122-23 (2d Cir. 2002)(same); *United States v. Hammond*, 286 F.3d 189, 192 (4th Cir. 2002) (same); *United States v. Footman*, 215 F.3d 145, 154-55 (1st Cir. 2000) (same); *Griggs-Ryan v. Smith*, 904 F.2d 112, 116-17 (1st Cir. 1990) (use of landlady's phone); *United States v. Rivera*, 292 F. Supp.2d 838, 843-45 (E.D.Va. 2003) (inmate use of prison phone monitored by private contractors); *see also, United States v. Conley*, 531 F.3d 56, 58-9 (1st Cir. 2008)(explicit consent as a condition for phone privileges).

[84] *Anthony v. United States*, 667 F.2d 870, 876 (10th Cir. 1981).

[85] *United States v. Antoon*, 933 F.2d 200, 203-204 (3d Cir. 1991). *But see*, *O'Ferrell v. United States*, 968 F.Supp. 1519, 1541 (M.D.Ala. 1997) (an individual who spoke to his wife on the telephone after being told by FBI agents who were then executing a search warrant at his place of business that he could only speak to her with the agents listening in consented to the interception, even if FBI's initial search was unconstitutional).

[86] 18 U.S.C. 2511(2)(d); *United States v. Lam*, 271 F.Supp.2d 1182, 1183-184 (N.D.Cal. 2003).

[87] *Caro v. Weintraub*, 618 F.3d 94, 100 (2d Cir. 2010)("We join the courts that have considered this question, and hold that a cause of action under §2511(2)(d) requires that the interceptor intend to commit a crime or tort independent of the act of recording itself"), citing, *Desnick v. American Broadcasting Co.*, 44 F.3d 1345, 1347-48 (7th Cir. 1995); *Sussman v. American Broadcasting Co*, 186 F.3d 1200, 1201 (9th Cir. 1999).

[88] S.Rept. 99-541, at 17-8 (1986); H.Rept. 99-647, at 39-40 (1986).

[89] "(g) It shall not be unlawful under this chapter or chapter 121 of this title for any person—(i) to intercept or access an electronic communication made through an electronic communication system that is configured so that such electronic communication is readily accessible to the general public;

"(ii) to intercept any radio communication which is transmitted—(I) by any station for the use of the general public, or that relates to ships, aircraft, vehicles, or persons in distress; (II) by any governmental, law enforcement, civil defense, private land mobile, or public safety communications system, including police and fire, readily accessible to the general public; (III) by a station operating on an authorized frequency within the bands allocated to the amateur, citizens band, or general mobile radio services; or (IV) by any marine or aeronautical communications system;

"(iii) to engage in any conduct which—(I) is prohibited by section 633 of the Communications Act of 1934; or (II) is excepted from the application of section 705(a) of the Communications Act of 1934 by section 705(b) of that Act;

"(iv) to intercept any wire or electronic communication the transmission of which is causing harmful interference to any lawfully operating station or consumer electronic equipment, to the extent necessary to identify the source of such interference; or

"(v) for other users of the same frequency to intercept any radio communication made through a system that utilizes frequencies monitored by individuals engaged in the provision or the use of such system, if such communication is not scrambled or encrypted," 18 U.S.C. 2511(2)(g).

[90] "*Except as otherwise specifically provided in this chapter* any person who (a) intentionally intercepts.... " 18 U.S.C. 2511(1)(emphasis added).

[91] "Notwithstanding any other provision of this chapter, any investigative or law enforcement officer, specially designated by the Attorney General, the Deputy Attorney General, the Associate Attorney General, or by the principal prosecuting attorney of any State or subdivision thereof acting pursuant to a statute of that State, who reasonably determines that—(a) an emergency situation exists that involves—(i) immediate danger of death or serious physical injury to any person, (ii) conspiratorial activities threatening the national

security interest, or (iii) conspiratorial activities characteristic of organized crime, [—] that requires a wire, oral, or electronic communication to be intercepted before an order authorizing such interception can, with due diligence, be obtained, and (b) there are grounds upon which an order could be entered under this chapter to authorize such interception, may intercept such wire, oral, or electronic communication if an application for an order approving the interception is made in accordance with this section within forty-eight hours after the interception has occurred, or begins to occur. In the absence of an order, such interception shall immediately terminate when the communication sought is obtained or when the application for the order is denied, whichever is earlier. In the event such application for approval is denied, or in any other case where the interception is terminated without an order having been issued, the contents of any wire, oral, or electronic communication intercepted shall be treated as having been obtained in violation of this chapter, and an inventory shall be served as provided for in subsection (d) of this section on the person named in the application," 18 U.S.C. 2518(7).

92 "(i) It shall not be unlawful under this chapter for a person acting under color of law to intercept the wire or electronic communications of a computer trespasser transmitted to, through, or from the protected computer, if—(I) the owner or operator of the protected computer authorizes the interception of the computer trespasser's communications on the protected computer; (II) the person acting under color of law is lawfully engaged in an investigation; (III) the person acting under color of law has reasonable grounds to believe that the contents of the computer trespasser's communications will be relevant to the investigation; and (IV) such interception does not acquire communications other than those transmitted to or from the computer trespasser," 18 U.S.C. 2511(2)(i).

93 "(e) Notwithstanding any other provision of this title or section 705 or 706 of the Communications Act of 1934, it shall not be unlawful for an officer, employee, or agent of the United States in the normal course of his official duty to conduct electronic surveillance, as defined in section 101 of the Foreign Intelligence Surveillance Act of 1978, as authorized by that Act," 18 U.S.C. 2511(2)(e).

94 "(h) It shall not be unlawful under this chapter—(I) to use a pen register or a trap and trace device (as those terms are defined for the purpose of chapter 206)…." 18 U.S.C. 2511(2)(h). Neither the stored communications sections in chapter 121 nor the pen register and trap and trace device in chapter 206 authorize the contemporaneous interception of the contents of a communication. For the citations to state statutes permitting judicial authorization of law enforcement interception of wire, oral, or electronic communications, for access to stored electronic communications, and for the use of pen registers and trap and trace devices, *see*, Appendix D.

95 "(a)(i) It shall not be unlawful under this chapter for an operator of a switchboard, or an officer, employee, or agent of a provider of wire or electronic communication service, whose facilities are used in the transmission of a wire orel ectronic communication, to intercept, disclose, or use that communication in the normal course of his employment while engaged in any activity which is a necessary incident to the rendition of his service or to the protection of the rights or property of the provider of that service, except that a provider of wire communication service to the public shall not utilize service observing or random monitoring except for mechanical or service quality control checks....

"(h) It shall not be unlawful under this chapter ...

"(ii) for a provider of electronic communication service to record the fact that a wire or electronic communication was initiated or completed in order to protect such provider, another provider furnishing service toward the completion of the wire or electronic communication, or a user of that service, from fraudulent, unlawful or abusive use of such service," 18 U.S.C. 2511(2)(a)(I), (h).

96 "(ii) Notwithstanding any other law, providers of wire or electronic communication service, their officers, employees, and agents, landlords, custodians, or other persons, are authorized to provide information, facilities, or technical assistance to persons authorized by law to

intercept wire, oral, or electronic communications or to conduct electronic surveillance, as defined in section 101 of the Foreign Intelligence Surveillance Act of 1978, if such provider, its officers, employees, or agents, landlord, custodian, or other specified person, has been provided with—
(A) a court order directing such assistance signed by the authorizing judge, or
(B) a certification in writing by a person specified in section 2518(7) of this title or the Attorney General of the United States that no warrant or court order is required by law, that all statutory requirements have been met, and that the specified assistance is required,
setting forth the period of time during which the provision of the information, facilities, or technical assistance is authorized and specifying the information, facilities, or technical assistance required. No provider of wire or electronic communication service, officer, employee, or agent thereof, or landlord, custodian, or other specified person shall disclose the existence of any interception or surveillance or the device used to accomplish the interception or surveillance with respect to which the person has been furnished a court order or certification under this chapter, except as may otherwise be required by legal process and then only after prior notification to the Attorney General or to the principal prosecuting attorney of a State or any political subdivision of a State, as may be appropriate. Any such disclosure, shall render such person liable for the civil damages provided for in section 2520. No cause of action shall lie in any court against any provider of wire or electronic communication service, its officers, employees, or agents, landlord, custodian, or other specified person for providing information, facilities, or assistance in accordance with the terms of a court order, statutory authorization, or certification under this chapter," 18 U.S.C. 2511(2)(a)(ii).

[97] "(b) It shall not be unlawful under this chapter for an officer, employee, or agent of the Federal Communications Commission, in the normal course of his employment and in discharge of the monitoring responsibilities exercised by the Commission in the enforcement of chapter 5 of title 47 of the United States Code, to intercept a wire or electronic communication, or oral communication transmitted by radio, or to disclose or use the information thereby obtained," 18 U.S.C. 2511(2)(b).

[98] *Pollock v. Pollock*, 154 F.3d 601, 611 (8th Cir. 1998); *Wagner v. Wagner*, 64 F.Supp.2d 895, 889-901 (D.Minn. 1999); *Campbell v. Price*, 2 F.Supp.2d 1186, 1191-192 (E.D.Ark. 1998); *Thompson v. Dulaney*, 838 F.Supp. 1535,1544-45 (D.Utah 1993); cf., *Babb v. Eagleton*, 616 F.Supp.2d 1195, 1205-206 (N.D.Okla. 2007).

[99] *Glazner v. Glazner*, 347 F.3d 1212, 1215-16 (11th Cir. 2003); *Heggy v. Heggy*, 944 F.2d 1537, 1539 (10th Cir. 1991); *Kempf v. Kempf*, 868 F.2d 970, 972 (8th Cir. 1989); *Pritchard v. Pritchard*, 732 F.2d 372, 374 (4th Cir. 1984); *UnitedStates v. Jones*, 542 F.2d 661, 667 (6th Cir. 1976); *Kratz v. Kratz*, 477 F.Supp. 463, 467-70 (E.D.Pa. 1979); *Heyman v.Heyman*, 548 F.Supp. 1041, 1045-47 (N.D.Ill.1982); *Lombardo v. Lombardo*, 192 F.Supp.2d 885, 809 (N.D.Ill. 2002).

[100] *Simpson v. Simpson*, 490 F.2d 803, 809 (5th Cir. 1974); *Perfit v. Perfit*, 693 F.Supp. 851, 854-56 (C.D.Cal. 1988); *see generally, Applicability, in Civil Action, of Provisions of Omnibus Crime Control and Safe Streets Act of 1968 Prohibiting Interception of Communications (18 USCS §2511(1)), to Interception by Spouse, or Spouse's Agent, of Conversations of Other Spouse*, 139 ALR Fed. 517, and the cases discussed therein.

[101] *Anonymous v. Anonymous*, 558 F.2d 677, 678-79 (2d Cir. 1977); *Scheib v. Grant*, 22 F.3d 149, 154 (7th Cir. 1994); *Newcomb v. Ingle*, 944 F.2d 1534, 1536 (10th Cir. 1991); cf., *Babb v. Eagleton*, 616 F.Supp.2d 1195, 1203-205 (N.D. Okla. 2007); *contra, United States v. Murdock*, 63 F.3d 1391, 1400 (6th Cir. 1995).

[102] 18 U.S.C. 2511(1)(c).

[103] *McCann v. Iroquois Memorial Hospital*, 622 F.3d 745, 753 (7th Cir. 2010), citing, *Nix v. O'Malley*, 160 F.3d 343, 348 (6th Cir. 1998); *Williams v. Poulos*, 11 F.3d 271, 284 (1st Cir. 1993); and *Thompson v. Dulaney*, 970 F.2d 744, 749 (10th Cir. 1992).

[104] *Bartnicki v. Vopper*, 532 U.S. 514, 533-34 (2001). Bartnicki was a union negotiator whose telephone conversations with the union's president concerning teachers' contract negotiations were surreptitiously intercepted and recorded. During the conversation, the possibility of using violence against school board members was mentioned. After the teachers' contract was signed, the unknown wiretapper secretly supplied Yocum, a critic of the union's position, with a copy of the tape. Yocum in turn played it for members of the school board and turned it over to Vopper, a radio talk show host, who played it on his show. Other stations and media outlets published the contents as well. Bartnicki sued Vopper and Yocum for use and disclosure in violation of sections 2511(1)(c) and 2511(1)(d). Vopper and Yocum offered a free speech defense, which the Supreme Court accepted. *But see*, *Quigley v. Rosenthal*, 327 F.3d 1044, 1067-68 (10th Cir. 2003) (denying First Amendment protection for those knowingly involved with interceptors of private matters (not public concerns)); *Boehner v. McDermott*, 484 F.3d 573, 577-81 (D.C.Cir. 2007)(Members of Congress do not have a First Amendment right to disclose unlawful wiretap information in violation of House rules).

[105] "Subparagraphs (c) and (d) prohibit, in turn, the disclosure or use of the contents of any intercepted communication by any person knowing or having reason to know the information was obtained through an interception in violation of this subsection. The disclosure of the contents of an intercepted communication that had already become 'public information' or 'common knowledge' would not be prohibited. The scope of this knowledge required to violate either subparagraph reflects existing law (*Pereira v. United States*, 347 U.S. 1 (1954))," S.Rept. 90-1097, at 93 (1967).

[106] "Any investigative or law enforcement officer who, by any means authorized by this chapter, has obtained knowledge of the contents of any wire, oral, or electronic communication, or evidence derived therefrom, may disclose such contents to another investigative or law enforcement officer to the extent that such disclosure is appropriate to the proper performance of the official duties of the officer making or receiving the disclosure," 18 U.S.C. 2517(1).

[107] "Any person who has received, by any means authorized by this chapter, any information concerning a wire, oral, or electronic communication, or evidence derived therefrom intercepted in accordance with the provisions of this chapter may disclose the contents of that communication or such derivative evidence while giving testimony under oath or affirmation in any proceeding held under the authority of the United States or of any State or political subdivision thereof," 18 U.S.C. 2517(3). This does not entitle private litigants to disclosure in the view of at least one court, *In re Motion to Unseal Electronic Surveillance Evidence*, 990 F.2d 1015 (8th Cir. 1993).

When court-ordered interception results in evidence of a crime other than the crime with respect to which the order was issued, the evidence is admissible only upon a judicial finding that it was otherwise secured in compliance with Title III/ECPA requirements, 18 U.S.C. 2517(5).

[108] 18 U.S.C. 2511(1)(e). When acting with a similar intent, disclosure of the *fact* of authorized federal wiretap or foreign intelligence gathering is proscribed elsewhere in title 18: "Whoever, having knowledge that a Federal investigative or law enforcement officer has been authorized or has applied for authorization under chapter 119 to intercept a wire, oral, or electronic communication, in order to obstruct, impede, or prevent such interception, gives notice or attempts to give notice of the possible interception to any person shall be fined under this title or imprisoned not more than five years, or both," 18 U.S.C. 2232(d).

"Whoever, having knowledge that a Federal officer has been authorized or has applied for authorization to conduct electronic surveillance under the Foreign Intelligence Surveillance Act of 1978 (50 U.S.C. 1801, et seq.), in order to obstruct, impede, or prevent such activity, gives notice or attempts to give notice of the possible activity to any person shall be fined under this title or imprisoned not more than five years, or both," 18 U.S.C. 2232(e).

[109] 18 U.S.C. 2511(1)(e), (4)(a), 2520(a), (g).

[110] 18 U.S.C. 2516(2).

[111] *Id.*

[112] 18 U.S.C. 2511(3)(a) ("Except as provided in paragraph (b) of this subsection, a person or entity providing an electronic communication service to the public shall not intentionally divulge the contents of any communication (other than one to such person or entity, or an agent thereof) while in transmission on that service to any person or entity other than an addressee or intended recipient of such communication or an agent of such addressee or intended recipient").

[113] 18 U.S.C. 2511(3)(b) ("A person or entity providing electronic communication service to the public may divulge the contents of any such communication—(i) as otherwise authorized in section 2511(2)(a) or 2517 of this title; (ii) with the lawful consent of the originator or any addressee or intended recipient of such communication; (iii) to a person employed or authorized, or whose facilities are used, to forward such communication to its destination; or (iv) which were inadvertently obtained by the service provider and which appear to pertain to the commission of a crime, if such divulgence is made to a law enforcement agency").

[114] Note that subsection 2520(d) establishes a good faith defense that specifically references the prohibition: "A good faith reliance on ... (3) a good faith determination that section 2511(3) ... of this title permitted the conduct complained of; is a complete defense against any civil or criminal action brought under this chapter.... "

[115] 18 U.S.C. 2511(1)(d).

[116] *See e.g., McCann v. Iroquois Memorial Hospital*, 622 F.3d 745, 753-54 (7th Cir. 2010).

[117] "Subparagraphs (c) and (d) prohibit, in turn, the disclosure or use of the contents of any intercepted communication by any person knowing or having reason to know the information was obtained through an interception in violation of this subsection," S.Rept. 90-1097, at 93 (1967).

[118] *Compare*, 18 U.S.C. 2517(1)("Any investigative or law enforcement officer who, by any means authorized by this chapter, has obtained knowledge of the contents of any wire, oral, or electronic communication, or evidence derived therefrom, may disclose such contents to another investigative or law enforcement officer to the extent that such disclosure is appropriate to the proper performance of the official duties of the officer making or receiving the disclosure"), *with* 18 U.S.C. 2517(2)("Any investigative or law enforcement officer who, by any means authorized by this chapter, has obtained knowledge of the contents of any wire, oral, or electronic communication or evidence derived therefrom may use such contents to the extent such use is appropriate to the proper performance of his official duties").

On the other hand, the Supreme Court in *Bartnicki* seemed to parse the constitutionally suspect ban on disclosure from the constitutionally permissible ban on use. *Bartnicki v. Vopper*, 532 U.S. 514, 526-27 (2001)("[T]he naked prohibition against disclosures is fairly characterized as a regulation of pure speech. Unlike the prohibition against the guse' of the contents of an illegal interception in §2511(1)(d), subsection (c) is not a regulation of conduct").

[119] *Forsyth v. Barr*, 19 F.3d 1527, 1541-545 (5th Cir. 1994); *United States v. Murdock*, 63 F.3d 1391, 1400-403 (6th Cir. 1995); *contra, United States v. Crabtree*, 565 F.3d 887, 889 (4th Cir. 2009); *Berry v. Funk*, 146 F.3d 1003, 1011-13 (D.C.Cir. 1998); *Chandler v. United States Army*, 125 F.3d 1296, 1300-302 (9th Cir. 1997); *In re Grand Jury*, 111 F.3d 1066, 1077 (3d Cir. 1997); *United States v. Vest*, 813 F.2d 477, 481 (1st Cir. 1987).

[120] 18 U.S.C. 2511(4), 2520(a), (g).

[121] "It shall not be unlawful under this section for—(a) a provider of wire or electronic communication service or an officer, agent, or employee of, or a person under contract with, such a provider, in the normal course of the business of providing that wire or electronic communication service ... to send through the mail, send or carry in interstate or foreign commerce, or manufacture, assemble, possess, or sell any electronic, mechanical, or other

device knowing or having reason to know that the design of such device renders it primarily useful for the purpose of the surreptitious interception of wire, oral, or electronic communications," 18 U.S.C. 2512(2)(a).

122 "(2) It shall not be unlawful under this section for ... (b) an officer, agent, or employee of, or a person under contract with, the United States, a State, or a political subdivision thereof, in the normal course of the activities of the United States, a State, or a political subdivision thereof, to send through the mail, send or carry in interstate or foreign commerce, or manufacture, assemble, possess, or sell any electronic, mechanical, or other device knowing or having reason to know that the design of such device renders it primarily useful for the purpose of the surreptitious interception of wire, oral, or electronic communications.
"(3) It shall not be unlawful under this section to advertise for sale a device described in subsection (1) of this section if the advertisement is mailed, sent, or carried in interstate or foreign commerce solely to a domestic provider of wire or electronic communication service or to an agency of the United States, a State, or a political subdivision thereof whichis duly authorized to use such device," 18 U.S.C. 2512(2)(b),(3).

123 *United States v. Spy Factory, Inc.*, 951 F.Supp. 450, 473-75 (S.D.N.Y. 1997); *United States v. Bast*, 495 F.2d 138, 141 (D.C.Cir. 1974).

124 *United States v. Simels*, 654 F.3d 161, 171 (2d Cir. 2011).

125 18 U.S.C. 2512.

126 S.Rept. 90-1097, at 95 (1968).

127 The two appellate panel decisions that found the devices beyond the bounds of section 2512, *United States v. Herring*, 933 F.2d 932 (11th Cir. 1991) and *United States v. Hux*, 940 F.2d 314 (8th Cir. 1991) were overturned en banc, *United States v. Herring*, 993 F.2d 784, 786 (11th Cir. 1993); *United States v. Davis*, 978 F.2d 415, 416 (8th Cir. 1992).

128 *United States v. Harrell*, 983 F.2d 36, 37-39 (5th Cir. 1993); *United States v. One Macom Video Cipher II*, 985 F.2d 258, 259-61 (6th Cir. 1993); *United States v. Shriver*, 989 F.2d. 898, 901-06 (7th Cir. 1992); *United States v. Davis*, 978 F.2d 415, 417-20 (8th Cir. 1992); *United States v. Lande*, 968 F.2d 907, 910-11 (9th Cir. 1992); *United States v. McNutt*, 908 F.2d 561, 564-65 (10th Cir. 1990); *United States v. Herring*, 993 F.2d 784, 786-89 (11th Cir. 1991).

129 *DirecTV, Inc. v. Treworgy*, 373 F.3d 1124, 1129 (11th Cir. 2004); *DirecTV, Inc. v. Robson*, 420 F.3d 532, 538-39 (5th Cir. 2005)(citing several district court cases that have reached the same conclusion). Proof that the possessor used the device to intercept satellite transmission evidences a violation of section 2511 and exposure to civil liability under section 2520, *DirecTV, Inc. v. Nicholas*, 403 F.3d 223, 227-28 (4th Cir. 2005); *DirecTV, Inc. v. Pepe*, 431 F.3d 162, 169 (3d Cir. 2005).

130 18 U.S.C. 2516-2518.

131 18 U.S.C. 2511(2)(c).

132 18 U.S.C. 2511(2)(i)("It shall not be unlawful under this chapter for a person acting under color of law to intercept the wire or electronic communications of a computer trespasser transmitted to, through, or from the protected computer, if—(I) the owner or operator of the protected computer authorizes the interception of the computer trespasser's communications on the protected computer; (II) the person acting under color of law is lawfully engaged in an investigation; (III) the person acting under color of law has reasonable grounds to believe that the contents of the computer trespasser's communications will be relevant to the investigation; and (IV) such interception does not acquire communications other than those transmitted to or from the computer trespasser").
A computer trespasser is a person who: (A) "accesses a protected computer without authorization and thus has no reasonable expectation of privacy in any communication transmitted to, through, or from the protected computer; and
(B) does not include a person known by the owner or operator of the protected computer to have an existing contractual relationship with the owner or operator of the protected computer for access to all or part of the protected computer," 18 U.S.C. 2510(21).

133 "The Attorney General, Deputy Attorney General, Associate Attorney General, or any Assistant Attorney General, any acting Assistant Attorney General, or any Deputy Assistant Attorney General or acting Deputy Assistant Attorney General in the Criminal Division specially designated by the Attorney General, may authorize an application to a Federal judge of competent jurisdiction for, and such judge may grant in conformity with section 2518 of this chapter an order authorizing or approving the interception of wire or oral communications by the Federal Bureau of Investigation, or a Federal agency having responsibility for the investigation of the offense as to which the application is made, when such interception may provide or has provided evidence of [the predicate offenses]...." 18 U.S.C. 2516(1).

Subsection 2516(1) "plainly calls for the prior, informed judgment of enforcement officers desiring court approval for intercept authority, and investigative personnel may not themselves ask a judge for authority to wiretap or eavesdrop. The mature judgment of a particular, responsible Department of Justice official is interposed as a critical precondition of any judicial order," *United States v. Giordano*, 416 U.S. 505, 515-16 (1974). Evidence generated without such senior approval must be suppressed, *id.* at 23. However, "suppression is not warranted ... when a wiretap application or order either misidentifies a DOJ official who could not legally authorize the wiretap or, ... identifies no official at all, so long as the record shows that a statutorily designated official actually gave the authorization," *United States v. Gray*, 521 F.3d 514, 526-27 (6th Cir. 2008), *citing in accord, United States v. Callum*, 410 F.3d 571, 576 (9th Cir. 2005); *United States v. Radcliff*, 331 F.3d 1153, 1160-163 (10th Cir. 2003); *United States v. Fudge*, 325 F.3d 910, 918 (7th Cir. 2003).

134 The list appears in 18 U.S.C. 2516(1).

135 18 U.S.C. 2516(1)(*l*).

136 "Any attorney for the Government (as such term is defined for the purposes of the Federal Rules of Criminal Procedure) may authorize an application to a Federal judge of competent jurisdiction for, and such judge may grant, inconformity with section 2518 of this title, an order authorizing or approving the interception of electronic communications by an investigative or law enforcement officer having responsibility for the investigation of the offense as to which the application is made, when such interception may provide or has provided evidence of any Federal felony," 18 U.S.C. 2516(3); *e.g., United States v. Benjamin*, 72 F.Supp.2d 161, 189 (W.D.N.Y. 1999).

137 18 U.S.C. 2516(2).

138 Identification of the place where, or facilities over which, the targeted communications are to occur may be excused where the court finds that the suspect has or will take steps to thwart interception, 18 U.S.C. 2518(11), (12); *United States v. Oliva*, 686 F.3d 1106, 1109-110 (9th Cir. 2012).

139 18 U.S.C. 2518(1), (2).

140 18 U.S.C. 2518(3). Paragraphs 2518(3)(a) and (b) mirror the probable demands of the Fourth Amendment, i.e., that the court find probable cause to believe that the interception will capture evidence of a specific offense, *United States v.Abu-Jihaad*, 630 F.3d 102, 122 (2d Cir. 2010), *citing, Dalia v. United States*, 441 U.S. 238, 255 (1979). Title III, however, provides its own particularity requirements relating to targets, facilities, locations, and crimes, *United States v. Gaines*, 639 F.3d 423, 430 (8th Cir. 2011), *citing inter alia, United States v. Donovan*, 429 U.S. 413, 427 n.15 (1977).

141 18 U.S.C. 2518(3). As for the necessity requirement of paragraph 2518(3)(c), the Supreme Court explained in the infancy of Title III that: "[I]t is at once apparent that [Title III] not only limits the crimes for which intercept authority may be obtained but also imposes important preconditions to obtaining any intercept authority at all. Congress legislated in considerable detail in providing for applications and orders authorizing wiretapping and evinced the clear intent to make doubly sure that the statutory authority be used with restraint and only where the circumstances warrant the surreptitious interception of wire and

oral communications. These procedures were not to be routinely employed as the initial step in criminal investigation. Rather, the applicant must state and the court must find that normal investigative procedures have been tried and failed or reasonably appear to be unlikely to succeed if tried or to be too dangerous. §§2518(1)(c) and (3)(c)," *United States v. Giordano*, 416 U.S. 505, 515 (1974).

Thus, "[t]he necessity requirement was intended to ensure that wiretaps are not used as the initial step in a criminal investigation. However, officials need not exhaust every conceivable investigative technique before obtaining a wiretap." *United States v. Forrester*, 616 F.3d 929, 944 (9th Cir. 2010)(internal citations omitted); *see also*, United States v. Long, 639 F.3d 293, 301 (7th Cir. 2011)(internal citations omitted)("While this necessity requirement discourages the use of wiretaps as a first-line investigative tool in the mine run of cases, it was not intended to ensure that wiretaps are used only as a last resort in an investigation. Hence, the government's burden of establishing necessity is not high, and whether it met the burden is reviewed in a practical, common-sense fashion"); *United States v. Glover*, 681 F.3d 411, 420 (D.C. Cir. 2012)("That [necessity] requirement is satisfied when traditional investigative techniques have proved inadequate to reveal the operation's full nature and scope"); *United States v. Perez*, 661 F.3d 568, 581 (1st Cir. 2011); *United States v. Foy*, 641 F.3d 455, 464 (10th Cir. 2011); *United States v. Wilson*, 484 F.3d 267, 281 (4th Cir. 2007).

142 Under subsection 2518(5), officers executing an interception order must make efforts to minimize the capture of communications that are outside the scope of the orders; *United States v. De La Cruz Suarez*, 601 F.3d 1202, 1215 (11th Cir. 2010). Whether their efforts are sufficient is matter governed by the circumstances surrounding the interception, *Scott v. United States*, 436 U.S. 128, 135-37 (1978); *United States v. Glover*, 681 F.3d 411, 420-21 (D.C. Cir. 2012);*United States v. West*, 589 F.3d 936, 939-40 (8th Cir. 2009); *United States v. Yarbrough*, 527 F.3d 1092, 1098 (10th Cir.2008)("In *United States v. Willis*, this court articulated the proper procedure for determining the reasonableness of governmental efforts to avoid monitoring non-pertinent calls. 890 F.2d 1099, 1102 (10th Cir. 1989). The government must make an initial prima facie showing of reasonable minimization. *Id.* 'Once the government has made a prima facie showing of reasonable minimization, the burden then shifts to the defendant to show more effective minimization could have taken place." *Id.* In determining whether the government has made a prima facie showing of reasonable efforts to minimize the interception of non-pertinent calls, we consider the factors identified by the Supreme Court in *Scott*: (1)whether a large number of the calls are very short, one-time only, or in guarded or coded language; (2) the breadth of the investigation underlying the need for the wiretap; (3) whether the phone is public or private; and (4) whether the non-minimized calls occurred early in the surveillance. 436 U.S. at 140-41. It is also appropriate to consider (5) the extent to which the authorizing judge supervised the ongoing wiretap. *United States v. Lopez*, 300 F.3d 46, 57 (1st Cir.2002); *United States v. Daly*, 535 F.2d 434, 442 (8th Cir. 1976); *United States v. Vento*, 533 F.2d 838, 853 (3d Cir.1976)").

143 18 U.S.C. 2518(4).

144 18 U.S.C. 2518(7). An observation made a quarter of a century ago remains true: "very little case-law inter pretation of the emergency requirement exists," *United States v. Crouch*, 666 F. Supp. 1414, 1416 (N.D. Cal. 1987)(holding that twenty-day-old information indicating the defendants would commit a bank robbery within the next sixty days did not constitute a sufficient emergency to justify invocation of subsection 2518(7)); *but see*, *Nabozny v. Marshall*, 781 F.2d 83, 84-5 (6th Cir. 1986)(holding with respect to a hostage situation "an emergency situation existed within the terms of the statute").

145 18 U.S.C. 2518(5).

146 18 U.S.C. 2518(6).

147 18 U.S.C. 2518(8)(a),(b). Paragraph 2518(8)(a) requires that court ordered interceptions be recorded and that the recording immediately be sealed by the court, upon expiration of the

interception authority. The seal or a satisfactory explanation for its absence is a prerequisite to the admissibility of the contents or anything derived from the contents as evidence.
"The 'absence' the Government must satisfactorily explain encompasses not only the total absence of a seal but also the absence of a timely applied seal," *United States v. Ojeda Rios,* 495 U.S. 257, 263 (1990). "[T]he 'satisfactory explanation' language in §2518(8)(a) must be understood to require that the Government explain not only why a delay occurred but also why it is excusable," *Id.* at 265; *United States v. Martin*, 618 F.3d 705, 716, 718 (7th Cir. 2010)(some internal citations omitted)("[W]hat should be deemed 'satisfactory' in the context of a statute aimed at preventing government tampering with electronic evidence must depend largely on the statutory objective. A satisfactory explanation must dispel any reasonable suspicion of tampering, and also must be both accurate and believable. Whether the explanation is satisfactory also may depend on the delay in sealing, unique pressure on the Government to obtain a conviction due to particularly notorious charges or defendants, the importance of the recordings to the Government's case and whether the Government has established a procedure for complying with its sealing obligations.... *Cf. United States v. Quintero*, 38 F.3d 1317, 1328-330 (3d Cir. 1994) (rejecting the prosecutor's heavy workload as a satisfactory explanation for a sealing delay because to do so 'would be rendering extraordinary that which is ordinary'); *United States v. Carson*, 969 F.2d 1480, 1498 (3d Cir. 1992) (rejecting the need to enhance the audibility of tapes as a satisfactory explanation for a sealing delay because that need was "readily foreseeable and could just as readily become routine"); *but see*, *United States v. Bansal*, 663 F.3d 634, 651-53 (3d Cir. 2011)(finding the government's reasonable mistake of fact a satisfactory explanation for its failure to seal in a timely manner).
The section does not preclude use or disclosure other than admissibility of the intercepted contents in judicial proceedings, *United States v. A manuel*, 615 F.3d 117, 125-28 (2d Cir. 2010)(uphold the admissibility of evidence secured under a warrant based on interceptions that were recorded in violation of section 2518(8)(a)).

148 18 U.S.C. 2518(8)(d), (9).

149 18 U.S.C. 2517(1), (2), (5), (7). This includes the disclosures to a criminal defendant required in 18 U.S.C. 2518(9), cf., *SEC v. Rajaratnam*, 622 F.3d 159, 172-87 (2d Cir. 2010)(holding that a government attorney may disclose wiretap communications to a criminal defendant under 18 U.S.C. 2517(2) and that under some circumstances the defendant may be compelled to disclose them in the context of a governmental civil enforcement action).

150 18 U.S.C. 2517(6). "'[F]oreign intelligence information,' for purposes of section 2517(6) of this title, means—(A) information, whether or not concerning a United States person, that relates to the ability of the United States to protect against—(i) actual or potential attack or other grave hostile acts of a foreign power or an agent of a foreign power; (ii) sabotage or intentional terrorism by a foreign power or an agent of a foreign power; or (iii) clandestine intelligence activities by and intelligence service or network of a foreign power or by an agent of a foreign power; or (B) information, whether or not concerning a United States person, with respect to a foreign power or foreign territory that relates to—(i) the national defense or the security of the United States; or (ii) the conduct of the foreign affairs of the United States," 18 U.S.C. 2510(19).

151 18 U.S.C. 2518(8).

152 18 U.S.C. 2517(3), (5).

153 18 U.S.C. 2517(4).

154 18 U.S.C. 2511(2)(c).

155 *United States v. Verdin-Garcia*, 516 F.3d 884, 894-95 (10th Cir. 2008) (inmate use of prison phone); *United States v. Friedman*, 300 F.3d 111, 122-23 (2d Cir. 2002)(same); *United States v. Hammond*, 286 F.3d 189, 192 (4th Cir. 2002) (same); *United States v. Footman*, 215 F.3d 145, 154-55 (1st Cir. 2000) (same); *Griggs-Ryan v. Smith*, 904 F.2d 112, 116-17 (1st Cir. 1990) (use of landlady's phone); *United States v. Rivera*, 292 F. Supp.2d 838, 843-45 (E.D. Va. 2003) (inmate use of prison phone monitored by private contractors); *see also*,

United States v. Conley, 531 F.3d 56, 58-9 (1st Cir. 2008)(explicit consent as a condition for phone privileges).

156 *Anthony v. United States*, 667 F.2d 870, 876 (10th Cir. 1981).

157 *United States v. Antoon*, 933 F.2d 200, 203-204 (3d Cir. 1991). *But see, O'Ferrell v. United States*, 968 F. Supp. 1519, 1541 (M.D. Ala. 1997) (an individual who spoke to his wife on the telephone after being told by FBI agents who were then executing a search warrant at his place of business that he could only speak to her with the agents listening in consented to the interception, even if FBI's initial search was unconstitutional).

158 *See, Clemnts-Jeffrey v. Springfield*, 810 F.Supp.2d 857, 871-72 (S.D. Ohio 2011)("As Plaintiffs correctly point out, §2511(2)(i) is completely inapposite because the Absolute Defendants, who intercepted Plaintiffs' electronic communications, were not 'acting under color of law'").

159 Section 217, P.L. 107-56, 115 Stat. 291 (2001).

160 *Implementation of the USA PATRIOT Act: Crime, Terrorism and the Age of Technology: Hearing Before the Subcomm. on Crime, Terrorism, and Homeland Security of the House Comm. on the Judiciary*, 109th Cong., 2d sess. 30-1 (2005)(prepared statement of FBI Dep. Ass't Director Steven M. Martinez).

161 "Except as provided in (b) of this subsection or in subsection (5), whoever violates subsection (1) of this section shall be fined under this title* or imprisoned not more than five years, or both." 18 U.S.C. 2511(4)(a).

* Section 3559 of title 18 classifies as a felony any offense with a maximum penalty of imprisonment of more than one year; and as a Class A misdemeanor any offense with a maximum penalty of imprisonment set at between six months and one year. Unless Congress clearly rejects the general fine ceilings it provides, section 3571 of title 18 sets the fines for felonies at not more than $250,000 for individuals and not more than $500,000 for organizations, and for class A misdemeanors at not more than $100,000 for individuals and not more than $200,000 for organizations. If there is monetary loss or gain associated with the offense, the offender may alternatively be fined not more than twice the amount of the loss or gain, 18 U.S.C. 3571.

162 116 Stat. 2158 (2002).

163 18 U.S.C. 2511(4)(b)(2000 ed.).

164 "(b) Conduct otherwise an offense under this subsection that consists of or relates to the interception of a satellite transmission that is not encrypted or scrambled and that is transmitted—(i) to a broadcasting station for purposes of retrains mission to the general public; or (ii) as an audio subcarrier intended for redistribution to facilities open to the public, but not including data transmissions or telephone calls, is not an offense under this subsection unless the conduct is for the purpose of direct or indirect commercial advantage or private financial gain," 18 U.S.C. 2511(4)(b).

165 "(5)(a)(I) If the communication is—(A) a private satellite video communication that is not scrambled or encrypted and the conduct in violation of this chapter is the private viewing of that communication and is not for a tortious orillegal purpose or for purposes of direct or indirect commercial advantage or private commercial gain; or (B) a radio communication that is transmitted on frequencies allocated under subpart D of part 74 of the rules of the Federal Communications Commission that is not scrambled or encrypted and the conduct in violation of this chapter is not fortortious or illegal purpose or for purposes of direct or indirect commercial advantage or private commercial gain, then the person who engages in such conduct shall be subject to suit by the Federal Government in a court of competent jurisdiction. (ii) In an action under this subsection—(A) if the violation of this chapter is a first offense for the person under paragraph (a) of subsection (4) and such person has not been found liable in a civil action under section 2520 of this title, the Federal Government shall be entitled to appropriate injunctive relief; and (B) if the violation of this chapter is a second or subsequent offense under paragraph (a) of subsection (4) or such person has been

found liable in any prior civil action under section 2520, the person shall be subject to a mandatory $500 civil fine.

"(b) The court may use any means within its authority to enforce an injunction issued under paragraph (ii)(A), and shall impose a civil fine of not less than $500 for each violation of such an injunction." 18 U.S.C. 2511(5).

Under 18 U.S.C. 2520, victims may recover the greater of actual damages or statutory damages of not less than $50 and not more than $500 for the first offense; those amounts are increased to $100 and $1000 for subsequent offenses.

[166] 18 U.S.C. 2513 ("Any electronic, mechanical, or other device used, sent, carried, manufactured, assembled, possessed, sold, or advertised in violation of section 2511 or section 2512 of this chapter may be seized and forfeited to the United States ... "); 18 U.S.C. 983(a)(3)(C)("In lieu of, or in addition to, filing a civil forfeiture complaint, the Government may include a forfeiture allegation in a criminal indictment ... ").

[167] "A good faith reliance on—(1) a court warrant or order, a grand jury subpoena, a legislative authorization, or a statutory authorization; (2) a request of an investigative or law enforcement officer under section 2518(7) of this title; or (3) a good faith determination that section 2511(3) [electronic communications provider authority to disclose content of an electronic communication "(i) as otherwise authorized in section 2511(2)(a) or 2517 of this title; (ii) with the lawful consent of the originator or any addressee or intended recipient of such communication; (iii) to a person employed or authorized, or whose facilities are used, to forward such communication to its destination; or (iv) which were inadvertently obtained by the service provider and which appear to pertain to the commission of a crime, if such divulgence is made to a law enforcement agency] or 2511(2)(I) [interception of communications of a trespasser in a computer system] of this title permitted the conduct complained of; is a complete defense against any civil or criminal action brought under this chapter or any other law," 18 U.S.C. 2520(d).

[168] The $10,000 lump sum for liquidated damages is limited to a single award per victim rather than permitting $10,000 multiples based on the number of violations or the number of types of violations, as long as the violations are "interrelated and time compacted," *Smoot v. United Transportation Union*, 246 F.3d 633, 642-645 (6th Cir. 2001); *Desilets v. Wal-Mart Stores, Inc.*, 171 F.3d 711, 713 (1st Cir. 1999); *see also, Dish Nework v. Delvecchio*, 831F.Supp.2d 595, 601 (W.D.N.Y. 2011)(""Although a range is given for violations under 2520(c)(1), Congress provided no such range under 2520(c)(2). Therefore, in the Court's view, the discretion provided to it allows it only to decide between no damages and $10,000").

[169] 18 U.S.C. 2520(b), (c).

[170] *Compare, e.g., DirecTV, Inc. v. Barczewski*, 604 F.3d 1004, 1006-1008 (7th Cir. 2010); *DirecTV, Inc. v. Brown*, 371 F.3d 814, 818 (11th Cir. 2004); *Dorris v. Absher*, 179 F.3d, 420, 429-30 (6th Cir. 1999); *Nalley v. Nalley*, 53 F.3d 649, 651-53 (4th Cir. 1995), *Reynolds v. Spears*, 93 F.3d 428, 433 (8th Cir. 1996); *DirecTV, Inc. v. Neznak*, 371 F.Supp.2d 130, 133-34 (D. Conn. 2005) (each concluding that courts have discretion), *with, Rodgers v. Wood*, 910 F.2d 444, 447-49 (7th Cir. 1990) and *Menda Biton v. Menda*, 812 F.Supp. 283, 284 (D. Puerto Rico 1993) (courts have no such discretion) (note that after *Menda*, the First Circuit in *Desilets v. Wal-Mart Stores, Inc.*, 171 F.3d at 716-17 treated as a matter for the trial court's discretion the question of whether the award of plaintiff's attorneys' fees should be reduced when punitive damages have been denied).

Section 2520(c) has a second statutory damage provision, available for violations involving private satellite videos or radio communications, 18 U.S.C. 2520(c)(1). This provision is more clearly mandatory (18 U.S.C. 2520(c)(1): "the court *shall* access damages" versus 18 U.S.C. 2520(c)(2): "the court *may* assess as damages")(emphasis added in both instances).

[171] *Adams v. Battle Creek*, 250 F.3d 980, 984 (6th Cir. 2001); *Organizacion JD Ltda. v. United States Department of Justice*, 18 F.3d 91, 94-5 (2d Cir. 1994); *Garza v. Bexar Metropolitan Water District*, 639 F.Supp.2d 770, 773-74 (W.D. Tex. 2009); *Connor v. Tate*, 130

F.Supp.2d 1370, 1374 (N.D. Ga. 2001); *Dorris v. Absher*, 959 F.Supp. 813, 820 (M.D. Tenn. 1997), *aff'd/rev'd in part on other grounds*, 179 F.3d 420 (6th Cir. 1999); *PBA Local No. 38 v. Woodbridge Police Department*, 832 F. Supp. 808, 822-23 (D.N.J. 1993) (each concluding that governmental entities may be held liable); *contra, Abbott v. Winthrop Harbor*, 205 F.3d 976, 980 (7th Cir. 2000); *Amati v. Woodstock*, 176 F.3d 952, 956 (7th Cir. 1999).

[172] *Narducci v. Moore*, 572 F.3d 313, 323 (7th Cir. 2009); *Tapley v. Collins*, 211 F.3d 1210, 1216 (11th Cir. 2000); *Blake v. Wright*, 179 F.3d 1003, 1011-13(6th Cir. 1999); *Babb v. Eagleton*, 614 F.Supp.2d 1232, 1237-238 (N.D. Okla. 2008); *contra, Berry v. Funk*, 146 F.3d 1003, 1013 (D.C. Cir. 1998); *see generally, Qualified Immunity as Defense in Suit Under Federal Wiretap Act (18 U.S.C.A. §§2510 et seq.)*, 178 ALR FED. 1.

[173] 18 U.S.C. 2520(d) ("A good faith reliance on—(1) a court warrant or order, a grand jury subpoena, a legislative authorization, or a statutory authorization; (2) a request of an investigative or law enforcement officer under section 2518(7) of this title; or (3) a good faith determination that section 2511(3) or 2511(2)(i) of this title permitted the conduct complained of; [—] is a complete defense against any civil or criminal action brought under this chapter or any other law"); *SEC v. Rajaratnam*, 622 F.3d 159, 175 (2d Cir. 2010); *Clements-Jeffrey v. Springfield*, 810 F.Supp.2d 857, 872 (S.D. Ohio 2011).

[174] *Williams v. Poulos*, 11 F.3d 271, 285 (1st Cir. 1993); *United States v. Wuliger*, 981 F.2d 1497, 1507 (6th Cir. 1992); *Rice v. Rice*, 951 F.2d 942, 944-45 (8th Cir. 1991); *but see, McCready v. eBay*, 453 F.3d 882, 892 (7th Cir. 2006).

[175] 50 U.S.C. 1885a("Notwithstanding any other provision of law, a civil action may not lie or be maintained in a Federal or State court against any person for providing assistance to an element of the intelligence community, and shall be promptly dismissed, if the Attorney General certifies to the district court of the United States in which such action is pending that - (1) any assistance by that person was provided pursuant to an order of the court established under section 1803(a) of this title [relating to electronic surveillance under FISA] directing such assistance; (2) any assistance by that person was provided pursuant to a certification in writing under section 2511(2)(a)(ii)(B)[relating to the Attorney General's assurance that no court approval is required] or 2709(b)[relating to a national security letter] of title 18; (3) any assistance by that person was provided pursuant to a directive under section 1802(a)(4)[relating to electronic surveillance without a court order under FISA] ... or 1881a(h)[relating to communications of overseas targets under FISA] of this title directing such assistance; [or] (4) in the case of a covered civil action, the assistance alleged to have been provided by the electronic communication service provider was—(A) in connection with an intelligence activity involving communications that was - (i) authorized by the President during the period beginning on September 11, 2001, and ending on January 17, 2007 ... ").

[176] 18 U.S.C. 2712.

[177] 18 U.S.C. 2712(a).

[178] "If a court or appropriate department or agency determines that the United States or any of its departments or agencies has violated any provision of this chapter, and the court or appropriate department or agency finds that the circumstances surrounding the violation raise serious questions about whether or not an officer or employee of the United States acted willfully or intentionally with respect to the violation, the department or agency shall, upon receipt of a true and correct copy of the decision and findings of the court or appropriate department or agency promptly initiate a proceeding to determine whether disciplinary action against the officer or employee is warranted. If the head of the department or agency involved determines that disciplinary action is not warranted, he or she shall notify the Inspector General with jurisdiction over the department or agency concerned and shall provide the Inspector General with the reasons for such determination," 18 U.S.C. 2520(f).

[179] *Ala. Opinion 84-22* (1984); *People v. Smith*, 778 P.2d 685, 686, 687 (Colo. 1989); *Haw. Formal Opinion No. 30* (1988); *Ind.State Bar Ass'n Op.No.1* (2000); *Iowa State Bar Ass'n v. Mollman*, 488 N.W.2d 168, 169-70, 171-72 (Iowa 1992); *Mo.Advisory Comm. Op. Misc. 30* (1978); *Tex S tat. Bar Op. 514* (1996); *Va. LEO #1635* (1995), *Va. LEO #1324*; *Gunter v. Virginia State Bar*, 238 Va. 617, 621-22, 385 S.E.2d 597, 600 (1989).
The federal courts seem to have been in accord, *Parrott v. Wilson*, 707 F.2d 1262 (11th Cir. 1983); *Moody v. IRS*, 654 F.2d 795 (D.C.Cir. 1981); *Ward v. Maritz, Inc*., 156 F.R.D. 592 (D.N.J. 1994); *Wilson v. Lamb*, 125 F.R.D. 142 (E.D.Ky. 1989); *Haigh V. Matsushita Electric Corp*., 676 F.Supp. 1332 (E.D.Va. 1987).

[180] *Ariz. Opinion No. 95-03* (1995); *Alaska Bar Ass'n Eth.Comm. Ethics Opinions No. 95-5 (1995) and No. 91-4* (1991); *Idaho Formal Opinion 130* (1989); *Kan.Bar.Ass'n Opinion 96-9* (1997); *Ky.Opinion E-279* (1984); *Minn.Law.Prof. Resp.Bd. Opinion No. 18* (1996); *Ohio Bd.Com.Griev.Disp. Opinion No. 97-3* (1997); *S.C. Ethics Advisory Opinion 92-17* (1992); *Tenn.Bd.Prof.Resp. Formal Ethics Opinion No. 86-F-14(a)* (1986).

[181] *D.C. Opinion No. 229* (1992) (recording was not unethical because it occurred under circumstances in which the uninformed party should have anticipated that the conversation would be recorded or otherwise memorialized); *Mississippi Bar v. Attorney ST*., 621 So.2d 229 (Miss. 1993)(context of the circumstances test); *Conn.Bar Ass''n Op. 98-9* (1998)(same); *Mich. State Bar Op. RI-309* (1998)(same); *Me. State Bar Op. No. 168* (1999)(same); *N.M. Opinion 1996-2* (1996)(members of the bar are advised that there are no clear guidelines and that the prudent attorney avoids surreptitious recording); *N.C. RPC 171* (1994)(lawyers are encouraged to disclose to the other lawyer that a conversation is being tape recorded); *Okla. Bar Ass'n Opinion* 307 (1994)(a lawyer may secretly recording his or her conversations without the knowledge or consent of other parties to the conversation unless the recording is unlawful or in violation of some ethical standard involving more than simply recording); *Ore. State Bar Ass'n Formal Opinion No. 1991-74* (1991) (an attorney with one party consent he or she may record a telephone conversation "in absence of conduct which would reasonably lead an individual to believe that no recording would be made"); *Utah State Bar Ethics Advisory Opinion No. 96-04* (1996) ("recording conversations to which an attorney is a party without prior disclosure to the other parties is not unethical when the act, considered within the context of the circumstances, does not involve dishonesty, fraud, deceit or misrepresentation"); *Wis. Opinion E-94-5* ("whether the secret recording of a telephone conversation by a lawyer involves gdishonesty, fraud, deceit or misrepresentation' under SCR 20:8.4(c) depends upon all the circumstances operating at the time"). In New York, the question of whether an attorney's surreptitiously recording conversations is ethically suspect is determined by locality, compare, *Ass'n of the Bar of City of N.Y. Formal Opinion No. 1995-10* (1995)(secret recording is per se unethical), with, *N.Y. County Lawyer's Ass'n Opinion No. 696* (1993)(secret recording is not per se unethical).

[182] *Cf., Nissan Motor Co., Ltd. v. Nissan Computer Corp*., 180 F.Supp.2d 1089, 1095-97 (C.D. Cal. 2002).

[183] *E.g., State v. Murtagh*, 169 P.3d 602, 617-18 (Alaska 2007)("undisclosed recording is not unethical"); *In re Crossen*, 450 Mass. 533, 558, 880 N.E.2d 352, 372 (2008) (undisclosed recording was unethical where it was part of scheme to coerce or manufacture testimony against the judge presiding over pending litigation); *Midwest Motor Sports v. Arctic Cat Sales, Inc*., 347 F.3d 693, 699 (8th Cir. 2003) (citing *ABA Comm. on Ethics and Prof'l Responsibility*, Formal Op. 01-422, which states that recording without consent should be prohibited when circumstances make it unethical); *United States v. Smallwood*, 365 F. Supp.2d 689, 697-98 (E.D. Va. 2005) (holding that a lawyer cannot ethically record a conversation without the consent of all parties, even though doing so is not illegal under Virginia law). Declaring the new ABA opinion to be an "overcorrection," one bar association explained that secret taping should not be routine practice, but that it should be permitted if it advances a "societal good." *Ass'n of the Bar of the City of New York Formal*

Opinion No. 2003-02 (2003). For a New York state bar opinion employing a similar line of reasoning, *see, Mena v. Key Food Stores Co-operative, Inc.*, 758 N.Y.S.2d 246, 247-50 (N.Y. Sup. Ct. 2003) (conduct of attorney who obtained a private investigator's services for a client and instructed the client on the use of recording equipment held *not* to warrant severe sanctions, because there was a compelling public interest in exposing the racial discrimination that was the subject of the secret recordings); *see also, S.C. Bar Ethics Advisory Op. 08-13* (November 14, 2008)(noting that the S.C. ethical prohibition on undisclosed recording by attorneys, based on the earlier ABA opinion, had not been withdrawn); *Tex. Ethics Op.* 575 (November 2006)(undisclosed recording by an attorney is not a per se violation of the Texas Disciplinary Rules of Professional Conduct); *Mo. Formal Advisory Op. 123* (March 8, 2006)(agreeing with ABA Formal Opinion 01-422); see generally, CRS Report R42650, *Wiretapping, Tape Recorders, and Legal Ethics: An Overview of Questions Posed by Attorney Involvement in Secretly Recording Conversation.*

184 "Whenever any *wire or oral communication* has been intercepted, no part of the contents of such communication and no evidence derived therefrom may be received in evidence in any trial, hearing, or other proceeding in or before any court, grand jury, department, officer, agency, regulatory body, legislative committee, or other authority of the United States, a State, or a political subdivision thereof if the disclosure of that information would be in violation of this chapter," 18 U.S.C. 2515 (emphasis added); *United States v. Chavez*, 416 U.S. 562, 570 (1974); *United States v. Lnu*, 575 F.3d 298, 301 (3d Cir. 2009); *United States v. Lam*, 271 F.Supp.2d 1182, 1183-184 (N.D. Cal. 2003). Note that suppression does not extend to unlawfully intercepted *electronic* communications, *United States v. Amanuel*, 615 F.3d 117, 125 (2d Cir. 2010); *United States v. Steiger*, 318 F.3d 1039, 1050-52 (11th Cir. 2003); *United States v. Jones*, 364 F. Supp.2d 1303, 1308-09 (D. Utah 2005); nor does it extend to evidence secured in violation the pen register/trap and trace provisions, *United States v. German*, 486 F.3d 849, 852-53 (5th Cir. 2007).

185 18 U.S.C. 2510(11)("'aggrieved person' means a person who was a party to any an intercepted wire, oral, or electronic communication or a person against whom the interception was directed"); *United States v. Oliva*, 686 F.3d 1106, 1108-109 (9th Cir. 2012).

186 *United States v. Lomeli*, 676 F.3d 734, 739 (8th Cir. 2012)(internal citations omitted)("Suppression is not justified if the facial insufficiency of the wiretap order is not more than a technical defect. According to *Moore*, our analysis is two tiered, first identifying the omission or defect at issue ... and second, determining whether that defect violates a core statutory requirement or whether it is a mere technical defect not warranting suppression"); *see also*, *United States v. Lopez*, 300 F.3d 46, 55-6 (1st Cir. 2002); *United States v. Staffeldt*, 451 F.3d 578, 582-85 (9th Cir. 2006); *United States v. Gray*, 521 F.3d 514, 522 (6th Cir. 2008); *United States v. Foy*, 641 F.3d 455, 463 (10th Cir. 2011). This is the case even where the court is clearly troubled by the government's failure to comply with the requirements of Title III, *United States v. Callum*, 410 F.3d 571, 579 (9th Cir. 2005)("Under the force of precedent, we uphold the challenged wiretap applications and orders. Still, we note that the Department of Justice and its officers did not cover themselves with glory in obtaining the wiretap orders at issue in this case. Title III is an exacting statute obviously meant to be followed punctiliously, yet the officers repeatedly ignored its clear requirements").

187 *Gelbard v. United States*, 408 U.S. 41, 52 (1972).

188 *United States v. Moore*, 41 F.3d 370, 376 (8th Cir. 1994); *United States v. Ambrosio*, 898 F.Supp. 177, 187 (S.D.N.Y. 1995); *United States v. Malelzadeh*, 855 F.2d 1492, 1497 (11th Cir. 1988); *United States v. Mullen*, 451 F.Supp.2d 509, 530-31 (W.D.N.Y. 2006); *contra, United States v. Rice*, 478 F.3d 704, 711-14 (6th Cir. 2007).

Gelbard held that a grand jury witness might claim the protection of section 2515 through a refusal to answer questions based upon an unlawful wiretap notwithstanding the fact that the Fourth Amendment exclusionary rule does not apply in grand jury proceedings. *Gelbard*, 408 U.S. at 51-52. The good faith exception to the Fourth Amendment exclusionary rule permits the admission of evidence secured in violation of the Fourth Amendment, if the officers responsible for the breach were acting in good faith reliance upon the apparent authority of a search warrant or some like condition negating the remedial force of the rule, *United States v. Leon*, 468 U.S. 897, 909 (1984).

189 *United States v. Simels*, 654 F.3d 161, 169-70 (2d Cir. 2011)(citing cases in accord); *Culbertson v. Culbertson*, 143 F.3d 825, 827-28 (4th Cir. 1998); *United States v. Echavarria-Olarte*, 904 F.2d 1391 (9th Cir. 1990); *United States v. Vest*, 813 F.2d 477, 484 (1st Cir. 1987); cf., *United States v. Crabtree*, 565 F.3d 887, 891-92 (4th Cir. 2009)(noting that the Circuit's recognition of admissibility for impeachment purposes does not require recognition of a clean hands exception under which the government may admit introduce illegal wiretap evidence as long as it was not involved in the illegal interception).

190 *United States v. Thompson*, 130 F.3d 676, 683 (5th Cir. 1997); *United States v. Panaro*, 241 F.3d 1104, 1111 (9th Cir. 2001); *United States v. Smith*, 242 F.3d 737, 741 (7th Cir. 2001).

191 *United States v. Webster*, 84 F.3d 1056, 1064 (8th Cir. 1996); *United States v. Green*, 175 F.3d 822, 830 n.3 (10th Cir. 1999); *United States v. Green*, 324 F.3d 375, 379 (5th Cir. 2003)(citing 4 of the 7 factors); cf., *United States v.Calderin-Rodriguez*, 244 F.3d 977, 986-87 (8th Cir. 2001). These seven factors have been fairly widely cited since they were first announced in *United States v. McKeever*, 169 F. Supp. 426, 430 (S.D.N.Y. 1958), *rev'd on other grounds*,271 F.2d 669 (2d Cir. 1959). They are a bit formalistic for some courts who endorse a more ad hoc approach to the assessment of whether the admission of what purports to be a taped conversation will introduce fraud or confusion into the court, e.g., *Stringel v. Methodist Hosp. of Indiana, Inc.*, 89 F.3d 415, 420 (7th Cir. 1996)(McKeever "sets out a rather formal, seven step checklist for the authentication of tape recordings, and we have looked to some of the features[in the past]"); *United States v. White*, 116 F.3d 903, 921 (D.C. Cir. 1997)("tapes may be authenticated by testimony describing the process or system that created the tape or by testimony from parties to the conversation affirming that the tapes contained an accurate record of what was said"); *United States v. Tropeano*, 252 F.3d 653, 661 (2d Cir.2001)("[T]his Circuit has never expressly adopted a rigid standard for determining the admissibility of tape recordings"); *United States v. Westmoreland*, 312 F.3d 302, 310-11 (7th Cir. 2002); *United States v. Dawson*, 425 F.3d389, 393 (7th Cir. 2005)("But there are no rigid rules, such as chain of custody, for authentication; all that is required is adequate evidence of genuineness. (There are such rules for electronic surveillance governed by Title III, but Title III is in applicable to conversations that, as here, are recorded with the consent of one of the participants)").

192 *E.g., State Analysis, Inc. v. American Financial Services Ass'n*, 621 F.Supp.2d 309, 317-18 (E.D.Va. 2009); *Pure Power Boot Camp v. Warrior Fitness Boot Camp*, 587 F.Supp.2d 548, 555 (S.D.N.Y. 2008).

193 *KLA-Tencor Corp. v. Murphy*, 717 F.Supp.2d 895, 905 (N.D.Cal. 2010); *Cardinal Health 414, Inc. v. Adams*, 582 F.Supp.2d 967, 976 (M.D. Tenn. 2008).

194 *Penrose Computer Marketgroup, Inc. v. Camin*, 682 F.Supp.2d 202, 210-12 (N.D.N.Y. 2010) citing cases on each side of the debate including cases under the Computer Fraud and Abuse Act (18 U.S.C. 1030) where the "access" terms are used, e.g., *Shurgard Storage Ctrs., Inc. v. Safeguard Self Storage, Inc.*, 119 F.Supp.2d 1121, 1125 (W.D. Wash. 2000)("[T]he authority of the plaintiff's ... employees ended when they allegedly became agents of the defendant [although still employed by the plaintiff] ... [T]hey lost their authorization and were without authorization when they allegedly obtained and sent the proprietary information to the defendant via email"); *Ass'n of Machinists and Aerospace Workers v. Werner*, 390 F.Supp.2d 479, 496 (D. Md. 2005)("Because section 2701 prohibits only unauthorized access and not the misappropriation or disclosure of information, there is no violation of section 2701 for a person with authorized access to the database no matter how malicious or larcenous his intended use of that access").

195 *KLA-Tencor Corp. v. Murphy*, 717 F.Supp.2d 895, 905-906 (N.D. Cal. 2010)("Finally, plaintiff has not established that Chen's conduct [of deleting her e-mails in her employer's

system] was unauthorized. Plaintiff asserts that Chen was 'without authorization or exceeded authorization to access these e-mails on KT's e-mail server in [her] last days at KT because [she] did not have any legitimate business reasons for doing so and [is] prohibited, as a condition of their employment, from unauthorized use of KT information.' However, this claim is not supported by the evidence. As an initial matter, it appears that employees were generally authorized to use their own e-mail account.... The agreements cited by plaintiff in its motion only restrict use of *confidential* information, and plaintiff has provided no evidence that the contents of the deleted e-mails were confidential or that deleting e-mails would constitute 'use.' In addition, Chen states that there was no company policy prohibiting her from deleting her own e-mail").In a case under the Computer Fraud and Abuse Act, that might as easily have been brought under the SCA, however, the court held that "if any conscious breach of a website's terms of service is held to be sufficient by itself to constitute intentionally accessing a computer without authorization or in excess of authorization, the result will be that section1030(a)(2)(C) becomes a law 'that affords too much discretion to the police and too little notice to citizens who wish to use the [Internet]' [and consequently is unconstitutionally vague]," *United States v. Drew*, 259 F.R.D. 449, 467(C.D. Cal. 2009).

[196] *Cardinal Health 414, Inc. v. Adams*, 582 F. Supp. 967, 977 (M.D. Tenn. 2008)("Adams used the log-in information for another person, a former co-worker, to spy on the activities of his former company. On these facts, to argue that continued access was 'authorized' is absurd"); *see also, State Analysis, Inc. v. American Financial Services Assoc.*, 621F.Supp.2d 309, 318 (E.D. Va. 2009).

[197] *Devine v. Kapasi*, 729 F.Supp.2d 1024, 1027-28 (N.D. Ill. 2010), *citing, Fraser v. Nationwide Mutual Ins. Co*, 352F.3d 107, 115 (3d Cir. 2003); *In re iPhone Application Litigation*, 844 F.Supp.2d 1040, 1057 (N.D .Cal. 2012)("To state a claim under the SCA, Plaintiffs must allege that Defendants accessed without authorization 'a facility through which an electronic communication service is provided.' 18 U.S.C. 2701(a)(1). An 'electronic communication service' ('ECS') is 'any service which provides to users thereof the ability to send and receive wire or electronic communications.' 18 U.S.C. 2510(15). While the computer systems of an e-mail provider, a bulletin board system, or an ISP are uncontroversial examples of facilities that provide electronic communications services to multiple users, less consensus surrounds the question presented here: whether an individual's computer, laptop, or mobile device fits the statutory definition of a 'facility through which an electronic communication service is provided.' The Court agrees with Defendants that it does not").

[198] 18 U.S.C. 2711(1)("As used in this chapter [18 U.S.C. 2701-2712]—(1) the terms defined in section 2510 of this title have, respectively, the definitions given such terms in that section"); 18 U.S.C. 2510(17)("'electronic storage' means—(A) any temporary, intermediate storage of a wire or electronic communication incidental to the electronic transmission thereof; and (B) any storage of such communication by an electronic communication service for purposes of backup protection of such communication").

[199] *See e.g., KLA-Tencor Corp. v. Murphy*, 717 F.Supp.2d 895, 904-905 (N.D. Cal. 2010)("As an initial matter, it is not clear to the court that e-mails on KT's server were in 'electronic storage' within the meaning of the SCA. In *Theofel v. Farey-Jones*, 359 F.3d 1066, 1075 (9th Cir. 2004), the Ninth Circuit held that messages remaining on an ISP's server after delivery could fall within the SCA. The court found that '[a]n obvious purpose for storing a message on an ISP's server after delivery is to provide a second copy of the message in the event that the user needs to download it again-if, for example, the message is accidentally erased from the user's own computer.' *Id*. However, 'the mere fact that a copy *could* serve as a backup does not mean it is stored for that purpose' *Id*. at 1076. The court noted that there would be instances where an ISP could hold messages not in electronic storage, such as 'messages a user has flagged for deletion from the server.' *Id*. In an apparent attempt to mirror *Theofel* language, plaintiff suggests that its server's storage of e-mail has a backup

purpose because a user could 'download them again when, for instance, his or her e-mails are accidentally deleted from the computer while working in an offline mode.' Gurule SJ Decl. ¶ 7. However, plaintiff also explains that the server's software 'is configured to synchronize a user's e-mail account so that the account contains the same set of e-mails regardless of where it is accessed.' *Id.* ¶ 10. It seems to the court that these two purposes cannot coexist. Either the server is linked to the computer and flags for deletion a message that is deleted on the computer, or it acts as a backup and would not automatically delete messages that are deleted on a computer. Under either theory, plaintiff's SCA claim fails. Even if the system's operation is as plaintiff describes, the fact that automatic deletion does not occur in the specific situation of a message being deleted while the computer is offline does not establish that the server stores e-mails for the purposes of backup protection rather than only for purpose of synchronization").

In re iPhone Application Litigation, 844 F.Supp.2d 1040, 1059 (N.D. Cal. 2012) ("The Court finds persuasive the reasoning in *In re Double click, Inc. Privacy Litigation*, 154 F.Supp.2d 497 (S.D.N.Y. 2001). There, the court dismissed an SCA claim upon finding that the identification numbers for browser cookies the defendants installed on the plaintiffs' computers were not in 'electronic storage' because they resided on the plaintiff's hard drives and thus were not in temporary electronic storage, as is required by the Act. In *In re Double Click*, the district court, after considering the plain language of the statute, concluded that '[the SCA] only protects electronic communications stored for a limited time in the middle of a transmission, i.e. when an electronic communication service temporarily stores a communication while waiting to deliver it.' 154 F.Supp.2d at 512 (quoting dictionary definitions of 'temporary' and 'intermediate'). The district court concluded that '[t]he cookies' long-term residence on plaintiffs' hard drives places them outside of §2510(17)'s definition of 'electronic storage' and, hence, Title II [of the ECPA's] protection.' *Id.* at 511").

[200] 18 U.S.C. 2701(c). Here, the word "user" means "any person or entity who—(A) uses an electronic communication service; and (B) is duly authorized by the provider of such service to engage in such use," 18 U.S.C. 2510(13), 2711(1); *Webapps v. Accelerize New Media, Inc.*, 847 F. Supp. 912, 917 (E.D. La. 2012).

[201] "(a) Except as provided in paragraph (b) of this subsection, a person or entity providing an electronic communication service to the public shall not intentionally divulge the contents of any communication (other than one to such person or entity, or an agent thereof) while in transmission on that service to any person or entity other than an addressee or intended recipient of such communication or an agent of such addressee or intended recipient.

"(b) A person or entity providing electronic communication service to the public may divulge the contents of any such communication—(i) as otherwise authorized in section 2511(2)(a) or 2517 of this title; (ii) with the lawful consent of the originator or any addressee or intended recipient of such communication; (iii) to a person employed or authorized, or whose facilities are used, to forward such communication to its destination; or (iv) which were inadvertently obtained by the service provider and which appear to pertain to the commission of a crime, if such divulgence is made to a law enforcement agency," 18 U.S.C. 2511(3).

[202] 18 U.S.C. 2702(a)(1), (2).

[203] 18 U.S.C. 2702(a)(3).

[204] 18 U.S.C. 2702(a)(1).

[205] 18 U.S.C. 2702(a)(2).

[206] 18 U.S.C. 2702(a)(3).

[207] 18 U.S.C. 2702(b)(emphasis added).

[208] "A provider described in subsection (a) may divulge a record or other information pertaining to a subscriber to or customer of such service (not including the contents of communications covered by subsection (a)(1) or (a)(2))—(1) as otherwise authorized in section 2703; (2) with the lawful consent of the customer or subscriber; (3) as may be necessarily incident to

the rendition of the service or to the protection of the rights or property of the provider of that service; (4) to a governmental entity, if the provider, in good faith, believes that an emergency involving danger of death or serious physical injury to any person requires disclosure without delay of information relating to the emergency; (5) to the National Center for Missing and Exploited Children, in connection with a report submitted there to under section 227 of the Victims of Child Abuse Act of 1990 (42 U.S.C. 13032); or (6) to any person other than a governmental entity," 18 U.S.C. 2702(c).[209] *Quon v. Arch Wireless Operating Co., Inc.*, 529 F.3d 892, 900-903 (9th Cir. 2008), *rev'd on other grounds sub nom.,City of Ontario v. Quon*, 130 S.Ct. 2619 (2010).

[210] *Id.* (ECS provider that supplied the city police department with pager service for some of its officers violated section2702 when it provided the department with the content of the officers' pager messages).

[211] 18 U.S.C. 2701-2712.

[212] The SCA also authorizes the issuance of national security letters for foreign intelligence gathering rather than law enforcement purposes, 18 U.S.C. 2709, *see generally*, CRS Report RL33320, *National Security Letters in Foreign Intelligence Investigations: Legal Background and Recent Amendments*, by Charles Doyle.

[213] 18 U.S.C. 2702(b)("A provider described in subsection (a) may divulge the contents of a communication ... (7) to a law enforcement agency—(A) if the contents—(i) were inadvertently obtained by the service provider; and (ii) appear to pertain to the commission of a crime").

[214] 18 U.S.C. 2702(b)("A provider described in subsection (a) may divulge the contents of a communication ... (8) to a governmental entity, if the provider, in good faith, believes that an emergency involving danger of death or serious physical injury to any person requires disclosure without delay of communications relating to the emergency").

[215] 18 U.S.C. 2702(c)("A provider described in subsection (a) may divulge the contents of a communication ... (4) to a governmental entity, if the provider, in good faith, believes that an emergency involving danger of death or serious physical injury to any person requires disclosure without delay of information relating to the emergency").

[216] 18 U.S.C. 2711("As used in this chapter ... (4) the term 'governmental entity' means a department or agency of the United States or State or political subdivision thereof"); *but see, United States v. Amawi*, 552 F.Supp.2d 679, 680 (N.D. Ohio 2008)(the Office of the Federal Public Defender is not a "governmental entity").

[217] Recall that "'electronic storage' means—(A) any temporary, intermediate storage of a wire or electronic communication incidental to the electronic transmission thereof; and (B) any storage of such communication by an electronic communication service for purposes of backup protection of such communication," 18 U.S.C. 2510(17).

[218] 18 U.S.C. 2703(a). At least one court has held that opened web-based e-mail stored on a service provider's server is no longer is "electronic storage," because the service provider storage is not necessary for backup purposes once the e-mail has been opened (i.e., after storage is not only incidental to transmission). The original remains on the web server and the service provider is simply supplying remote storage. Consequently, a governmental entity may secure access using a subpoena, *United States v. Weaver*, 636 F.Supp.2d 769, 770-72 (C.D. Ill. 2009)(distinguishing and finding unpersuasive *Theofel v. Farey-Jones*, 359 F.3d 1066 (9th Cir. 2004), thought to support a contrary view).

[219] 18 U.S.C. 2703(a)(" ... A governmental entity may require the disclosure by a provider of electronic communications services of the contents of a wire or electronic communication that has been in electronic storage in an electronic communications system for more than one hundred and eighty days by the means available under subsection (b) of this section").

18 U.S.C. 2703(b)("(1) A governmental entity may require a provider of remote computing service to disclose the contents of any wire or electronic communication to which this paragraph is made applicable by paragraph (2) of this subsection—(A) without required notice to the subscriber or customer, if the governmental entity obtains a warrant issued

using the procedures described in the Federal Rules of Criminal Procedure by a court with jurisdiction over the offense under investigation or equivalent State warrant; or (B) with prior notice from the governmental entity to the subscriber or customer if the governmental entity—(i) uses an administrative subpoena authorized by a Federal or State statute or a Federal or State grand jury or trial subpoena; or (ii) obtains a court order for such disclosure under subsection (d) of this section; except that delayed notice may be given pursuant to section 2705 of this title").

220 *Compare*, 18 U.S.C. 2703(d)("A court order for disclosure under subsection (b) or (c) may be issued by any court that is a court of competent jurisdiction...."); 18 U.S.C. 2711(3)("As used in this chapter ... (3) the term 'court of competent jurisdiction' has the meaning assigned by section 3127, and includes any Federal court within that definition, without geographic limitation"); 18 U.S.C. 3127(2)(emphasis added) ("As used in this chapter ... (2) the term "court of competent jurisdiction" means—(A) any district court of the United States (*including a magistrate of such a court*) or a United States Court of Appeals having jurisdiction over the offense being investigated ..."), *with*, 18 U.S.C. 2516(3)("Any attorney for the Government ... may authorize an application to a Federal judge of competent jurisdiction for, and such judge may grant ... an order authorizing or approving the interception of electronic communications ..."); 18 U.S.C. 2510(9)(" As used in this chapter ... 'Judge of competent jurisdiction' means—(a) a judge of a United States district court or a United States court of appeals").

221 *United States v. Berkos*, 543 F.3d 392, 397 (7th Cir. 2008), *quoting* 18 U.S.C. 2703(a), ("[W]hen 'a court with jurisdiction over the offense' issues an out-of-district warrant for the seizure of electronic communications, it must do so 'using the procedures described in the Federal Rules of Criminal Procedure'"); *see also*, 18 U.S.C. 2711(3)(above).

222 18 U.S.C. 2705(a)(1)(A), (4).

223 18 U.S.C. 2705(a)(1)(B), (4).

224 18 U.S.C. 2705(a)(2), (b).

225 18 U.S.C. 2703(d)("A court order for disclosure under subsection (b) or (c) may be issued by any court that is a court of competent jurisdiction and shall issue only if the governmental entity offers specific and articulable facts showing that there are reasonable grounds to believe that the contents of a wire or electronic communication, or the records or other information sought, are relevant and material to an ongoing criminal investigation. In the case of a State governmental authority, such a court order shall not issue if prohibited by the law of such State. A court issuing an order pursuant to this section, on a motion made promptly by the service provider, may quash or modify such order, if the information or records requested are unusually voluminous in nature or compliance with such order otherwise would cause an undue burden on such provider").

226 *United States v. Warshak*, 631 F.3d 266, 288 (6th Cir. 2010)(internal quotation marks and citations omitted) ("Accordingly, we hold that a subscriber enjoys a reasonable expectation of privacy in the contents of emails that are stored with, or sent or received through, a commercial ISP. The government may not compel a commercial ISP to turn over the contents of a subscriber's emails without first obtaining a warrant based on probable cause. Therefore, because they did not obtain a warrant, the government agents violated the Fourth Amendment when they obtained the contents of Warshak's emails. Moreover, to the extent that the SCA purports to permit the government to obtain such emails warrant lessly, the SCA is unconstitutional"); *see also, In re Application of the United States*, 620 F.3d 304, 313 (3d Cir.2010)("We also conclude that this [§2703(d)] standard is a lesser one than probable cause").

227 *United States v. Warshak*, 631 F.3d at 283-88.

228 *Id.* at 288-92 (exception for good faith reliance on the SCA); *see also, United States v. Ferguson*, 508 F.Supp.2d 7, 8-10 D.D.C. 2007)(even if a Fourth Amendment violation occurred, officers could rely in good faith on the magistrate's order issued before any court had raised the specter of constitutional suspicion which surfaced later in *Warshak*).

[229] 18 U.S.C. 2703(f)(1)("A provider of wire or electronic communication services or a remote computing service, upon the request of a governmental entity, shall take all necessary steps to preserve records and other evidence in its possession pending the issuance of a court order or other process").

[230] *United States v. Warshak*, 631 F.3d 266, 283, 290 n.21 (6th Cir. 2010)(internal citations omitted)("Warshak had a number of email accounts with various ISPs, including an account with NuVox Communications. In October 2004, the government formally requested that NuVox prospectively preserve the contents of any emails to or from Warshak's email account. The request was made pursuant to 18 U.S.C. §2703(f) and it instructed NuVox to preserve all future messages. NuVox acceded to the government's request and began preserving copies of Warshak's incoming and outgoing emails—copies that would not have existed absent the prospective preservation request. Per the government's instructions, Warshak was not informed that his messages were being archived. In January 2005, the government obtained a subpoena under §2703(d) and compelled NuVox to turn over the emails that it had begun preserving the previous year. In May 2005, the government served NuVox with an *ex parte* court order under §2703(d) that required NuVox to surrender any additional email messages in Warshak's account. In all, the government compelled NuVox to reveal the contents of approximately 27,000 emails. Warshak did not receive notice of either the subpoena or the order until May 2006.... Some courts and commentators have suggested that §2703(f) applies only retroactively. However, the language of the statute, on its face, does not compel this reading").

[231] 18 U.S.C. 2704(b)(4)("If the court finds that the applicant is not the subscriber or customer for whom the communications sought by the governmental entity are maintained, or that there is a reason to believe that the law enforcement inquiry is legitimate and that the communications sought are relevant to that inquiry, it shall deny the motion or application and order such process enforced. If the court finds that the applicant is the subscriber or customer for whom the communications sought by the governmental entity are maintained, and that there is not a reason to believe that the communications sought are relevant to a legitimate law enforcement inquiry, or that there has not been substantial compliance with the provisions of this chapter, it shall order the process quashed").

[232] 18 U.S.C. 2704(a)(1), (2)(emphasis added)("A governmental entity acting under section 2703(b)(2) may include in its subpoena or court order a requirement that the service provider to whom the request is directed create a backup copy of the contents of the electronic communications sought in order to preserve those communications. Without notifying the subscriber or customer of such subpoena or court order, such service provider shall create such backup copy as soon as practicable consistent with its regular business practices and shall confirm to the governmental entity that such backup copy has been made. *Such backup copy shall be created within two business days after receipt by the service provider of the subpoena or court order.* (2) Notice to the subscriber or customer shall be made by the governmental entity within three days after receipt of such confirmation, unless such notice is delayed pursuant to section 2705(a)").

[233] 18 U.S.C. 2703(c)(1).

[234] 18 U.S.C. 2703(c)(2)("A provider of electronic communication service or remote computing service shall disclose to a governmental entity the (A) name; (B) address; (C) local and long distance telephone connection records, or records of session times and durations; (D) length of service (including start date) and types of service utilized; (E) telephone or instrument number or other subscriber number or identity, including any temporarily assigned network address; and (F) means and source of payment (including any credit car or bank account number), of a subscriber to or customer of such service, when the governmental entity uses an administrative subpoena authorized by a Federal or State statute or a Federal or State grand jury or trial subpoena or any means available under paragraph (1)"); *United States v. Cray*, 673 F.Supp.2d 1368, 1378-379 (S.D. Ga. 2009).

[235] 18 U.S.C. 2703(c)(3); *In re Application of the United States*, 830 F.Supp.2d 114, 127-28 (E.D. Va. 2011).

[236] *See, In re Application of the United States*, 733 F.Supp.2d 939, 940 n.1 (N.D. Ill. 2009)(listed cases decided up to that point).

[237] *In re Application of the United States*, 620 F.3d 304, 313-19 (3d Cir. 2010); *see also*, *In re Application of the United States*, 747 F.Supp.2d 827, 838-40 (S.D.Tex. 2010)(access to provider records relating to cell phone location over the course of an earlier two month period requires a warrant); *In re Application of the United States*, 727 F.Supp.2d 571,583-84 (W.D. Tex. 2010)(access to provider records relating to cell phone location either historically or prospectively should be only be available under a warrant, at least until a circuit court rules otherwise).

[238] *United States v. Jones*, 132 S. Ct. 945 (2012).

[239] *Id.* at 949; *id.* at 957 (Alito, J., with Ginsburg, Breyer, and Kagan)(concurring in the judgment).

[240] *United States v. Jones*, 132 S. Ct. at 949.

[241] *Id.* at 964 (Alito, J., with Ginsburg, Breyer, and Kagan)(concurring in the judgment)("[T]he longer term GPS monitoring in investigations of most offenses impinges on expectations of piracy").

[242] *Id.* at 945-55 (Sotomayor, J.)(concurring).

[243] *See*, *United States v. Skinner*, ___ F.3d ___, ___ (6th Cir. August 14, 2012)("Justice Alito's concurrence and the majority in *Jones* both recognize that there is little precedent for what constitutes a level of comprehensive tracking that would violate the Fourth Amendment. Skinner's case, however, comes nowhere near that line"); *In re Application of the United States*, 849 F.Supp.2d 177, 179 (D. Mass. 2012)(declining to undo district precedent concerning the collection of "cumulative historical cell site location records ... [u]ntil either the First Circuit Court of Appeals or the Supreme Court rule otherwise, or Congress enacts legislation dealing with the problem").

[244] "The punishment for an offense under subsection (a) of this section is—(1) if the offense is committed for purposes of commercial advantage, malicious destruction or damage, or private commercial gain, or in furtherance of any criminal or tortious act in violation of the constitution and laws of the United States or any state—(A) a fine under this title or imprisonment for not more than 5 years, or both, in the case of a first offense under this subparagraph; and (B) a fine under this title or imprisonment for not more than 10 years, or both, for any subsequent offense under this subparagraph; and (2)(A) a fine under this title or imprisonment for not more than 1 year or both, in the case of a first offense under this paragraph; and (B) a fine under this title or imprisonment for not more than 5 years, or both, in the case of an offense under this subparagraph that occurs after a conviction of another offense under this section," 18 U.S.C. 2701(b).

[245] "(a) Cause of action—Except as provided in section 2703(e)[relating to immunity for compliance with judicial process], any provider of electronic communication service, subscriber, or customer aggrieved by any violation of this chapter in which the conduct constituting the violation is engaged in with a knowing or intentional state of mind may, in a civil action, recover from the person or entity other than the United States which engaged in that violation such relief as may be appropriate.

"(b) Relief—In a civil action under this section, appropriate relief includes—(1) such preliminary and other equitable or declaratory relief as may be appropriate; (2) damages under subsection(c); and (3) a reasonable attorney's fee and other litigation costs reasonably incurred;

"(c) Damages—The court may assess as damages in a civil action under this section the sum of the actual damages suffered by the plaintiff and any profits made by the violator as a result of the violation, but in no case shall a person entitled to recover receive less than the sum of $1,000...." 18 U.S.C. 2707.

To be eligible for statutory damages, a plaintiff must show actual damage, but attorneys' fees and punitive damages may be award without proof of actual damages, *Van Alystyne v. Electronic Scriptorium, Ltd.*, 560 F.3d 199, 202 (4th Cir. 2009).

[246] "Any person who is aggrieved by any willful violation this chapter or of chapter 119 of this title [18 U.S.C. 2510-2520] ... may commence an action in United States District Court.... If ... any of the departments or agencies has violated any provision of this chapter ... the department or agency shall ... promptly initiate a proceeding to determine whether disciplinary action ... is warranted...."18 U.S.C. 2712(a),(c).

[247] *Cardinal Health 414, Inc. v. Adams*, 582 F.Supp.2d 967, 976 (M.D. Tenn. 2008).

[248] *United States v. Perrine*, 518 F.3d 1196, 1202 (10th Cir. 2008); *United States v. Clenney*, 631 F.3d 658, 667 (11th Cir. 2011); *United States v. Navas*, 640 F.Supp.2d 256, 262 (S.D.N.Y. 2009), rev'd on other grounds, 597 F.3d 492 (2d Cir. 2010).

[249] *See e.g., United States v. Warshak*, 631 F.3d 266, 282-89 (6th Cir. 2010).

[250] No liability under section 2707 accrues, however, as a consequence of aiding or abetting a provider's violation of section 2702, *Freeman v. DirecTV*, 457 F.3d 1001, 1009 (9th Cir. 2006).

[251] "(3) [T]he term 'pen register' means a device which records or decodes electronic or other impulses which identify the numbers dialed or otherwise transmitted on the telephone line to which such device is attached, but such term does not include any device used by a provider or customer of a wire or electronic communication service for billing, or recording as an incident to billing, for communications services provided by such provider or any device used by a provider or customer of a wire communication service for cost accounting or other like purposes in the ordinary course of its business; (4) the term 'trap and trace device' means a device which captures the incoming electronic or other impulses which identify the originating number of an instrument or device from which a wire or electronic communication was transmitted," 18 U.S.C. 3127(3),(4). Although clone pagers are not considered pen registers, *Brown v. Waddell*, 50 F.3d 285, 290-91 (4th Cir. 1995), "caller id" services have been found to constitute trap and trace devices by some courts, *United States v. Fregoso*, 60 F.3d 1314, 1320 (8th Cir. 1995), but not others, *Sparshott v. Feld Entertainment, Inc.*, 311 F.3d 425, 432-33 (D.C. Cir. 2003).

[252] *United States v. New York Telephone Co.*, 434 U.S. 159 (1977).

[253] 18 U.S.C. 3121-3127.

[254] "'Post-cut-through dialed digits' are any numbers dialed from a telephone after the call is initially setup or 'cut through.' Sometimes these digits are other telephone numbers, as when a party places a credit card call by first dialing the long distance carrier access number and then the phone number of the intended party. Sometimes these digits transmit real information, such as bank account numbers, Social Security numbers, prescription numbers, and the like. In the latter case, the digits represent communications content; in the former, they are non-content call processing numbers," *In re United States*, 441 F.Supp.2d 816, 818 (S.D. Tex. 2006); *see also*, *In re United States for Orders (1)Authorizing Use of Pen Registers and Trap and Trace Devices*, 515 F.Supp.2d 325, 328-38 (E.D.N.Y. 2007); *In re United States*, 622 F.Supp.2d 411, 419-22 (S.D. Tex. 2007); *In re Application of the United States*, 632 F.Supp.2d 202,203-204 (E.D.N.Y. 2008)(granting a pen register/trap and trace application that would capture post-cut-through numbers after the government assured the court that its computers would be configured to delete them upon receipt).

[255] 115 Stat. 288-91 (2001).

[256] 18 U.S.C. 3121 ("Except as provided in this section, no person may install or use a pen register or a trap and trace device without first obtaining a court order under section 3123 of this title or under the Foreign Intelligence Surveillance Act of 1978 (50 U.S.C. 1801 et seq.)").

[257] 18 U.S.C. 3121(b)("The prohibition of subsection (a) does not apply with respect to the use of a pen register or a trap and trace device by a provider of electronic or wire communication service—(1) relating to the operation, maintenance, and testing of a wire or electronic

communication service or to the protection of the rights or property of such provider, or to the protection of users of that service from abuse of service or unlawful use of service; or (2) to record the fact that a wire or electronic communication was initiated or completed in order to protect such provider, another provider furnishing service toward the completion of the wire communication, or a user of that service, from fraudulent, unlawful or abusive use of service; or (3) where the consent of the user of that service has been obtained").

[258] 18 U.S.C. 3125(a)("Notwithstanding any other provision of this chapter, any investigative or law enforcement officer, specially designated by the Attorney General, the Deputy Attorney General, the Associate Attorney General, any Assistant Attorney General, any acting Assistant Attorney General, or any Deputy Assistant Attorney General, or by the principal prosecuting attorney of any State or subdivision thereof acting pursuant to a statute of that State, who reasonably determines that—(1) an emergency situation exists that involves—(A) immediate danger of death or serious bodily injury to any person; (B) conspiratorial activities characteristic of organized crime; (C) an immediate threat to a national security interest; or (D) an ongoing attack on a protected computer (as defined in section 1030) that constitutes a crime punishable by a term of imprisonment greater than one year [—] that requires the installation and use of a pen register or a trap and trace device before an order authorizing such installation and use can, with due diligence, be obtained, and (2) there are grounds upon which an order could be entered under this chapter to authorize such installation and use [—] may have installed and use a pen register or trap and trace device if, within forty-eight hours after the installation has occurred, or begins to occur, an order approving the installation or use is issued in accordance with section 3123 of this title").

[259] 18 U.S.C. 3122.

[260] 18 U.S.C. 3123.

[261] 18 U.S.C. 3122(a), 3127(2); *In re United States*, 10 F.3d 931, 935-36 (2d Cir. 1993).

[262] 18 U.S.C. 3125(a).

[263] 18 U.S.C. 3121(b).

[264] *E.g., In re Application of the United States*, 849 F.Supp.2d 526 (D. Md. 2011); *In re Application of the United States*, 733 F.Supp.2d 939 (N.D. Ill. 2009); *In re Application of the United States*, 534 F.Supp.2d 585 (W.D. Pa. 2008); In *re Application of the United States*, 497 F.Supp.2d 301 (D. P.R. 2007); *In re United States*, 441 F.Supp.2d 816 (S.D. Tex. 2006); *In re Application of the United States*, 416 F. Supp. 390 (D. Md. 2006); *In re Application of the United States*, 415 F.Supp.2d 211 (W.D.N.Y. 2006); *In re Application of the United States*, 412 F.Supp.2d 947 (E.D. Wis. 2006); *In re Application of the United States*, 407 F.Supp.2d 134 (D.D.C. 2006) (each denying the application); *but see*, *In re Application of the United States*, 632 F.Supp.2d 202 (E.D.N.Y. 2008); *In re Application of the United States*, 509 F.Supp.2d 76 (D. Mass. 2007); *In re Application of the United States*, 460 F.Supp.2d 448 (S.D.N.Y. 2006); *In re Application of the United States*, 433 F.Supp.2d 804 (S.D. Tex. 2006); *In re Application of the United States*, 411 F.Supp.2d 678 (W.D. La. 2006)(each granting the application).

[265] 18 U.S.C. 3121(d), 3571.

[266] 18 U.S.C. 3124(e).

[267] *United States v. Forrester*, 512 F.3d 500, 512-13 (9th Cir. 2008); *United States v. German*, 486 F.3d 849, 852-53 (5th Cir. 2007); *United States v. Fregoso*, 60 F.3d 1314, 1320 (8th Cir. 1995); *United States v. Thompson*, 936 F.2d 1249, 1249-250 (11th Cir. 1991). To the extent that the unlawful use captures content, the Fourth Amendment exclusionary rule may apply, *cf., In re United States for Orders (1) Authorizing Use of Pen Registers and Trap and Trace Devices*, 515 F.Supp.2d 325, 328-38 (E.D.N.Y. 2007).

[268] Subsection 3124(d) makes the denial of a cause of action explicit for service providers and others assisting in execution of an order or emergency request. Subsection 3124(e) provides a good faith defense to civil liability on other grounds.

[269] *In re Sealing and Non-Disclosure of Pen/Trap/2703(d) Orders*, 562 F.Supp.2d 876, 879, 886-87 (S.D. Tex. 2008) ("Section 3123(d)(2) provides that the 'the person owning or leasing

the line or other facility to which the pen register or a trap and trace device is attached, or applied, or who is obligated by the order to provide assistance to the applicant' shall be directed not to disclose to any other person the existence of the pen/trap or the investigation 'unless or until otherwise ordered by the court.' Again, no particular showing by the government is required to justify non-disclosure, and no minimum time period is imposed or even suggested. In fact, the 'unless' clause implies that the court may refuse to enjoin disclosure even in the first instance. In the end, the duration of any gag order remains subject to the court's discretion.

An indefinite non-disclosure order is tantamount to a permanent injunction of prior restraint. To the extent such an order enjoins speech beyond the life of the underlying investigation, it must be narrowly tailored to serve a compelling governmental interest in order to pass muster under the First Amendment. The governmental interests considered here—the integrity of an ongoing criminal investigation, the reputational interests of targets, and the sensitivity of investigative techniques—are not sufficiently compelling to justify a permanent gag order. And because the statutes authorizing these non-disclosure orders must be construed whenever possible in a manner that avoids constitutional infirmity, it follows that neither 18 U.S.C. §2705(b) nor §3123 may be interpreted to permit a gag order of indefinite duration").

[270] *e.g.*, ARIZ. REV. STAT. ANN. §13-3005; FLA. STAT. ANN. §934.31; IOWA CODE ANN. §808B.10; N.H. RV. STAT. ANN. §570-B:2; UTAH CODE ANN. §77-23-13.

[271] *But see*, MINN. STAT. ANN. §626A.391. **Appendix E** contains the citations of state statutes that authorized court ordered installation and use of pen registers and trap and trace devices. **Appendix C** lists the citations of state statutes that create a separate cause of action for unlawful interception.

In: Electronic Communications Privacy Act ISBN: 978-1-62948-826-4
Editor: Marissa G. Haul

Chapter 2

STATEMENT OF JUDICIARY COMMITTEE CHAIRMAN BOB GOODLATTE. ''HEARING ON ELECTRONIC COMMUNICATIONS PRIVACY ACT (ECPA) PART 1: LAWFUL ACCESS TO STORED CONTENT''*

The dawn of the digital age and the explosive development of communication methods has brought with it faster ways to compile, transmit and store information. These developments have produced faster and more efficient ways to do everything from conducting commerce to connecting with friends.

Unfortunately, criminals have found ways to convert the benefits offered by new technology into new ways to commit crimes. At the intersection of these activities are the privacy rights of the public, society's interest in encouraging and expanding commerce, the investigative needs of law enforcement professionals, and the demands of the Constitution.

The Electronic Communications Privacy Act (ECPA) was designed to provide rules for government surveillance in the modern age. The technology of 1986 now seems ancient in comparison to today's. The interactive nature of the Internet, now including elements such as home banking and telecommuting, has produced an environment in which many people may spend hours each day "on-line." In this context, a person's electronic

---

* This is an edited, reformatted and augmented version of a statement, presented March 19, 2013 before the House Judiciary Committee, Subcommittee on Crime, Terrorism, Homeland Security, and Investigations.

communications encompass much more today than they did in 1986. Indeed in 2013, a person's electronic communications encompass much more than they did in 2000, when Congress acknowledged that much had changed since the original ECPA of 1986. ECPA reform must be undertaken so that despite the evolution of technology and its use in the world, the constitutional protections reinforced by ECPA will endure.

ECPA was intended to establish a balance between privacy and law enforcement. In addition, ECPA sought to advance the goal of supporting the development and use of new technologies and services. Those original tenets must and will be upheld as this law is improved.

There are many investigations in which ECPA is working, and working well. Pedophiles who sexually assault children and distribute video recordings over the Internet have become increasingly savvy. They encrypt their communications and use technologies to hide their identities and whereabouts. Investigators routinely use court orders under ECPA to identify these offenders, uncover caches of child pornography that has been stored remotely "in the cloud," and develop probable cause to execute warrants and arrest them.

ECPA reform is one of the top priorities of the House Judiciary Committee. Technology will help us solve many of the pressing problems our nation currently faces. We need to make sure that the federal government's efforts are focused on creating incentives that encourage innovation and eliminating policies that hinder it. In updating a law passed before the creation of the Internet, the modernization of ECPA needs to provide electronic communications with protection comparable to their more traditional counterparts and take into account the recent boom in new technologies like cloud computing, social networking sites and video streaming. That's why we will modernize the decades-old Electronic Communications Privacy Act to reflect our current digital economy while preserving constitutional protections.

This particular hearing focuses on issues related to the lawful access to stored communications under the current law. It is becoming clear that some reforms are necessary, but this committee will move toward modernization and reform after a thorough review and with input from all stakeholders.

I look forward to working with all members on both sides of the aisle to modernize the Electronic Communications Privacy Act.

In: Electronic Communications Privacy Act
Editor: Marissa G. Haul
ISBN: 978-1-62948-826-4

Chapter 3

STATEMENT OF ELANA TYRANGIEL, ACTING ASSISTANT ATTORNEY GENERAL, OFFICE OF LEGAL POLICY, DEPARTMENT OF JUSTICE. HEARING ON "ELECTRONIC COMMUNICATIONS PRIVACY ACT (ECPA) PART 1: LAWFUL ACCESS TO STORED CONTENT"*

Chairman Sensenbrenner, Ranking Member Scott, and Members of the Subcommittee, thank you for the opportunity to testify on behalf of the Department of Justice regarding the Electronic Communications Privacy Act (ECPA). This topic is particularly important to the Department because of the wide-ranging impact the statute has on public safety and both criminal and civil law enforcement operations. We are pleased to engage with the Subcommittee in discussions about how ECPA is used and how it might be updated and improved.

ECPA includes the Pen Register Statute and the Stored Communications Act (SCA), as well as amendments to the Wiretap Act. These statutes are part of a set of laws that control the collection and disclosure of both content and non-content information related to electronic communications, as well as content that has been stored remotely. Although originally enacted in 1986,

* This is an edited, reformatted and augmented version of a statement, presented March 19, 2013 before the House Judiciary Committee, Subcommittee on Crime, Terrorism, Homeland Security, and Investigations.

ECPA has been updated several times since, with significant revisions occurring in both 1994 and 2001.

I intend to focus the majority of my testimony on the SCA, which contains three primary components that regulate the disclosure of certain communications and related data. First, section 2701 of Title 18 prohibits unlawful access to certain stored communications: anyone who obtains, alters, or prevents authorized access to those communications is subject to criminal penalties. Second, section 2702 of Title 18 regulates voluntary disclosure by service providers of customer communications and records, both to government and non-governmental entities. Third, section 2703 of Title 18 regulates the government's ability to compel disclosure of both stored content and non-content information from a service provider; it creates a set of rules that all governmental entities must follow in order to compel disclosure of stored communications and other records.

Since its inception, the SCA has served multiple purposes. It provides the rules governing how providers of communications services disclose stored information—including contents of communications, such as the body of an email, and non-content information—to a wide variety of government entities. In doing so, it imposes requirements on the government and providers to ensure that the privacy of individuals is protected. The statute thus seeks to ensure public safety and other law enforcement imperatives, while at the same time ensuring individual privacy. It is important that efforts to amend the SCA remain focused on maintaining both of these goals.

I. The Stored Communications Act Has a Broad Scope

Any consideration of the SCA must begin with an understanding of the statute's extremely broad scope. The paradigm that generally comes to mind in discussions of the SCA is a law enforcement agency conducting a criminal investigation and seeking a target's email from a service provider that makes its services available to the public. And, indeed, the SCA is critical to all sorts of criminal investigations into murder, kidnapping, organized crime, sexual abuse or exploitation of children, identity theft, and more. As technology has advanced, appropriate governmental access to certain electronic communications, including both content and non-content information, has become even more important to upholding our law enforcement and national security responsibilities.

Even within these criminal investigations, it is important to understand the kind of information that the government obtains under the SCA as well as how that information is used. Under the SCA, the government may compel service providers to produce both content and non-content information related to electronic communications. It is clear that the contents of a communication—for example, a text message related to a drug deal, an email used in a fraud scheme, or an image of child pornography—can be important evidence in a criminal case. But non-content information can be equally important to building a case.

Generally speaking, service providers use non-content information related to a communication to establish a communications channel, route a communication to its intended destination, or bill customers or subscribers for communications services. Non-content information about a communication may include, for example, information about the identity of the parties to the communication, and the time and duration of the communication. During the early stages of an investigation, it is often used to gather information about a criminal's associates and eliminate from the investigation people who are not involved in criminal activity. Importantly, non-content information gathered early in investigations is often used to generate the probable cause necessary for a subsequent search warrant. Without a mechanism to obtain non-content information, it may be impossible for an investigation to develop and reach a stage where agents have the evidence necessary to obtain a warrant.

For example, the SCA has been critical to tracking down violent criminals. In one case, a suspected serial killer who had killed more than ten people sent an anonymous letter to a newspaper reporter that identified the location of a victim's body with an "X" drawn on a map. Investigators recognized the mapping website on which the serial killer generated the map. They obtained from that website the IP address of the user who had generated the map and then used ECPA process served on the user's internet service provider to obtain the physical address of the subscriber who had visited the mapping website. Using this information, the FBI and local police were able to arrest the suspect and stop his killing spree. ECPA process thus allowed law enforcement to trace an anonymous printout from the Internet back to the physical location of the target, in an extremely time-sensitive setting.

The SCA has broad effect in other ways as well. The statute applies not only to public and widely accessible service providers but also to non-public providers, such as companies or governments that provide email to their employees. Moreover, criminal investigations are only a subset of the circumstances in which the SCA applies. The statute applies to *all* government entities—federal, state, and local—when they seek to obtain content or non-content information from a service provider. This means that the statute also applies when the government is acting as a civil regulator—or even as an ordinary civil litigant. For instance, the SCA applies in all of the following circumstances that could arise, just within the Department of Justice:

- *Civil Rights Enforcement:* DOJ's Civil Rights Division brings a civil suit against a landlord who is sending racially harassing text messages to tenants. The target of the messages deletes them, and the landlord denies ownership of the account from which they were sent. The SCA governs the Division's ability to obtain those messages from the provider during civil discovery.
- *False Claims Act:* The DOJ Civil Division investigates a business for submitting fraudulent claims to the Federal government. The Division has reason to believe that the defendant's employees used email messages sent via the business's customer service email accounts to orchestrate the fraud. However, the defendant claims that it did not use email for business purposes. The SCA governs the ability of the Division to compel the internet service provider that hosted the company's website to disclose the contents of the business's email account.
- *Environmental Litigation:* The Department's Environment and Natural Resources Division brings a civil enforcement suit under the Superfund statute, a company relevant to the litigation has gone bankrupt, and the company's cloud provider has the only copies of that company's relevant corporate email. The SCA governs the Division's ability to obtain that email during civil discovery.
- *Antitrust Investigations:* The Department's Antitrust Division is conducting a civil investigation of several companies for engaging in an unlawful agreement to restrain trade. During the course of the investigation, DOJ attorneys discover that executives of those companies are using their personal email accounts to continue communications about the agreement. The SCA governs the Division's ability to obtain that email from the service provider.
- *Tax Enforcement:* The DOJ Tax Division investigates a tax preparation service that advertises via social networking sites. The

company fraudulently inflates the amount of refunds due to the taxpayer and profits from taking a significant share of the fraudulent refund. Based on complaints about the preparer, the social networking site closes the company's account. The SCA governs the Tax Division's ability to obtain the posts advertising the company's tax preparation services.

During any discussions of possible changes to the SCA and ECPA more broadly, it is important to keep in mind its wide-ranging application and scope.

II. Modernizing the Rules for Compelled Disclosure of Email and Other Similar Stored Content Information

As I mentioned, ECPA was originally enacted in 1986—a time when the internet was still a nascent technology and landline telephones predominated. Although ECPA has been updated several times since its enactment, the statute—and specifically the portion of the SCA addressing law enforcement's ability to compel disclosure of the stored contents of communications from a service provider—has been criticized for making outdated distinctions and failing to keep up with changes in technology and the way people use it today.

Many have noted—and we agree—that some of the lines drawn by the SCA that may have made sense in the past have failed to keep up with the development of technology, and the ways in which individuals and companies use, and increasingly rely on, electronic and stored communications. We agree, for example, that there is no principled basis to treat email less than 180 days old differently than email more than 180 days old. Similarly, it makes sense that the statute not accord lesser protection to opened emails than it gives to emails that are unopened.

Acknowledging that the so-called "180-day rule" and other distinctions in the SCA no longer make sense is an important first step. The harder question is how to update those outdated rules and the statute in light of new and changing technologies while maintaining protections for privacy and adequately providing for public safety and other law enforcement imperatives.

Personal privacy is critically important to all Americans—including those of us who serve in the government. It is also of increasing importance to individuals around the world, many of whom use communications services provided by U.S. companies. All of us use email and other technologies to share personal and private information, and we want it to be protected appropriately. We also know that companies in the United States and elsewhere depend on privacy as a driver of innovation and competitiveness. Some have suggested that the best way to enhance privacy under the SCA would be to require law enforcement to obtain a warrant based on probable cause to compel disclosure of stored email and similar stored content information from a service provider. We appreciate the appeal of this approach and believe that it has considerable merit, provided that Congress consider contingencies for certain, limited functions for which this may pose a problem.

For example, civil regulators and litigators do extremely important work. But they typically are investigating conduct that, while unlawful, is not a crime. Criminal search warrants are only available if an investigator can show probable cause that a crime has occurred. Lacking warrant authority, civil investigators enforcing civil rights, environmental, antitrust, and a host of other laws would be left unable to obtain stored contents of communications from providers. As increasing amounts of information are stored electronically, the amount of information that would be unobtainable to government regulators and litigators will only increase. It is also not the case that these civil regulators and litigators can ask criminal law enforcement officers to obtain a warrant on their behalf. For them to do so would be inappropriate because it would require the opening of a criminal investigation—a step that would be impermissible unless the underlying conduct appeared to be criminal in nature.

Nor could civil litigators and regulators reliably obtain email and other content information solely by serving a subpoena directly on a subscriber (rather than a provider). As several of the examples described above demonstrate, serving a subpoena on a provider may be the only way for civil law enforcement to obtain certain stored communications. For example, where the subscriber no longer exists—as in the case of a bankrupt corporation or a deceased individual—or a purported subscriber denies ownership of the communications and therefore refuses to comply with a subpoena, civil litigators and investigators without the ability to subpoena a provider would be unable to obtain relevant evidence. Moreover, many individuals who violate the law may be tempted to destroy their communications rather than turn them over. Serving a subpoena on the individual, rather than the provider, could serve to encourage such illegal obstruction of justice. Thus, it is important that any proposed changes to ECPA take into account the ability of civil regulators and litigators to compel disclosure of information from providers.

Reform efforts must also account for existing practices as to entities, such as corporations, that provide email to their employees. Investigations of corporate malfeasance— both civil and criminal—have long been conducted by subpoena. For example, it is settled law that a government investigator may use a subpoena to obtain corporate records such as memoranda, letters, or even printed emails. It would be anomalous for the SCA to afford greater protection to electronic corporate records than to the identical records in hard copy. In fact, the voluntary disclosure provision of the SCA already recognizes that this context is different: nonpublic providers may voluntarily disclose user communications without restriction. To be clear, it is decidedly not our view that subpoenas are blanket substitutes for warrants. But, in the narrow context of corporate investigations, it is important to remember that subpoenas are the norm for obtaining business records, and creating a different standard for different means of communications would hamper many such investigations.

Efforts to update ECPA can account for these considerations and, at the same time, incorporate strong mechanisms that protect individual privacy and ensure appropriate judicial oversight of government access to individual's communications.

III. The Need for Additional Updates to the SCA and ECPA

Although discussions about updating ECPA have often focused on the standard for governmental access to stored content information, we also believe there are a number of other parts of the statute that may merit further examination during any process updating and clarifying the statute.

A. Clarifying Exceptions to the Pen Register Statute

First, Congress could consider clarifying the exceptions to the Pen Register statute. The Pen Register statute governs the real-time collection of non-content "dialing, routing, addressing, or signaling information" associated with wire or electronic communications. This information includes phone numbers dialed as well as the "to" and "from" fields of email. In general, the statute requires a court order authorizing such collection on a prospective basis, unless the collection falls within a statutory exception. The exceptions to the Pen Register statute, however, are not coextensive with the exceptions to the Wiretap Act. This creates an unnecessarily complicated scheme where non-content information associated with a communication is subject to more extensive protection than the content itself. Congress could consider harmonizing the exceptions in these two sections of the statute. Moreover, the Pen Register Act's consent provision could helpfully be clarified to allow the user to provide direct, express consent for implementation of a pen/trap device by the government.

B. Clarifying the Standard for Issuing 2703(d) Orders

Second, Congress could consider clarifying the standard for the issuance of a court order under § 2703(d) of the SCA, which can be used by criminal law enforcement authorities to compel disclosure of various types of stored records. According to that provision of the statute, "[a] court order for disclosure ... may be issued by any court that is a court of competent jurisdiction and shall issue only if the governmental entity offers specific and articulable facts showing that there are reasonable grounds to believe that the [records] sought are relevant and material to an ongoing criminal investigation."

Until recently, no court had questioned that the United States was entitled to a 2703(d) order when it made the "specific and articulable facts" showing specified by § 2703(d).

However, the Third Circuit has held that because the statute says that a § 2703(d) order "may" be issued if the government makes the necessary showing, judges may choose not to sign an application even if it provides the statutory showing. *See In re Application of the United States*, 620 F.3d 304 (3d Cir. 2010). The Third Circuit's approach makes the issuance of § 2703(d) orders unpredictable and potentially inconsistent; some judges may impose additional requirements, while others may not.

C. Treating Civil Discovery Subpoenas Like Other Subpoenas

Third, Congress could consider ensuring that—where and to the extent subpoenas are already an acceptable means of obtaining information—courts treats civil discovery subpoenas just like they already treat grand jury subpoenas, trial subpoenas, and administrative subpoenas, in order to avoid unnecessarily impeding the government's ability to conduct civil litigation.

D. Making the Standard for Non-content Records Technology-Neutral

Fourth, Congress could consider modernizing the SCA so that the government can use the same legal process to compel disclosure of addressing information associated with modern communications, such as email addresses, as the government already uses to compel disclosure of telephone addressing information. Historically, the government has used a subpoena to compel a phone company to disclose historical dialed number information associated with a telephone call, and ECPA endorsed this practice. However, ECPA treats addressing information associated with email and other electronic communications differently from addressing information associated with phone calls. Therefore, while law enforcement can obtain records of calls made to and from a particular phone using a subpoena, the same officer can only obtain "to" and "from" addressing information associated with email using a court order or a warrant, both of which are only available in criminal investigations. This results in a different level of protection for the same kind of information (*e.g.*, addressing information) depending on the particular technology (*e.g.*, telephone or email) associated with it. Congress could consider updating the SCA to set the same standard for addressing information related to newer technologies as that which applies in traditional telephony.

E. Clarifying that Subscribers May Consent to Law Enforcement Access to Communications Content

Fifth, Congress could consider clarifying the consent provision of the SCA. Under section 2702, a provider *may* disclose the contents of communications with the consent of a user or customer, but the provider is not required to do so. This has the impact of allowing the provider to overrule its customer's direction to disclose content associated with the customer's account. Thus when the victim of a crime seeks to share his or her own emails or other messages that may provide evidence, providers can refuse to disclose that information to law enforcement, even when provided with a written release from the account owner or subscriber.

F. Appellate Jurisdiction for Ex Parte Orders in Criminal Investigations

Sixth, Congress could consider clarifying that higher courts have appellate jurisdiction over denials of warrants or other ex parte court orders in criminal investigations. Under existing law, the government may have no mechanism to obtain review of the denial of a court order or search warrant, even when the denial is based primarily on questions of law rather than questions of fact. Congress may wish to consider clarifying that these denials are appealable so that the disagreements among courts are resolved and the law becomes standardized.

* * *

In conclusion, I would like to reemphasize that in discussing any efforts to modernize ECPA, it is important to take into account the statute's broad application. As technology continues to advance, ECPA's importance to both criminal and civil law enforcement will only increase.

The Department of Justice stands ready to work with the Subcommittee as it considers potential changes to ECPA. We appreciate the opportunity to discuss this issue with you, and we look forward to continuing to work with you.

This concludes my remarks. I would be pleased to answer your questions.

In: Electronic Communications Privacy Act
Editor: Marissa G. Haul
ISBN: 978-1-62948-826-4

Chapter 4

TESTIMONY OF RICHARD LITTLEHALE, ASSISTANT SPECIAL AGENT IN CHARGE OF THE TECHNICAL SERVICES UNIT, TENNESSEE BUREAU OF INVESTIGATION. HEARING ON "ELECTRONIC COMMUNICATIONS PRIVACY ACT (ECPA) PART 1: LAWFUL ACCESS TO STORED CONTENT"*

Chairman Sensenbrenner, Ranking Member Scott, and members of the subcommittee,

My name is Richard Littlehale, and I am the Assistant Special Agent in Charge of the Technical Services Unit of the Tennessee Bureau of Investigation. We are the high-tech investigative unit of Tennessee's statewide criminal investigation agency. One of my unit's most important responsibilities is to help law enforcement agencies at all levels of government throughout Tennessee use communications records in support of their criminal investigations. I have used these techniques for the better part of eighteen

* This is an edited, reformatted and augmented version of a testimony, presented March 19, 2013 before the House Judiciary Committee, Subcommittee on Crime, Terrorism, Homeland Security, and Investigations.

years in support in cases ranging from searches for violent fugitives to efforts to recover abducted children.

I am grateful to the subcommittee for giving me the opportunity to share a law enforcement electronic surveillance practitioner's perspective on how access to stored communications evidence can be invaluable in the most critical of law enforcement investigations, and how improvements in the law can help my colleagues and I work faster and more efficiently to bring the guilty to justice and exonerate the innocent. My fellow practitioners and I especially appreciate the signal sent by your invitation to today's hearing, because state and local law enforcement conducts the vast majority of investigations in this country. Our community appreciates your recognition that our expert perspective should be a central consideration of any update to ECPA.

I offer testimony here today both on behalf of my agency, and as a representative of the Association of State Criminal Investigative Agencies (ASCIA), led by President Ron Sloan, the Director of the Colorado Bureau of Investigation. My agency's chief executive, TBI Director Mark Gwyn, is a member of ASCIA's Executive Board and a member of ASCIA's Technology Committee. He and the ASCIA Technology Committee chairman Steve Schierholt, Assistant Superintendent of the Ohio Bureau of Criminal Investigation, have asked me to serve as the ASCIA's subject matter expert on issues such as those before this subcommittee today.

Access to Evidence in the Digital Crime Scene

The crime scene of the 21st century is filled with electronic records and other digital evidence. The contents of this digital crime scene, including electronic communications records, often hold the key to solving the case. They also hold the key to ruling out suspects and exonerating the innocent. Law enforcement's ability to access those records quickly and reliably under the law is fundamental to our ability to carry out our sworn duties to protect the public and ensure justice for victims of crime.

To date, much of the scholarly and media attention given to the question of lawful access to stored content has focused almost entirely on the level of proof required for law enforcement to obtain it, and to a lesser extent on accountability considerations like customer notification and reporting requirements. From the law enforcement perspective, a set of concerns that is critical to our ability to use these records has been largely absent from the

ECPA reform debate. If Congress desires to update ECPA, it must do so in a way that addresses these concerns.

The simple truth is that legal barriers are not the only ones that keep communications records out of law enforcement hands. In many instances, we are unable to utilize evidence that would be of enormous value in protecting the public because the technologies used to carry and store that information are not accessible to us, no matter what legal process we obtain. That may be because of technological problems, but even more frequently it is because of logistical hurdles.

The companies that retain these records are many times unable or unwilling to respond to law enforcement's lawful demands in a timely manner. The primary emergency disclosure provision in the section of ECPA that we use to obtain stored content is *voluntary* for the providers, not mandatory, and even where emergency access is granted to law enforcement, in some instances, there is insufficient service provider compliance staff to process legitimate emergency requests quickly.

If you or a member of your family were a victim of a crime, and law enforcement needed timely access to electronic communications records to identify and apprehend the offender, would you be satisfied with this reality?

As Congress considers simplifying the legal requirements for obtaining communications records, and whether or not to change the standards law enforcement must meet to obtain those records, these other barriers to access must have a place in the discussion. *I urge Congress to ensure that regardless of the level of process it ultimately decides is appropriate, steps are taken to guarantee that law enforcement will be able to access the required communications transactional records reliably and quickly once that process is obtained.*

As we consider various law enforcement concerns, we must keep in mind a simple fact that is nevertheless often overlooked in the public discourse on this topic: we are talking about law enforcement's ability to gather *evidence*. Not "information" or "content" or "communications records," but *evidence*. All hammers are tools; a hammer only becomes *evidence* if it is relevant to a criminal investigation.

Similarly, law enforcement has no interest in communications records unless they advance a criminal investigation, whether to prove guilt or exonerate the innocent. The complete lack of a demonstrated pattern of misuse or abuse by law enforcement to access electronic communications records bears out this truth.

A LAW ENFORCEMENT PERSPECTIVE ON LAWFUL ACCESS TO STORED CONTENT

Timeliness and quality of service provider response. The timeliness and quality of service provider responses to lawful demands is of primary importance to the law enforcement community. We continue to encourage a thorough review of constructive measures to enhance service provider responsiveness to legitimate law enforcement process requests to ensure that investigative timelines are as short as possible. That is what we owe to the citizens we protect. There is no requirement in current law – including search warrant practice – for providers to respond in a timely fashion to lawful process requests by governmental entities. Some providers routinely respond in a timely way, but others do not. This has resulted in unnecessary investigative delays that adversely impact public safety.

Any contemplated change in the law that would result in a lengthening of the investigative timeline – including moving to a probable cause standard where it is not currently required – should be accompanied by provisions that ensure accountability and prompt response by service providers to legitimate law enforcement requests. These responsiveness issues are important to address even in the absence of an enhanced standard.

Service providers will often cite the high volume of law enforcement requests as a reason for response times that stretch on into months, threatening the underlying investigation. They say they do not have the staff necessary to process the volume of requests more quickly. We would urge the committee to consider that many of these companies are in the business of finding technological solutions to just this sort of problem. Further, they are well acquainted with monitoring customer service centers and determining adequate staffing levels. It is not a matter of capability, but rather a matter of will. Responding to law enforcement legal demands costs service providers money and does not generate revenue, however, and so there is little financial incentive to innovate or increase staffing levels. Therefore, a reasonable legal mandate for responsiveness may be the best solution to this problem. Such a solution need not be overly costly or burdensome to the providers. In a time when Congress is reluctant to impose new regulations on private industry, I would argue that this is one type of regulation that has a clear positive impact for the public. It protects citizens and allows victims of crime to see justice done. It should be addressed in any reform of ECPA, and we look forward to working with the providers and this subcommittee to consider the best way forward.

Notification provisions may put a greater burden on law enforcement than an increased proof requirement. Several ECPA reform proposals have borrowed language from wiretap law requiring notification of customers of legal demands, or securing a series of separate court orders delaying notification. These provisions risk diverting critical law enforcement resources from investigations simply to comply with burdensome notification provisions or delay orders that do not offer any additional constitutional protections, and may actually threaten ongoing investigations. We urge the committee to carefully balance the need for notification and reporting against the resources it will drain away from a range of investigative priorities.

CONCERNS ABOUT THE VOLUME OF LAW ENFORCEMENT LEGAL DEMANDS

As I address the issue of volume of legal process and its effect on timeliness of service provider response, I must also address a common talking point used by those who would further restrict law enforcement access to stored content: namely, that the number of law enforcement requests for this information is growing. Our response is simple: of course it is. That is because in the digital age, a growing percentage of the available evidence in any criminal case is going to exist in the digital crime scene. Communications records have taken their place alongside physical evidence, biological evidence, testimonial evidence, and the other traditional categories. Laws and policy should reflect this reality and ensure law enforcement access to evidence that by its nature can't make a mistaken identification in a lineup or testify untruthfully.

Google has provided an excellent example of how law enforcement demands truly relate to the new digital reality. Google now regularly publishes statistics on the number of government requests for information that it receives, broken down by the rate that it complies, proof standard, and a number of other factors. Public reporting on these statistical releases has tended to focus on the perception that law enforcement agencies are seeking access to this information at an excessive rate.

I applaud Google for this transparency initiative, but I believe some context is appropriate for the subcommittee's understanding. In June of 2012, Google claimed 425 million individual account holders for its Gmail product alone. In 2012, it reported receiving over 40,000 government requests for communications records worldwide, affecting about 68,000 users or accounts globally. In the U.S., Google reported a total of just over 16,000 government requests affecting just over 31,000 accounts. That means just a tiny fraction of one percent of Google's accounts were affected by government demands.

Consider that in the context of more than 17,000 law enforcement agencies in the United States. This means that on average, there was less than one request for information per law enforcement agency per year for Google records. Contrast that with crime reporting statistics, which reflect that in 2011, more that 14,000 Americans were murdered, more than 83,000 were forcibly raped, and there were over 350,000 robberies. It is hard to conclude from these numbers that law enforcement demands for records are excessive.

My fellow professionals and I deal with cases like that every day, and stored communications are a critical part of the constellation of evidence that allows us to identify the guilty and keep the public safe. I encourage the committee to keep these numbers in mind when some parties claim that law enforcement is "snooping" without regard to privacy. When we request these records, it is for a reason – we believe that the records constitute evidence that will lead to identification of sexual predators, the recovery of kidnapping victims, or the successful prosecution of a murderer. Any consideration of changes to ECPA that will make obtaining communications records more time-consuming and laborious should reflect an understanding of how those changes will impact our ability to do our job, and whether or not the public would truly be upset about the balance as it is currently struck.

Current emergency provisions within ECPA are not adequate to allow law enforcement to respond effectively in all cases. Few dispute that law enforcement should have rapid access to communications records in a life-threatening emergency, but few outside of our community truly understand how flawed the current emergency options are. The "emergency" provision in current law (18 USC 2702(b)(8)) puts the decision to release records before legal process is obtained, and about whether a situation is an "emergency," in the hands of the provider, rather that the law enforcement experts with their boots on the ground. This has led to situations where responses to legitimate law enforcement requests have been delayed. In some cases, providers make a decision never to provide records in the absence of legal process, no matter the circumstances.

We would further point out that 18 USC 2258, which has been erroneously cited as an emergency option for law enforcement in child exploitation cases, is in fact a requirement that service providers send information about online child exploitation to the National Center for Missing and Exploited Children. Law enforcement cannot use it as a means to obtain records directly. The service providers still require legal process or an emergency declaration under 2702 before they will provide the evidence that generated the referral to law enforcement.

Records retention is an issue that should be considered in any effort to update ECPA. Certain types of widely used electronic communications are not retained by some providers, which can hinder law enforcement investigations. In particular, most cellular service providers do not retain stored text messages accessible to law enforcement for any time at all. Billions of texts are sent every day, and some surely contain key evidence about criminal activity. In some cases, this means that critical evidence is lost. Text messaging often plays a big role in investigations related to domestic violence, stalking, menacing, drug trafficking, and weapons trafficking. I am well aware that retention means a cost for service providers. I would urge Congress to find a balance that is not overly burdensome to service providers, but that ensures that law enforcement can obtain access to critical evidence with appropriate legal process for at least some period of time.

Preservation provisions under current law should be revisited to ensure that law enforcement could prevent service providers from notifying customers of the existence of the request. Some proposals for ECPA reform would cause prior notification to law enforcement before a provider notifies a customer or subscriber about the existence of a warrant, order, or subpoena, and we believe that provision is important.

However, a similar provision relating to preservation should be considered. There are service providers who have stated a policy of notifying customers of any government inquiry unless they are in receipt of process ordering them not to do so. The principle behind their stance is laudable, but the real-world impact can be harmful to criminal investigations. Section 2705 offers a delay of notification scheme for court orders and subpoenas, but does not address preservation letters directly. If there is reason to believe that customer notification of the existence of a warrant, subpoena, or court order may result in:

1. endangering the life or physical security of an individual;
2. flight from prosecution;
3. destruction of or tampering with evidence;
4. intimidation of potential witnesses; or
5. otherwise seriously jeopardizes and investigation or unduly delays a trial,

then it seems that the ability to prevent early notification of the existence of a preservation letter issued in the early stages of an investigation with the intent to assemble a quantum of proof – such as probable cause – would be essential.

The definition of content must be clear and carefully considered. Definitions of "content" and "non-content" information need to be clear and comprehensive. Efforts to update ECPA should constrain the definition of content so that it does not expand over time to cover parts of an electronic communication that are ancillary to the actual purport, idea or intent of the writing, such as signaling, addressing, routing or URL information.

Any move to alter the standard of proof required to access stored content should be carefully considered in the broader context of the concerns identified above. If governing law is changed to require probable cause for any type of location information, there will be a negative impact on the time required for law enforcement to conduct certain types of investigations. Some of this impact can be balanced by changes in the law with respect to records retention and quality of service in response to law enforcement legal demands. Any effort to modify the standard of proof for access to stored content that does not address the concerns outlined above will lengthen law enforcement's investigative timeline, and therefore reduce our effectiveness and negatively impact our ability to bring criminals to justice.

CONCLUSION

A robust debate about balancing personal privacy and security is beneficial to all Americans, but the people and their representatives must be able to make an educated judgment about what they are giving up and what they are getting. There is no question that a growing number of personal details about all Americans are moving around the digital world, and some of those details make their way into digital crime scenes. Just as there is no question that people have an interest in preserving the privacy of that information, there can be no question that some of that information holds the keys to finding an abducted child, apprehending a dangerous fugitive, or preventing a terrorist attack. Whenever we move forward with the privacy/safety debate, we should be mindful that any restriction of law enforcement's access to that information, whether by redefining legal barriers or allowing service providers to erect new technological barriers, may well come at a price, and some of that price could be paid by our most vulnerable citizens. We should be sure we are willing to require them to pay it.

The thousands of law enforcement officers across this country who utilize communications evidence in the course of their duties recognize that we are guardians of a free society, a society that embraces in its founding law the decision to elevate the rights of the individual above incremental increases in public safety. The truth is that no one has put forward any evidence of pervasive law enforcement abuse of ECPA provisions. Law enforcement professionals also recognize that times are changing, and as a profession we are moving forward to utilize all available evidence in a responsible and effective way.

Ours is also a society that requires an open exchange of ideas on topics critical to the public interest, however, and we believe that the ECPA reform debate has been largely one-sided to date. As I hope to have shown, redrafting the laws governing law enforcement access to communications records raises significant implications for law enforcement's ability to protect the public. I urge the members of this subcommittee to ensure that the law enforcement community is given the opportunity to continue to share its perspective on the potential human implications of any proposed reform of the Electronic Communications Privacy Act, so that all the competing factors may be balanced appropriately.

I have always been proud of the Tennessee Bureau of Investigation motto, borrowed from the United States Supreme Court in *Berger v. United States.* It seems particularly appropriate in this context. The evidence in the digital crime scene, now more than ever, will help law enforcement to ensure "that guilt shall not escape, nor innocence suffer."

Thank you for the invitation to testify and I look forward to working with you on these important issues.

In: Electronic Communications Privacy Act ISBN: 978-1-62948-826-4
Editor: Marissa G. Haul

Chapter 5

STATEMENT OF ORIN S. KERR, FRED C. STEVENSON RESEARCH PROFESSOR, GEORGE WASHINGTON UNIVERSITY LAW SCHOOL. HEARING ON "ELECTRONIC COMMUNICATIONS PRIVACY ACT (ECPA) PART 1: LAWFUL ACCESS TO STORED CONTENT"*

It is my pleasure to testify this morning about the Electronic Communications Privacy Act ("ECPA"), and specifically about the provisions of ECPA that regulate government access to stored contents held by Internet providers. In my view, these important provisions are badly flawed and badly outdated.

My testimony will focus on five major problems with the statute governing access to stored contents under ECPA. First, the statute provides very weak protection for contents of communications held for more than 180 days.

Second, the statute appears to offer no protection for search engine queries. Third, the scope of the statute's warrant protection is uncertain. Fourth, part of the existing statute does not satisfy the Fourth Amendment.

* This is an edited, reformatted and augmented version of a Statement, presented March 19, 2013 before the House Judiciary Committee, Subcommittee on Crime, Terrorism, Homeland Security, and Investigations.

And fifth, the statute imposes no requirements of minimization, particularity, or non-disclosure for contents obtained under its provisions.[1]

These five problems point to a pressing need for Congress to revisit ECPA's provisions on lawful access to stored contents. My testimony will begin by summarizing the existing provisions of the law as they were enacted in 1986. I will then turn to the five major problems with those provisions from the perspective of 2013.

UNDERSTANDING ECPA'S CURRENT PROVISIONS ON COMPELLED ACCESS TO CONTENTS OF COMMUNICATIONS

The provisions of ECPA governing lawful access to stored content are found in 18 U.S.C. § 2703(a)-(b), which was enacted in 1986. These provisions create statutory privacy rights for "subscribers or customers" of two kinds of computer network services that existed at the time. The first kind of service is an "electronic communications service" provider ("ECS"), which is defined as "any service which provides to users thereof the ability to send or receive wire or electronic communications." 18 U.S.C. § 2510(15). Translated into plain English, an ECS is any service that provides connectivity, e-mail, or text messaging services. 18 U.S.C. § 2703(a) identifies the rules that the government must follow to compel contents of communications held by ECS providers. According to its provisions, the government needs a warrant to compel contents from an ECS provider if the contents have been stored for 180 days or less. If the contents have been stored for more than 180 days, however, the government can use lesser process pursuant to 18 U.S.C. § 2703(b).

The second type of Internet service regulated by the law is a "remote computing service" ("RCS"), defined as "the provision to the public of computer storage or processing services by means of an electronic communications system." 18 U.S.C. § 2711(2). In layman's terms, an RCS is a remote storage service that any member of the public can use, such as a cloud storage service. 18 U.S.C. § 2703(b) offers three ways that the government can compel contents held by an RCS or contents held by an ECS for more than 180 days. First, investigators can use a subpoena with either prior notice or delayed notice. Second, investigators can use a "specific and articulable facts" court order under 18 U.S.C. § 2703(d) with either prior notice or delayed notice. Third, investigators can use a warrant to obtain contents and do not need to satisfy a notice requirement.

Problem 1: No Warrant Protection for Storage More Than 180 Days

The current language of 18 U.S.C. § 2703(a)-(b) has five major problems. The first problem is that the statute does not require a warrant for remotely–stored contents held for more than 180 days. The government can compel contents held for more than 180 days with a mere subpoena. This is a strange result because most people use their e-mail accounts as a permanent storage site akin to a virtual home online. According to one recent report, a typical user of the popular Gmail e-mail service stores more than 17,000 e-mails in her account at any given time.[2] Almost 12,000 of those e-mails are received e-mails stored in the inbox, and almost 6,000 are sent e-mails directed elsewhere.[3] It is likely that most of those communications have been stored for more than 180 days. Under ECPA, however, only e-mails stored 180 days or less can receive statutory warrant protection. Anything stored for a longer time can be accessed by the government without a warrant. I find that aspect of the statute impossible to justify. It is a puzzling result that makes no sense for today's Internet and today's Internet users.

Problem 2: No Protection for Search Engine Requests

A second problem with the current statute is that private communications held by Internet services that do not fit within the definition of ECS or RCS receive no protection at all. Search engine requests provide the most important example. According to one study, search engines analyzed about 18.4 billion search requests from the United States in the month of March 2012 alone.[4] Search engine requests can reveal a person's innermost thoughts, and as a result such requests contain highly sensitive information. But it appears likely that search queries stored with services like Google are not protected under current law because they provide neither ECS nor RCS.

Search engines plainly do not provide ECS. They are destinations for communications, not providers of connectivity or messaging. And search queries do not appear to provide RCS, either. Recall that a remote computing service is defined by ECPA as a service that provides the public "computer storage or processing services by means of an electronic communications system."[5] Users do not send their search queries to search engines for storage purposes. Storage is a bug for users, not a feature. Whether ECPA protects search queries therefore hinges on whether search engines provide "processing services." The relevant text and legislative history suggests that they do not. In the context of computer data, the word "process" suggests operations on that data rather than a response to a query. The Senate Report accompanying ECPA clarifies the point: remote processing meant the outsourcing of tasks, such as number-crunching, that a computer of the 1980s might not be able to complete easily.[6] Search engines do not appear to fit the mold, as users do not use search engines as substitutes for the storage or processing powers of their own machines. For those reasons, it appears that likely that search engine queries are not protected by current law. The issue is not free from doubt, and courts have not ruled definitely on the issue.[7] But it appears that likely that search queries receive no statutory protection at all from the compelled storage provisions of ECPA.

Problem 3: The Scope of the Warrant Requirement Is Uncertain

A third important problem with the current statute is its uncertain scope. The most important example is opened e-mail stored for 180 days or less. Courts are presently divided on whether opened e-mails stored on a server will generally be covered by the ECS rules (which require a warrant) or the RCS rules (which do not).

The source of the difficulty is the complex definition of "electronic storage" in 18 U.S.C. § 2510(17), which is critical because only contents in "electronic storage" receive ECS protections. Some courts read the definition to include opened e-mails in the statute's ECS coverage on the theory that they are copies of e-mails stored "for backup purposes" under § 2510(17)(b). *See Theofel v. Farey–Jones*, 359 F.3d 1066, 1075-76 (9th Cir. 2004). On the other hand, other courts have concluded that opened e-mails are not covered by the ECS rules but rather are covered under the RCS rules on the theory that a user stores opened e-mails like other remotely stored files. The disagreement is presently the subject of a petition for certiorari before the United States Supreme Court seeking review of a decision from the Supreme Court of South Carolina. *See Jennings v. Jennings*, 736 S.E.2d 242 (S.C. 2012).[8]

Problem 4: The Statute Fails to Satisfy the Required Constitutional Standard

The fourth problem is the Fourth Amendment – or, more specifically, the statute's failure to measure up to constitutional standards. Existing lower court caselaw indicates that the provisions of 18 U.S.C. § 2703(b) fail to satisfy constitutional standards because they allow the government to obtain access to the contents of communications with less protection than a warrant based on probable cause.

The leading case is *United States v. Warshak*, 631 F.3d 266 (6th Cir. 2010), a Sixth Circuit decision involving government access to e-mails held by Yahoo!.

Investigators relied on 2703(b) to subpoena Yahoo! for the contents of stored e-mails relating to a criminal enterprise. Yahoo! complied, and it gave investigators copies of thousands of e-mail messages without a warrant.

The Sixth Circuit held that obtaining the contents of e-mails without a warrant was unconstitutional because users have a reasonable expectation of privacy in their e-mails just like their letters and phone calls. As a result, the provision of the SCA permitting the government to obtain e-mails with less process than a warrant did not satisfy the required Fourth Amendment standard. *See id.* at 288 ("[T]o the extent that the SCA purports to permit the government to obtain such emails warrantlessly, [that portion of] the SCA is unconstitutional.").

A number of courts have agreed with the Sixth Circuit since *Warshak*, including federal courts in Kansas[9] and the District of Columbia,[10] and the state of Washington Court of Appeals.[11] Other courts have applied *Warshak* to find a reasonable expectation of privacy in stored Facebook messages,[12] text messages,[13] faxes,[14] and password-protected websites.[15] The case law is not entirely settled, to be sure. Only one federal court of appeals has squarely addressed the issue. But the trend in the case law is to recognize fairly broad Fourth Amendment protection, backed by a warrant requirement, for stored contents such as e-mails.

Further, in my view *Warshak* is correct. Government access to remotely stored contents generally requires a warrant, meaning that the standards of § 2703(b) do not satisfy the constitutional floor provided by the Fourth Amendment. *See generally* Orin S. Kerr, *Applying the Fourth Amendment to the Internet: A General Approach*, 62 Stan. L. Rev. 1005, 1017-31 (2010).

Problem 5: Disclosure to Law Enforcement Allows All Disclosure Without Limits

The fifth problem with the current statute is that permitted disclosure comes without limits. When a provider must disclose the contents of communications, there are no limits on how many contents it can disclose or what the government can do with the contents it receives. Recall that a typical Gmail user stores more than 17,000 e-mails in his account at any given time.[16] If the government obtains a subpoena or even a warrant requiring a provider to disclose contents in a suspect's account, current law contains no limits on what gets disclosed or used. The provider will send the government the entire contents of the account. The government then has access to all of those contents. Investigators can scan through all of the contents of a person's digital life without limit.

To phrase this problem in legal jargon, the existing statutory provisions contain no requirement of particularity, minimization, or non-disclosure. Particularity requires the government to specify which records it is seeking. Minimization requires the government to set up a filtering system: One person can go through the records and pass on the pertinent communications to investigators. And non-disclosure rules limit what the government can do with communications it has obtained. The current statute contains no such limits. That absence may be explained by the statute's relatively ancient origin. In 1986, few remotely stored records were kept. But today it is common for computer users to store tens of thousands of records of their daily life online. Remote storage has become cheap, allowing users to store everything.

As a result, government access to stored records raises a needle-in-a-haystack problem. The current statute allows the providers to simply hand over the entire haystack to investigators. Investigators can then look through the haystack at their leisure without limits and can use or disclose whatever they find regardless of its relevance to the investigation. Given the highly sensitive information commonly found in a personal e-mail account, the statute should take more care to protect the non-pertinent communications that ordinarily will make up the bulk of the contents of communications found in an e-mail account. The Fourth Amendment may already impose some of these limits, and statutory authorities from the Wiretap Act adopt other limits when the government obtains a wiretap order.[17] The same protections should be written into the provisions for lawful access to stored content.

Thank you for the opportunity to testify. I look forward to your questions.

End Notes

[1] Parts of my testimony are adapted from a forthcoming article on ECPA reform that will be published in Volume 162 of the University of Pennsylvania Law Review.

[2] See Mike Barton, How Much Is Your Gmail Account Worth?, Wired, available at http://www.wired.com/insights/2012/07/gmail-account-worth/

[3] See id.

[4] See Press Release, comScore Releases March 2012 U.S. Search Engine Rankings, http://www.comscore.com/Insights/Press_Releases/2012/4/comScore_Releases_March_2012_U.S._Search_Engi ne_Rankings

[5] 18 U.S.C. § 2711(2).

[6] The Senate Report accompanying the passage of ECPA offered the following explanation of the concept of a "remote computing service" :

In the age of rapid computerization, a basic choice has faced the users of computer technology. That is, whether to process data inhouse on the user's own computer or on someone else's equipment. Over the years, remote computer service companies have developed to provide sophisticated and convenient computing services to subscribers and customers from remote facilities. Today businesses of all sizes—hospitals, banks and many others—use remote computing services for computer processing. This processing can be done with the customer or subscriber using the facilities of the remote computing service in essentially a time-sharing arrangement, or it can be accomplished by the service provider on the basis of information supplied by the subscriber or customer.

S. Rep. No. 99-541 (1986), at 10-11.

[7] Notably, Google has claimed that its search engine queries are covered by ECPA on the ground that it provides RCS. In litigation over the disclosure of Google search queries, Google made the following argument that its services are protected by the SCA:

Google processes search requests as directed by, and for, its users who in turn retrieve the search results of their choosing from Google's index, or Google sends the results by email or text messages to individuals, to wireless phones or other designated mobile devices. Said in plain language, users rely on the remote computer facilities of Google to process and store their search requests and to retrieve by electronic transmission their search results.

See Google's Opposition to the Government's Motion to Compel in Gonzales v. Google, 234 F.R.D. 674 (N.D. Cal. 2006), available at 2006 WL 543697.

[8] The Petition for Certiorari, Brief in Opposition, and an amicus brief filed before the United States Supreme Court are available at http://www.scotusblog.com/case-files/cases/jennings-v-broome/.

[9] In re Applications for Search Warrants for Information Associated with Target Email Address, 2012 WL 4383917 at *5 (D.Kan. 2012) ("The Court finds the rationale set forth in Warshak persuasive and therefore holds that an individual has a reasonable expectation of privacy in emails or faxes stored with, sent to, or received thorough an electronic communications service provider.")

[10] United States v. Ali 870 F.Supp.2d 10 (D.D.C. 2012)

[11] State v. Hinton, 280 P.3d 476, 483(Wash.App. Div. 2 2012) ("While Warshak does not aid Hinton, its comparison of e-mails with traditional forms of communication is helpful and we adopt it to hold that text messages deserve privacy protection similar to that provided for letters.")

[12] R.S. ex rel. S.S. v. Minnewaska Area School Dist. No. 2149 --- F.Supp.2d ----, 2012 WL 3870868 at 12 (D.Minn. 2012).

[13] State v. Hinton, 280 P.3d 476, 483(Wash.App. Div. 2 2012) ("While Warshak does not aid Hinton, its comparison of e-mails with traditional forms of communication is helpful and we adopt it to hold that text messages deserve privacy protection similar to that provided for letters.")

[14] In re Applications for Search Warrants for Information Associated with Target Email Address, 2012 WL 4383917 at *5 (D.Kan. 2012)

[15] United States v. D'Andrea, 497 F. Supp.2d 117, 121 (D. Mass. 2007).

[16] See Mike Barton, How Much Is Your Gmail Account Worth?, Wired, available at http://www.wired.com/insights/2012/07/gmail-account-worth/

[17] See, e.g., In re Applications for Search Warrants for Information Associated with Target Email Address, 2012 WL 4383917 (D. Kan. 2012) (imposing particularity requirements on a warrant for the contents of an e-mail account under the Fourth Amendment); See United States v. McGuire, 307 F.3d 1192 (9th Cir. 2002) (discussing minimization requirements for electronic communications under the Wiretap Act).

In: Electronic Communications Privacy Act
Editor: Marissa G. Haul
ISBN: 978-1-62948-826-4

Chapter 6

TESTIMONY OF RICHARD SALGADO, DIRECTOR, LAW ENFORCEMENT AND INFORMATION SECURITY, GOOGLE, INC.. HEARING ON "ELECTRONIC COMMUNICATIONS PRIVACY ACT (ECPA) PART 1: LAWFUL ACCESS TO STORED CONTENT"*

Chairman Sensenbrenner, Ranking Member Scott, and members of the Subcommittee, thank you for the opportunity to appear before you this morning to discuss updating the Electronic Communications Privacy Act (ECPA).

My name is Richard Salgado. As the Director for Law Enforcement and Information Security at Google, I oversee the company's response to government requests for user information under various authorities including ECPA. I am also responsible for working with teams across Google to protect the security of our networks and user data. I have served as a Senior Counsel in the Computer Crime and Intellectual Property Section in the U.S. Department of Justice, and have taught and lectured on these issues at Georgetown University Law Center, George Mason University Law School, and Stanford Law School.

---

* This is an edited, reformatted and augmented version of a testimony, Presented March 19, 2013 before the House Judiciary Committee, Subcommittee on Crime, Terrorism, Homeland Security, and Investigations.

Google is a member of the Digital Due Process Coalition, which supports updating ECPA. More than 80 organizations, trade associations, and corporations, including a number of which have joined in recent months, are now members of the Digital Due Process Coalition. Digital Due Process Coalition members include the American Civil Liberties Union, Americans for Tax Reform, the Center for Democracy & Technology, the Competitive Enterprise Institute, and the Electronic Frontier Foundation. Notably, these entities span the political spectrum. The diverse array of organizations, trade associations, and corporations that comprise the Digital Due Process Coalition is a testament to the recognition across the political spectrum and in the corporate community that there is a need to update ECPA.

The statute, though ahead of its time in many ways when enacted, needs to be brought in line with how people use the Internet today, provide them with the privacy they reasonably should expect, and allow the growth of the Internet — and the job creation and economic opportunity that such growth brings — to continue. Google believes this can be done while also ensuring that government agencies have the legal tools they need to efficiently and effectively protect public safety.

ECPA Reflects the Pre-Internet Computing Landscape of the 1980s

ECPA was enacted in 1986 — well before the web as we know it today even existed. The ways in which people use the Internet in 2013 are dramatically different than 25 years ago.

- In 1986, there was no generally available way to browse the World Wide Web, and commercial email had yet to be offered to the general public. Only 340,000 Americans subscribed to cell phone service, and not one of them was able to send a text message, surf the web, or download applications. To the extent that email was used, users had to download messages from a remote server onto their personal computer, holding and storing data was expensive, and storage devices were limited by technology and size.
- In 2013, hundreds of millions of Americans use the web every day — to work, learn, connect with friends and family, entertain themselves, and more. Data transfer rates are significantly faster than when ECPA

became law — making it possible to share richer data, collaborate with many people, and perform more complicated tasks in a fraction of the time. Video sharing sites, video conferencing applications, search engines, and social networks — all the stuff of science fiction in 1986 — are now commonplace. Many of these services are free.

The distinctions that ECPA made in 1986 were foresighted in light of technology at the time. But in 2013, ECPA frustrates users' reasonable expectations of privacy. Users expect, as they should, that the documents they store online have the same Fourth Amendment protections as they do when the government wants to enter the home to seize documents stored in a desk drawer. There is no compelling policy or legal rationale for this dichotomy.

THE INTERNET IS NOW PART OF EVERYDAY LIFE

New forms of Internet computing, more popularly known as "cloud computing," have emerged since ECPA was first signed into law. This computing model is used today by significant numbers of consumers, businesses, and the public sector. Companies like Google offer users the ability to store, process and access their data from servers located in offsite data centers, rather than on the user's premises. We provide our users with the ability to get work done on any device, store important documents, easily share and collaborate, and receive a service's latest innovations just by refreshing your browser.

For example, Google's services, including Google Search, Gmail, YouTube, Blogger, Google Drive, and Google Calendar, allow our users to run programs and store data on our geographically distributed and secured data centers. Businesses are increasingly choosing to use such data centers — managed by Google and many other technology companies — the same way they once used their desktop computers or on-premise file servers. In the process, they are saving money, becoming more efficient, and improving their security.

More than five million businesses are now running on Google Apps and benefiting from more modern technology at a lower cost. These include Global 500 companies, top American universities, and state and local agencies in 45 states. Everyday processes and information that are typically run and stored on local computers — such as email, documents, and calendars — can now be accessed securely anytime, anywhere, and with any device through an Internet connection.

Internet computing also enables services like online video and shared document collaboration among people across the country or around the world. As customer needs grow, the services they use can be expanded on demand, without requiring slow and burdensome procurement processes.

These services have created enormous and tangible value in the economy, spawning new businesses and spurring innovation and further growth in the tech sector. As communications and networks become faster and more data intensive, this sector will continue to create new jobs and more opportunities for investors, innovators, and small businesses.

It is increasingly difficult for individual business and organizations to keep up with the growing sophistication of cyber attacks. However, web services leverage significant economies of scale to bring both human and technology resources to bear in defense against such attacks. Google's services are delivered on a multi-billion dollar infrastructure that is designed and maintained with security as a top priority. The latest security updates can be pushed quickly across all of our data centers globally, protecting all of our customers in a more effective and uniform way than traditional software would allow. We've also made the Internet safer for millions of users by providing them with with free, strong-authentication mechanisms — such as two-step verification — and secured connections through SSL encryption.

Information technology (IT) departments within companies and other organizations are vulnerable to sophisticated attackers. Often underfunded and undermanned, these IT departments are further susceptible to cuts when financial constraints require it. Removing artificial and counterproductive legal standards that hinder movement to services offered by providers like Google will help strengthen our nation's network security.

ECPA Should be Updated

As the benefits of Internet computing become more obvious and widespread, its growth shouldn't be artificially slowed by the outdated technology assumptions that are currently baked into parts of ECPA. Nor should the progression of innovation and technology be hobbled by pre-Internet ECPA provisions that no longer reflect the way people use the services or the reasonable expectations they have about government access to information they store on Internet services. ECPA worked well for many years, and much of it remains vibrant and relevant. In significant places, however, a large gap has grown between the technological assumptions made in ECPA and the reality of how the Internet works today. This leaves us, in some circumstances, with complex and baffling rules that are both difficult to explain to users and difficult to apply.

The current complexity can be demonstrated by the requirements to compel production of communications content such as email. ECPA provides that the government can compel a service provider to disclose the contents of an email that is older than 180 days with nothing more than a subpoena (and notice to the user, which can be delayed in certain circumstances). If the email is 180 days or newer, the government will need a search warrant. The Department of Justice also takes the position that a subpoena is appropriate to compel the service provider to disclose the contents of an email even if it is not older than 180 days if the user has already opened it. The Ninth Circuit Court of Appeals has rejected this view. In 2010, the Sixth Circuit held in *United States v. Warshak* that ECPA violates the Fourth Amendment to the extent that it does not require law enforcement to obtain a warrant for email content. Google believes the Sixth Circuit's interpretation in *Warshak is* correct, and we require a search warrant when law enforcement requests the contents of Gmail accounts and other services.

Warshak lays bare the constitutional infirmities with the statute and underscores the importance of updating ECPA to ensure that a warrant is uniformly required when government entities seek to compel production of the content of electronic communications. The inconsistent, confusing, and uncertain standards that currently exist under ECPA illustrate how the law fails to preserve the reasonable privacy expectations of Americans today. Moreover, providers, judges, and law enforcement alike have difficulty understanding and applying the law to today's technology and business practices. By creating inconsistent privacy protection for users of cloud services and inefficient, confusing compliance hurdles for service providers, ECPA has created an unnecessary disincentive to move to a more efficient, more productive method of computing. ECPA must be updated to help encourage the continued growth of the cloud and our economy.

IMPROVING TRANSPARENCY

We believe that better data about the requests that governmental entities make under ECPA can help inform the broader debate around updating ECPA.

We are the first Internet company to launch a Transparency Report, which provides data about government requests we have received since 2009. Google's Transparency Report provides data about the volume of requests we receive from governments around the world. Other companies, including Twitter, Dropbox, Linkedin, and Sonic.net, are now publishing their own transparency reports. These efforts to provide transparency to users are important, and we hope others will join them. Over the three years that we've provided these reports, government requests for user data issued to Google in criminal matters in the U.S. have increased by 136%. We recognize that local, state, and federal law enforcement agencies have legitimate needs for data. We also recognize the need to ensure that disclosure laws such as ECPA properly honor the privacy that users of communications services reasonably expect. Our hope is that the Transparency Report will inform that discussion.

In 2013 alone, we've taken several steps to be more transparent with our users about government requests that we receive:

- On January 23, we began publishing more detailed data about the types of government requests that we receive in the United States pursuant to ECPA.
- On January 28, we published a new section to our Transparency Report and a blog post that explains how we handle and respond to government requests.
- On March 5, we began including some data about the number of National Security Letters (NSLs) that we receive.

Going forward, we're committed to exploring ways to surface more data and provide greater insight into the government requests we receive. Transparency in this context has had a salutary effect in encouraging a broader discussion about the importance of updating ECPA.

* * * * *

We look forward to working with this Subcommittee, the full Judiciary Committee, and Congress as a whole to strengthen the legal protections for individuals and businesses that rely on our services so that technological innovation can continue to drive economic growth, while ensuring that law enforcement continues to have the legal tools needed to investigate and prosecute crime.

Thank you for your time and consideration.

In: Electronic Communications Privacy Act
Editor: Marissa G. Haul
ISBN: 978-1-62948-826-4

Chapter 7

STATEMENT OF JUDICIARY COMMITTEE CHAIRMAN BOB GOODLATTE. "HEARING ON ELECTRONIC COMMUNICATIONS PRIVACY ACT (ECPA), PART 2: GEOLOCATION PRIVACY AND SURVEILLANCE"*

The Electronic Communications Privacy Act or "ECPA" provides a myriad of protections. Keep in mind that it was enacted well before our everyday use of cell phones and the Internet. Yet ECPA sets forth the rules which prevent unauthorized government access to certain electronic records. Even when it became law in 1986, ECPA, perhaps unintentionally, set the standards for the court-authorized disclosure of geolocation information.

A suspect's location is often only a piece of the puzzle for law enforcement, but sometimes that piece is a matter of life or death. In 2001, enhanced or "E" 9-1-1, was deployed in the U.S. to associate a location with the origin of a phone call. Geolocation is critical in cases of child abductions, lost hikers, and missing Alzheimer's patients where every minute counts. In many other investigations, geolocation is a vital building block in order to prevent or curtail a crime. Many criminals use false identities to impede law enforcement so they may complete their crimes and commit more. In every

* This is an edited, reformatted and augmented version of a statement, Presented April 25, 2013 before the House Judiciary Committee, Subcommittee on Crime, Terrorism, Homeland Security, and Investigations.

case, the identity of the criminal is essential for the investigation to move forward. The geolocation of dangerous fugitives is crucial, particularly after they are convicted of crimes like rape and murder.

Today, many civil liberty concerns center on the abundance of new technological devices and a lag in the law keeping pace with this new technology. For instance, the law is well-settled when it comes to police entering a home to arrest someone or conduct a search. However, complexities arise when, by the use of cell phones, we are permitting communications providers to record our location to route a phone call. We also allow them to record our location in order to advertise to us or send us instant coupons on our cell phones when we subscribe to a certain “app”. Cellular providers often use cell tower data but also use GPS technology and our public Wi-Fi connections to determine where we are. In updating our federal surveillance laws, Congress must weigh our privacy interests with the needs of law enforcement without stifling commerce and innovation.

Last week, the Department of Justice briefed Judiciary staff on its current practices in seeking geolocation data. I was encouraged to learn that the Department seeks a court order for every type of geolocation information it acquires. At a minimum, the Department obtains what is called a 2703(d) federal court order when it seeks historical cell site data on a particular cell phone. This cell site data only provides very general location information which can vary widely.

On the other side of the spectrum, the Department of Justice obtains a search warrant from a federal judge when it seeks very accurate, real-time location information based on GPS satellite technology. Such search warrants are based on probable cause, the same standard specified in the Fourth Amendment to our Constitution. While these practices are encouraging, current DOJ practices do not carry the same weight as federal statutes. The privacy interests we have in our cell phones are being protected today through a patchwork of federal laws. Our task is to re-examine current laws and give clarity to individuals, corporations, innovators and law enforcement.

I look forward to working with my colleagues to examine geolocation privacy and surveillance. Our efforts must protect individual liberties by providing clear guidelines for when and how geolocation information can be accessed and used.

In: Electronic Communications Privacy Act
Editor: Marissa G. Haul
ISBN: 978-1-62948-826-4

Chapter 8

STATEMENT OF MARK ECKENWILER, SENIOR COUNSEL, PERKINS COIE, LLP. HEARING ON "ELECTRONIC COMMUNICATIONS PRIVACY ACT (ECPA) PART 2: GEOLOCATION PRIVACY AND SURVEILLANCE"*

I. INTRODUCTION

Chairman Sensenbrenner, Ranking Member Scott, and distinguished members of the Subcommittee, thank you for convening this hearing. It is an honor to appear before you today to discuss the important legal and technical issues raised by law enforcement access to wireless user location data.

Let me say at the outset that these comments reflect my personal views. I am not speaking for or on behalf of any client or group of clients, nor for my former colleagues at the Department of Justice. Instead, I offer my personal observations, drawn from over 16 years of working with the Electronic Communications Privacy Act (ECPA) while with the Justice Department and, more recently, in the course of representing service providers in private practice.

---

* This is an edited, reformatted and augmented version of a statement, presented April 25, 2013 before the House Judiciary Committee, Subcommittee on Crime, Terrorism, Homeland Security, and Investigations.

II. Types of Location Data Available from Wireless Carriers

To understand the issues surrounding law enforcement access to carrier-held location data, it is essential to start with the technology, not the law. Law enforcement typically seeks two distinct types of location data from wireless carriers: cell-site location information and precision location data.

A. Cell-Site Location Information (CSLI)

As you know, cellular providers rely upon a network of antennas to provide service across large coverage areas. Whenever a user places or receives a voice call (or sends or receives a text message), the radio portion of that communication is transmitted between the customer's handset and a nearby tower. If the user moves in the course of a voice call—such as when traveling on the highway—the call may be seamlessly "handed off" to one or more other towers in sequence as the handset moves through different coverage areas.

Spacing between towers is determined primarily by the amount of network activity (and thus by the number of users) in a given area. In sparsely populated regions, cell towers are widely spaced, with each typically serving a coverage area several miles in radius. In suburban areas with moderate population density, carriers place towers closer together, with each having a service radius of a mile or less. Antennas in center cities are clustered even more tightly, with cell towers in the most densely populated areas (such as midtown Manhattan) spaced every 200 meters or less.

In suburban and urban areas, the coverage area for a given cell tower is typically subdivided into multiple sectors (or tower "faces"). In these cases, there are typically three 120-degree sectors, each with its own antenna. (To visualize this configuration, imagine a clock face divided into thirds from 10 to 2, 2 to 6, and 6 to 10. Each "pie slice" represents the coverage area for a given antenna.) Towers in sparsely populated areas, by contrast, normally have a single omnidirectional antenna.

Whenever a user places or receives a voice call (or sends or receives a text message), the network handling that communication—which may be the customer's home network, or another network with which the customer's carrier has a roaming agreement—creates a record of the first cell tower that handles the call or text message. If the tower coverage area is divided into multiple sectors, the stored cell-site location information (CSLI) record also indicates which particular antenna handled the communication. Most, but not all, carriers also record the last tower (and, where applicable, sector) handling a voice call. Because text messages are short, and thus are transmitted almost instantaneously, they pass through only a single antenna.

The degree to which CSLI reveals the location of a user's phone varies for several reasons. First, these records *do not* provide grid coordinates for the phone itself; rather, they indicate which nearby antenna transmitted a communication associated with that handset. Because tower spacing varies enormously, the radius of corresponding tower coverage does as well, and therefore the projected area from where a call was placed will likewise vary.

In heavily populated urban areas, CSLI can—subject to the further limitations discussed below— place a handset in an area of approximately 1,000 square meters. In suburban areas with towers spaced further apart, CSLI may suggest an area of a square mile or more. Tower data from rural areas, by contrast, provides only very broad location data often covering dozens of square miles or more.

Other factors also contribute to the general imprecision of CSLI. For example, the boundaries between the sectors of an individual cell tower, as well as the boundaries between areas served by different towers, are neither precise nor fixed. Records showing communications activity alternating between two adjacent coverage areas may indicate handset movement back and forth between the areas, or may instead result from the activity of a non-moving user in an area of overlapping coverage.

More importantly, a particular communication is not always handled by the closest tower. Both natural terrain features (*e.g.*, hills and valleys) and man-made structures interfere with line-ofsight radio transmission. Weather conditions, including precipitation or even humidity level, also may affect signal propagation.

At times, the carrier antenna closest to the user's handset may even be entirely unavailable. This can result from local, temporary equipment or network outages, or simply from network congestion. For example, when highway traffic backs up at a toll plaza or accident scene, the nearest tower's capacity may be saturated by unusually high activity levels. In these circumstances, the next user trying to make a call may only be able connect to a more distant, less burdened tower; the resulting CSLI record will indicate usage of the latter, creating the misleading impression that the handset was closer to that tower than to any other.

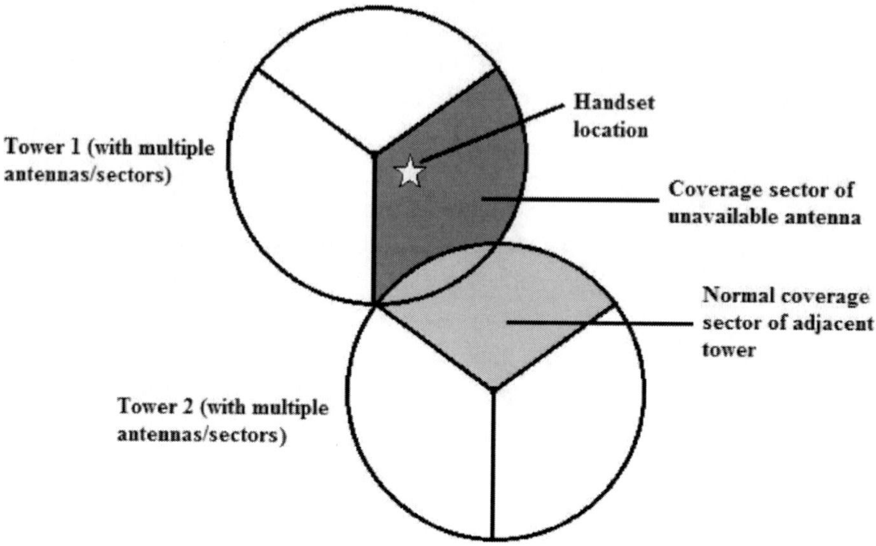

Figure 1.

In Figure 1 above, the star represents a hypothetical handset location; the dark area represents the normal, but temporarily unavailable, coverage area for the closest antenna on Tower 1; and the light gray area depicts the normal coverage area for an adjacent tower's sector. Activity handled by Tower 2 would create a record associating the handset with the light gray area, even though the phone was outside that sector and closer to Tower 1.

Some commentators assert that the increasing use of "microcells" with smaller coverage areas renders CSLI functionally equivalent to GPS or other more precise location technologies. These claims are misleading. User-owned microcells – such as those purchased and installed by home customers – do not expand the network of towers available to the general population. Rather, these microcells are usable only by their owners, and therefore cannot provide service to, let alone identify the location of, the millions of other cell phone users.

B. Laws Restricting Disclosure of CSLI to Government Agencies:

The Electronic Communications Privacy Act (ECPA) is the main federal statute regulating communications privacy. ECPA draws numerous distinctions between

- real-time (prospective) collection and access to historical records;
- communications content and non-content records; and
- transactional non-content records and more limited subscriber records.

Depending on the type of information sought and the manner in which it is to be collected, ECPA requires varying forms of compulsory process. These range from subpoenas—issued by a prosecutor (or, in some cases, an investigative agency) on the comparatively low standard of relevance—up through various types of increasingly demanding court orders—with wiretap orders (based on probable cause and other special requirements) at the other end of the spectrum.

1. Access to Stored CSLI

As originally enacted in 1986, ECPA allowed the government to obtain any stored non-content record about a communications provider's customer using a grand jury, trial, or administrative subpoena. As part of the 1994 Communications Assistance for Law Enforcement Act (CALEA), however, Congress amended ECPA to divide non-content records into two categories.

The first of these categories, often referred to informally as "basic subscriber information," remains available in response to a subpoena.[1] These records—explicitly enumerated in an exhaustive list of six categories—include the customer's name, address, account identifier, length of service, and method of payment. Except for "local and long distance telephone connection records, or records of session times and durations," however, this category does not include records about specific user activity.

Instead, when law enforcement seeks to compel a service provider to disclose other stored non-content records, it must apply for a unique type of court order that was created in the 1994 amendment to ECPA.[2] To obtain this so-called "2703(d) order" (named for the section of the statute where it resides), the government must

> offer[] specific and articulable facts showing that there are reasonable grounds to believe that ... the records or other information sought, are relevant and material to an ongoing criminal investigation.

As explained in the report from this Committee, "[t]he intent of raising the standard for access to transactional data is to guard against 'fishing expeditions' by law enforcement."[3] Advocating strongly in favor of this raised standard during an August 11, 1994 joint House-Senate committee hearing on the legislation,[4] the Executive Director of the Electronic Frontier Foundation described the proposal as follows:

> Chief among these new protections is an enhanced protection for transactional records from indiscriminate law enforcement access.
>
> ... Provisions in the bill recognize that this transactional information created by new digital communications systems is extremely sensitive and deserves a high degree of protection from casual law enforcement access which is currently possible without any independent judicial supervision. ...
>
> In order to gain access to transactional records ... law enforcement will have to prove to a court, by the showing of "specific and articulable facts" that the records requested are relevant to an ongoing criminal investigation. This means that the government may not request volumes of transactional records merely to see what it can find through traffic analysis. Rather, law enforcement will have to prove to a court that it has reason to believe that it will find specific information relevant to an ongoing criminal investigation in the records it requested. ...
>
> Court order protection will make it much more difficult for law enforcement to go on "fishing expeditions" through online transactional records, hoping to find evidence of a crime by accident. ...
>
> The most important change that these new provisions offer is that law enforcement will: (a) have to convince a judge that there is reason to look at a particular set of records, and; (b) have to expend the time and energy necessary to have a United States Attorney or District Attorney actually present a case before a court.

An overwhelming majority of courts, including the federal Third Circuit Court of Appeals, has found that historical "CSLI from cell phone calls is obtainable under a § 2703(d) order."[5] Although a handful of lower courts have held that section 2703(d) does not apply to stored CSLI, this view has failed to win broader acceptance.[6]

Many of these same lower court judges have also argued that historical CSLI is protected by the Fourth Amendment, and that a warrant is therefore necessary to compel such third-party records. Here, too, this represents a minority position; so far as I am aware, no federal court has ever granted a motion to suppress CSLI on these or any other grounds, despite attempts by numerous criminal defendants.[7]

2. Prospective Collection of CSLI

CSLI acquired in real time is qualitatively the same (and thus its value is subject to the same practical limitations) as historical CSLI. The rules governing real-time government acquisition of CSLI from wireless carriers are, however, much less clear.

The pen register statute permits the government to obtain a court order authorizing ongoing collection of non-content "dialing, routing, addressing, or signaling information,"[8] information that would normally include CSLI. However, CALEA states that

> with regard to information acquired solely pursuant to the authority for pen registers and trap and trace devices (as defined in section 3127), such call-identifying information [delivered by a carrier to the government] shall not include any information that may disclose the physical location of the subscriber (except to the extent that the location may be determined from the telephone number) ....[9]

This restriction creates a gap in the statutory framework: although it declares which type of process may not be used (*i.e.*, a bare pen register order), it does not prescribe the types of court orders that may be used. (Moreover, the other major federal statute governing real-time surveillance—the far more demanding Wiretap Act—does not apply because it regulates only the collection of communications *contents.*[10])

In an effort to fill this gap, prosecutors began to apply for court orders under the combined authority of the pen register statute and section 2703(d) (which, as discussed above, requires a higher showing) on the grounds that such orders are not "solely pursuant" to pen register authority. Beginning in 2005, however, lower court judges started to reject these so-called "hybrid" orders. While some of these courts based their objections on obvious misunderstandings of the technology and kinds of data involved,[11] others reasoned that section 2703(d)—located in the Stored Communications Act,[12] and lacking provisions that address duration and other aspects of real-time surveillance—could not be used to collect information prospectively. These courts concluded that the government needs to use a search warrant, not because the Fourth Amendment requires it, but rather because a search warrant is the only available mechanism.[13]

Courts remain sharply divided on this question, with practices varying from district to district (and, in some cases, from one judge to another within a single federal district). Even courts endorsing the hybrid theory have called upon Congress to resolve the issue.[14]

C. Precision Location Information (PLI)

Beginning in 1997, the FCC adopted regulations requiring cellular carriers to be able to locate wireless 911 callers. Phase I of this rulemaking— known as Enhanced 911 or simply E-911—required carriers to be able to deliver a 911 caller's cell-site and sector information (*i.e.*, CSLI) to the "public safety answering point" (*i.e.*, the 911 call center). Because of the inherent limits on the precision of CSLI, E-911 Phase II (in effect today) requires carriers to be able to deliver more precise location information.

In imposing these obligations, the FCC permitted carriers to choose either of two different methodologies for complying:

1. *Handset-based location technology* relying on special hardware or software in the mobile phone itself. U.S. carriers opting for such a "handset solution" have chosen to use Global Positioning System (GPS) technology, in which the phone calculates its position based on signals received from overhead GPS satellites.
2. *Network-based location technology* in which the work of calculating a phone's position occurs not on the handset, but rather in the carrier's network. This "network solution" typically involves measuring the time required for a test signal to travel between the handset and detection devices on cell towers in the vicinity. Using the known locations of those towers and the different timing information, software in the carrier's network is able to calculate a position for the phone. (This process, technically known as "multilateration," is often referred to informally as "triangulation.")

Generally speaking, the regulations require such E-911 Phase II location information to be accurate to within 50-300 meters.[15]

Contrary to popular belief, carriers do not collect these types of precise location information (PLI) on consumer-level users in the ordinary course of business.[16] As a result, historical PLI from these technologies is not available to law enforcement.

However, law enforcement may nevertheless seek PLI on a prospective basis. Because ECPA itself provides no clear mechanism for compelling this type of information, it is common for prosecutors to obtain a search warrant under Federal Rule 41 or a state equivalent. In doing so, some prosecutors rely on the explicit "tracking device" provisions of Rule 41, while others rely upon the Rule's well-established history of use as a general means of conducting ongoing evidence collection.[17] These may appear either in the form of stand-alone warrants, or as supplemental authority incorporated into a wiretap order.[18]

III. Issues Deserving Congressional Attention

As suggested above, there are several areas in which the current legal framework is not entirely satisfactory. These include the following:

1. *Hybrid orders.* Easily the source of greatest controversy, the government's use of hybrid orders—*i.e.,* court orders combining the authority of the pen register statute and the "specific and articulable facts" test of section 2703(d) —has led to a sharp divide among lower federal courts. Greater clarity in this area would be an enormous benefit to the service provider community; providers have a substantial interest in knowing with certainty the boundaries of what is lawful, in protecting their customers' privacy, and in avoiding potential civil liability.
2. *"Tower dumps".* Instead of seeking historical CSLI for the identified phone of a specific target, prosecutors sometimes use a section 2703(d) order to seek all records associated with calls handled by a given tower for a specified interval of time (usually corresponding to the date and time of an unsolved crime). These so-called "tower dumps" can be essential to identifying suspects in certain kinds of crimes such as bank robberies,[19] but almost invariably involve disclosure of large numbers of user records. The volume of information varies enormously according to time of day, the size of the requested time frame, and the type of area (rural, suburban, or urban) at issue, but can reveal thousands or even tens of thousands of records.[20]

Given the potential for disclosure of such customer information, the Committee may wish to consider the desirability of additional statutory protections such as limits on the number of records or the length of the time window requested, or protocols for sealing or destroying voluminous non-pertinent records.

3. *Warrants or orders to surveil unidentified phones contacting a target phone.* Prosecutors at the state level sometimes apply for warrants or court orders that authorize monitoring the location not only of a named target phone (as to which they must establish probable cause),

but also of *any other* phone that contacts (or is contacted by) the target phone during the authorized period of surveillance. This is a troubling practice: it allows for location monitoring of an undetermined number of phones not identified in the warrant, and on the questionable assumption that even a single contact with the target phone constitutes evidence of criminal activity.

In light of the potential for significant, unjustified privacy invasions—for example, from misdialed numbers or calls from family members or others uninvolved in criminal activity—the Committee should carefully consider whether additional safeguards are required to limit or prohibit these types of orders.

4. *Legal framework for real-time PLI monitoring.* More generally, the Committee may wish to examine the adequacy of the current, somewhat ad hoc use of Rule 41 to authorize real-time law enforcement access to PLI. Specific areas for potential review include the following:

   a) *Whether the "tracking device" provisions are adequate for use in this area.* Rule 41 requires that a "tracking device" warrant be issued in the district where the device is "install[ed]."[21] Although this poses no problems in the case of the physical tracking devices clearly contemplated by the Rule's drafters, it is a potentially serious obstacle in situations where (1) the court believes the tracking device provisions strictly apply to cell phone location and (2) the applicant cannot attest that the phone is within the district at the time of application. Indeed, since the objective of such applications is to *learn* the location of the target phone through court-authorized electronic surveillance, this requirement generally creates a Catch-22.

   b) *Burden on service providers, and compensation therefor.* Rule 41 does not impose any explicit limit on how often law enforcement may request PLI in the course of executing a prospective warrant. In many instances, manual intervention by carrier personnel is necessary, often on nights and weekends, making frequent requests extremely burdensome. Moreover, Rule 41 contains no provisions for compensating carriers for their often substantial compliance costs.

   c) *Emergency requests.* Both the Wiretap Act and the pen register statute include express language allowing law enforcement to conduct surveillance in emergencies without first obtaining court authorization.[22] Each of these statutes requires the government to apply to a court for retroactive authorization within 48 hours. By contrast, Rule 41 contains no such emergency compulsion provision.

CONCLUSION

ECPA and its companion statutes currently provide significant privacy protection for wireless customers' location data. However, at least one gap in the statute has provoked widespread disagreement among federal judges, and other practical and procedural difficulties have emerged over time. Because these problem areas have a direct impact on user privacy, on service providers' compliance practices, and on our Nation's law enforcement efforts, the Committee deserves great credit for recognizing the need to re-examine the existing legal authorities and consider potential solutions.

Thank you for this opportunity to testify. I look forward to your questions.

End Notes

[1] See 18 U.S.C. § 2703(c)(2).

[2] See § 2703(d).

[3] H. Rep. No. 827, 103d Cong., 2d Sess., at 31 (Oct. 4, 1994).

[4] Digital Telephony and Law Enforcement Access to Advanced Telecommunications Technologies and Services, 1994: Joint Hearings on H.R. 4922 and S. 2375 Before the Subcomm. on Technology and the Law of the Senate Comm. on the Judiciary and the Subcomm. on Civil and Constitutional Rights of the House Comm. on the Judiciary, 103d Cong., 2d Sess. 160-61 (1994) (prepared statement of Jerry J. Berman, Executive Director, Electronic Frontier Foundation).

[5] In re Application, 620 F.3d 304, 313 (3d Cir. 2010).

[6] Courts adopting this minority view point to the exclusion of "any communication from a tracking device (as defined in section 3117 of this title)" from ECPA's definition, at 18 U.S.C. § 2510(12)(C), of "electronic communication." (As noted by the Third Circuit, this view fails to distinguish between a communication itself – such as a phone call – and data about the communication, such as CSLI.) The minority view has the perverse consequence of excluding CSLI entirely from ECPA's protections, meaning that the government could compel CSLI using lesser compulsory process such as a subpoena.

[7] See, e.g., United States v. Graham, 846 F. Supp. 2d 384 (D. Md. 2012) (finding no Fourth Amendment interest); see also United States v. Jones, 2012 WL 6443136 at *5 & n.9 (D.D.C. Dec. 14, 2012) (collecting cases).

[8] 18 U.S.C. § 3127(3).

[9] 47 U.S.C. § 1002(a)(2).

[10] See 18 U.S.C. §§ 2510(4) (defining "intercept" to mean "the aural or other acquisition of the contents" of a protected communication) & 2510(8) (defining "contents" to mean "any information concerning the substance, purport, or meaning of [a] communication").

[11] The most obvious example of this phenomenon is In re Application, 402 F. Supp. 2d 597 (D. Md. 2005), in which the court confuses CSLI with GPS data. See id. at 599.

[12] Chapter 121 of Title 18 is entitled "Stored Wire and Electronic Communications and Transactional Records Access."

[13] Typical of this line of cases is In re Application, 497 F. Supp. 2d 301 (D.P.R. 2007).

[14] See In re Application, 632 F. Supp. 2d 202, 211 (E.D.N.Y. 2008) ("District courts across the country are divided on an issue that requires balancing the Government's investigatory needs with citizens' right to privacy. Absent clarity from Congress, this division and inconsistency in outcomes will continue because the issue is one about which reasonable judges can, and obviously do, disagree."); In re Application, 460 F. Supp. 2d 448, 450 (S.D.N.Y. 2006).

[15] The applicable regulation (47 C.F.R. § 20.18(h)) lays out a complex set of criteria, including several deadlines for compliance across increased geographic areas. In general, handset-solution phone location data must be more precise than network-solution data.

[16] Many carriers do, however, offer so-called "fleet management" services to business customers at additional cost. In some cases, these services—intended for locating a company's delivery drivers, construction site supervisors, and the like—permit not only real-time monitoring but also review of historical PLI.

[17] Prior to the 2006 addition of tracking device provisions, prosecutors used Rule 41 to obtain warrants when needed to authorize the use of such devices. This practice flowed directly from the Supreme Court's directive in United States v. Karo, 468 U.S. 705, 718 (1984), to seek a warrant for certain tracking device uses. Prior to the 1986 enactment of the pen register statute, the Supreme Court likewise read Rule 41 as "sufficiently flexible" for use in authorizing prospective surveillance of dialed telephone numbers. United States v. New York Telephone Co., 434 U.S. 159, 169 (1977). And the federal circuits are unanimous in relying on Rule 41 as authority for issuance of surreptitious video surveillance warrants, even though the Rule contains no explicit provisions contemplating this use. See, e.g., United States v. Koyomejian, 970 F.2d 536, 542 (9th Cir. 1992) (en banc); United States v. Cuevas-Sanchez, 821 F.2d 248, 252 (5th Cir. 1987).

[18] See, e.g., United States v. Ortega-Estrada, 2008 WL 4716949 at *14 (N.D. Ga. Oct. 22, 2008).

[19] See, e.g., Criminal Complaint, United States v. Capito (D. Ariz. Mar. 12, 2010) (describing, at pp. 12-15, the use of tower dump data to identify the phones used by suspects at four separate armed bank robberies), available at http://tinyurl.com/towerdump.

[20] According to the Capito complaint, "[i]nvestigators used the four most rural [bank robbery] locations in order to minimize the amount of extraneous telephone data that would likely be obtained ...." Id. at 13.

[21] Fed. R. Crim. P. 41(b)(4).

[22] See 18 U.S.C. §§ 2518(7) (wiretap emergency authority) & 3125 (pen register).

In: Electronic Communications Privacy Act
Editor: Marissa G. Haul
ISBN: 978-1-62948-826-4

Chapter 9

STATEMENT OF PETER A. MODAFFERI, CHAIR, POLICE INVESTIGATIVE OPERATIONS COMMITTEE OF THE INTERNATIONAL ASSOCIATION OF CHIEFS OF POLICE. HEARING ON "ELECTRONIC COMMUNICATIONS PRIVACY ACT (ECPA) PART 2: GEOLOCATION PRIVACY AND SURVEILLANCE"*

INTRODUCTION

Good Morning Chairman Sensenbrenner, Ranking Member Scott, and distinguished members of the subcommittee. Thank you for this opportunity to speak to you this morning to discuss geolocation information, the role that information plays as evidence in criminal investigations, and its importance in law enforcement's effort to seek justice and public safety in the 21st century.

My name is Peter A. Modafferi and I am the Chief of Detectives of the Rockland County, New York District Attorney's Office. I also Chair the Police Investigative Operations Committee of the International Association of

* This is an edited, reformatted and augmented version of a Statement, Presented April 25, 2013 before the House Judiciary Committee, Subcommittee on Crime, Terrorism, Homeland Security, and Investigations.

Chiefs of Police and I have worked on a number of boards, working groups and committees concerned with issues related to criminal investigations.

I have been a detective for 41 years. For many years I conducted investigations into all types of criminal activity and I now lead, direct and coordinate these investigations. Today I wish to share with you what I have learned about investigations both from my experiences in Rockland County and from the exposure to the field which I have gained through various committees and working groups.

It is from this vantage point that I have seen the great potential that lies in law enforcement's utilization of the innovations in geolocation information. Utilizing this information in the early stages of an investigation often provides fundamental building blocks on which cases may rest. Requiring probable cause in the initial stage of an investigation to gain access to geolocation information would make it significantly more difficult to solve crimes.

It is my observation that, today, there is a digital evidence aspect to nearly every crime scene. Increasingly, those scenes are filled with digital evidence and, inevitably, to fully benefit from that evidence we must gather geolocation information. Some of this valuable evidence that is crucial in generating leads and ruling out suspects is in jeopardy if we are held to a probable cause standard to access every aspect of geolocation data.

There are issues of time, technology and process that must be addressed in such a manner that will allow us to proceed with an investigation from its initial stages, where little is known and nothing can be assumed, to a point where we go in the direction of establishing probable cause. From this point, we will hopefully proceed to an arrest that will withstand the rigors of due process and the judicial system and lead with 100% accuracy to a conviction beyond a reasonable doubt.

My Perspective

Crime is and always will be one of the most serious issues confronted by civilization.

Today's communications systems, worldwide information services, massive participation in social media services and multi-national economic partnerships have dramatically impacted our society. It is to this "globalized" environment that law enforcement must adapt, culturally and technologically in order to address crime.

THE INVESTIGATIVE PROCESS

Why Is Geolocation Information Valuable to Law Enforcement?

In the initial stages of an investigation, law enforcement seeks to quickly develop leads and theories that incorporate answers to classic questions presented: Who, What, Where, When, Why and How. Geolocation evidence can inform the answer to each question. The unique value of geolocation information is found in its two components – an accurate location and an accurate time the location was determined.

When investigators start working a case, little may be known and nothing should be assumed. To know pertinent facts and make valid assumptions, investigators use available geolocation evidence as a filter. This process allows investigators to winnow out and prioritize leads from the unorganized mass of related and unrelated information that surrounds a crime and a crime scene.

This process is the beginning of the effort to assemble an offering of probable cause to believe that a certain person or persons committed the crime, and that particular evidence will be found in specific locations.

Through the lens of geolocation evidence, investigators press to correctly determine an answer to Who, When and Where - what witnesses, victims, knowledgeable persons and perpetrators – were in the vicinity of the crime at about the time it occurred.

How Is Geolocation Evidence Used in an Investigation?

In addition to providing clarity by answering some or all of the initial questions presented, the time and place components of geolocation information can be of use to corroborate or refute statements and conclusions offered at any time during the investigation.

Geolocation information can be used to confirm or dismiss alibi statements that are offered to show that a subject was not present at the time and place the crime occurred, or to confirm or dismiss the claim of a witness or another knowledgeable person who was present at a certain time or place.

A location-enabled digital device can be a “witness” to a crime. In fact, in cases where a human witness does not exist or is not discovered, the stored contents of the device may be the only initial “witness” available to investigators. In this case, the geolocation information components of time and place are of upmost importance.

JUSTICE AND PUBLIC SAFETY IN THE 21ST CENTURY

Evidence is the basic foundation for addressing crime and criminals. The investigative process is how we secure the evidence we need to protect society and attain justice and public safety in the 21st century. Today we are part of a digital world and in that world digital evidence abounds.

Geolocation evidence is essential to obtain in the early stages of investigations when probable cause has not been established. Requiring probable cause to get basic, limited information about a person's historical location would make it significantly more difficult to solve crimes and seek justice for victims.

We do not have the luxury of setting the pace at a crime scene or in conducting an investigation. If we are constrained by a process that slows our progress in pursuing justice by extending the timeline of an investigation, the digital evidence at a crime scene may well go unexplored, evidence not be seized and analyzed, and our investigation will not meet our needs or the expectations of victims or civilized society as a whole.

The court room and judicial process are the safety net for a free and just society. That wrongful convictions have occurred is tragic and everything must be done to avoid them in the future. The process starts at the crime scene or with knowledge that a crime may have been committed and proceeds ahead. In the end, the basic fact is that you cannot have a wrongful conviction without a wrongful arrest. A wrongful arrest is the result of an inadequate investigation.

We have found that wrongful arrests occur because what we thought was proof wasn't always concrete, and what we thought was science was not always definitive. Some of our investigations, based on flawed conclusions, were neither necessarily accurate nor conclusive.

Geolocation information offers tremendous factual data that can be used to remedy these failures. Geolocation information can confirm or refute identifications, confessions and inaccurate testimony.

Added to the issues raised through the examination of wrongful convictions is globalization. The "usual suspects" are not just from the "old neighborhood" anymore. Globalization has, in the words of Thomas Friedman "unleashed the energies of hundreds of millions of people"[1]. Unfortunately some of those people and their energies result in crime. Criminal activity and the location of criminals is not restricted by the limits and boundaries of an earlier era. Many of those boundaries have evaporated. The only boundaries that now limit globalization are governmental, which for criminals are easy obstacles to overcome.

To learn from this and better ourselves we must take full advantage of all that is available in today's world. Processes, guidelines and standards must be developed that will allow law enforcement to gain from technological evolution and attain what Friedman refers to as "productivity impact." Utilizing all that can be found at a crime scene or directly from a device recovered through a crime scene will not simply result in an increase in arrests but also an increase in accuracy and effectiveness, which will lead to justice and public safety in the 21st century.

An investigation is a process. It starts with the basics of who, what, when and where which may lead to a suspect, facts, evidence and probable cause to believe a suspect committed the crime. Utilizing geolocation information will offer substantial facts which will assist in obtaining a conviction beyond a reasonable doubt.

Law enforcement in the 21st century must combine new technologies with new ways of doing business to maximize investigative potential, create productivity "breakthroughs" and bring criminals to justice. "Productivity impact" in law enforcement investigations can be achieved in part through effective use of geolocation information.

A recent investigation into a series of bank robberies in the tri state area around New York City offers a significant example of how geolocation information can help solve a case and avoid a possible wrongful conviction.

Two brothers, residents of New York City, had robbed seven banks in the suburbs outside of the city. Utilizing standard investigative methods, detectives developed a suspect. Bank employees however were not able to identify the individual because he wore a mask. As the investigation progressed, a teller from one of the banks that were robbed believed she had seen the defendant at a gas station and photographed the vehicle he was driving. However, none of the employees at the banks could identify the individual from the gas station as the robber.

Utilizing a range of legal process from a subpoena to a court order, detectives obtained basic geolocation information, which eventually led to development of probable cause and the placing of a GPS system on the vehicle. Once probable cause was established the suspect's location was monitored by tracking his cell phone.

The geolocation information obtained without a warrant at the beginning of the investigation when probable cause was not determined led to the arrest of two individuals immediately after a bank robbery. At the time of arrest they had the proceeds of the robbery in their possession.

As it turned out the original suspect was not the individual who entered the banks during the robberies. He was a cousin. If not for the teller seeing one of the brothers and photographing the vehicle he has just purchased (it had dealer license plates at that time) the actual robbers would not have been traced. Though similar in appearance, the man at the gas station was the person who entered the bank not the person the police were focusing on.

The right persons were arrested due to the effective use of geoloaction information at the early stages of the investigation when probable cause was not evident. Standard identification procedures were of no value.

FOLLOWING THE DIGITAL FOOTPRINT

The essentials to ensure the effectiveness of law enforcement lie in establishing a basic foundation from which we can pursue investigations. Investigations don't start with probable cause; they *lead us* to probable cause. Through investigations we discover facts. From these facts we start to build our case, which will hopefully lead to building probable cause and a fact-filled evidentiary case that leads to guilt beyond a reasonable doubt.

What is a "digital footprint" and how can investigators benefit from it? The science and technology behind geolocation has opened a new world filled with data that can corroborate or refute human observations. Geolocation information is part of a person's "digital footprint."

Evidence garnered through geolocation information can be established through of all types of equipment and records. Phones, mobile devices, trackers, and preinstalled (OnStar) technology are available today with more specific technology evolving at a rapid pace. Also from this technology comes the historical data and business records from which location information can be derived – EZ Pass, Credit Card / Debit Transactions, etc.

To establish probable cause we need a reasonable, manageable balance between legal process and investigative responsiveness.

As an example, an anonymous tip was offered to the Rockland County Drug Task Force. The tip included the name of an individual and a phone number connected to that individual. The caller stated that this person was operating a clandestine laboratory manufacturing illegal drugs.

The person offering the information stated that the principals involved in this criminal conspiracy had met recently at the location of the laboratory. The caller also stated an approximate date and time of that meeting. As is often the case, the initial information available to the investigators could not be confirmed and the person offering the information wished to remain anonymous.

The first step in the investigation was to subpoena basic subscriber information and limited call detail records. These subpoenas were issued in an effort to further identify the user of the given phone number and to display incoming and outgoing calls to and from associate numbers. This was done in an attempt to propose that certain associate phone numbers pointed to other members of the group and to discern a communications pattern between the conspirators. Any other associate numbers were ignored.

The boundaries of the information sought were confined to the proposed date/time window suggested by the caller.

Once a group of apparently related associate phone calls was established at the date and time proposed, historical geolocation information associated with the interacting phone numbers was obtained. This stored historical geolocation information is created and retained by the service provider during the operation of the cellular phone system. The boundary of this information was limited to the narrowed date/time in hopes that it might suggest a possible location of the meeting and the laboratory.

The use of this geolocation information led to the possible location of the lab and this information combined with standard police surveillance procedures led to a search warrant for the lab based on probable cause. We would not have been able to establish probable cause without the geolocation information provided in response to the initial subpoenas.

The technologies and records that can lead to geolocation of a criminal or exoneration of an innocent party varies between situations where geolocation is already "turned on" and recorded, and geolocation that results form a real time effort to obtain geolocation information. We can subpoena previously obtained records data or, following proper legal process, we can "turn on" appropriate technology.

CONCLUSION

Very little, if any, construction begins with out a foundation. Geolocation information is an essential building block in "the construction" of a criminal investigation. Often it will prove to be the concrete that cements eyewitness identification and the crime scene together. Geolocation puts us in an area where evidence and possibly a criminal or fugitive can be found.

To gather up and cement these building blocks together in the initial stages of an investigation we must determine a reasonable, manageable balance between legal process and investigative responsiveness. (Note, an emergency situation initiates a different, more expeditious process). In a criminal investigation, or a public safety/security event, access to geolocational information and records is an essential requirement to the determination of true facts. Likewise, it is essential to receive these facts in a rapid and complete response from the holder of that information or record.

I have not attempted to address the science and techniques used to derive geolocation information because I am not a technologist. What I have addressed in my testimony are the needs, the logistics and the processes that relate to the use of technology that helps law enforcement make accurate, effective and efficient decisions in the course of an investigation. Requiring probable cause to get basic, limited information about a person's historical location would make it significantly more difficult to solve crimes and seek justice.

Thank you for your time and the opportunity to address this issue.

End Note

[1] The World is Flat, Thomas Friedman, Farrar, Straus & Giroux, April 2005.

In: Electronic Communications Privacy Act
Editor: Marissa G. Haul
ISBN: 978-1-62948-826-4

Chapter 10

STATEMENT OF CATHERINE CRUMP, STAFF ATTORNEY, AMERICAN CIVIL LIBERTIES UNION. HEARING ON "ELECTRONIC COMMUNICATIONS PRIVACY ACT (ECPA) PART 2: GEOLOCATION PRIVACY AND SURVEILLANCE"*

Good morning Chairman Sensenbrenner, Ranking Member Scott and Members of the Subcommittee. Thank you for the opportunity to testify on behalf of the American Civil Liberties Union, its more than half a million members, countless additional activists and supporters, and fifty-three affiliate organizations nationwide.

Over the past week and a half, our nation has been gripped by the horrific events in Boston. Today our thoughts remain with the victims of this tragedy, with their families and with the diverse spectators and athletes that comprise the Boston Marathon community. Although details of the investigation are still unfolding, it is apparent that electronic surveillance played an important role in locating and tracking the suspected perpetrators. This is as it should be. No one denies that electronic surveillance such as access to mobile phone location data is a valuable law enforcement tool—and indeed, in horrific and rare events such as the Boston Marathon bombings, an essential one. That is why

* This is an edited, reformatted and augmented version of a statement, Presented April 25, 2013 before the House Judiciary Committee, Subcommittee on Crime, Terrorism, Homeland Security, and Investigations.

the ACLU has supported and continues to support an exemption in the law, permitting the immediate disclosure of location data to law enforcement agencies in such life and death situations.

However, in routine investigations, law enforcement agencies such as local police and the FBI should secure a warrant based upon probable cause to obtain mobile phone location data.

The ACLU supports the Geolocation Privacy and Surveillance Act because the framework it establishes allows law enforcement to access the tools they need, while providing an independent check and balance through a review by a judge which will ensure that innocent Americans do not have their privacy violated.

I. INTRODUCTION

Mobile phone technology provides law enforcement agents with an invasive yet inexpensive method of tracking individuals over extended periods of time and unlimited expanses of space as they traverse public and private areas.

It also makes it possible for law enforcement agents to identify all individuals located in a specific area—a valuable tool, but one that by necessity reveals the location of vast numbers of innocent Americans. In many parts of the country, the police have been obtaining mobile phone location data for days, weeks, or months at a time, without ever having to demonstrate to an independent judge that they have a good reason to believe that tracking will turn up evidence of wrongdoing.

Congress should reform our electronic privacy laws to require law enforcement agents to secure a warrant based upon probable cause to obtain mobile phone location data.

The warrant and probable cause requirements ensure that an objective magistrate determines that there is a good reason to believe that a search will turn up evidence of wrongdoing before mobile phone location data is disclosed.

The application of this standard as a routine matter, coupled with immediate disclosure of location data to law enforcement agencies in true emergencies, would ensure that legitimate law enforcement investigations can proceed and that Americans will not suffer undue invasions of their privacy.

II. Mobile Phone Technology Enables Invasive Tracking of Americans' Movements

Today mobile phone technology makes it possible to obtain location data about the vast majority of Americans with great precision, in both real time and historically. As of June 2012, there were 321.7 million wireless subscriber accounts in the United States—a number greater than the total U.S. population.[1] Mobile phone technology has given law enforcement an unprecedented new surveillance tool. With assistance from mobile phone carriers, the government now has the technical capability to covertly track any one of the nation's hundreds of millions of mobile phone owners, for 24 hours a day, for as long as it likes. Through so-called "tower dumps," it can also identify all of the individuals whose mobile phones used a particular tower—allowing law enforcement agents to infer who was present at a location days, weeks or months after the fact.

A. Types of Mobile Phone Location Data Available to Law Enforcement Agents

Mobile phones yield several types of information about their users' past and present locations and movements: cell site location data, triangulation data, and Global Positioning System data. The most basic type of mobile phone location information is "cell site" data or "cell site location information," which refer to the identity of the cell tower from which the phone is connected and the sector of the tower facing the phone. This data is generated because whenever individuals have their mobile phones on, the phones automatically and frequently scan for nearby cell towers that provide the best reception. The carriers keep track of the registration information to identify the cell tower through which calls can be made and received. The towers also monitor the strength of the telephone's signal during the progress of the call to manage the hand-off of calls from one adjacent tower to another if the caller is moving during the call.[2]

The precision of cell site location information depends, in part, on the size of the coverage area of each cell tower. This means that as the number of cell towers installed in cities and towns has increased and the coverage area for each cell tower has shrunk, cell site location information has become more precise. As Professor Matt Blaze has testified, the latest generation of cellular towers now may cover an area as small as a tunnel, a subway, a specific roadway, a particular floor of a building, or even an individual home or office.[3] Customers with poor cell phone coverage in their homes can request that their carrier provide them a "femtocell," a small cellular base station, which can cover just one home.[4] As consumers embrace data-hungry devices such as smartphones, the carriers have installed more towers, each with smaller coverage areas in order to cope with the demand for data.

Further improvement in precision can be expected given the explosive demand for wireless technology and its new services, to the point that "[t]he gap between the locational precision in today's cellular call detail records and that of a GPS tracker is closing, especially as carriers incorporate the latest technologies into their networks."[5] In the words of Professor Blaze, "[i]t is no longer valid to assume that the cell sector recorded by the network will give only an approximate indication of a user's location."[6]

In addition to cell site information, law enforcement agents can obtain location data at a high level of accuracy by requesting mobile phone carriers to engage in "triangulation," which entails collecting and analyzing data of the precise time and angle at which the mobile phone's signal arrives at multiple cell towers. Current technology can pinpoint the location of a mobile phone to an accuracy of within 50 meters or less anytime the phone is on, and the accuracy will improve with newer technology.[7]

Finally, a mobile phone that has GPS receiver hardware built into it can determine its precise location by receiving signals from global positioning satellites. Current GPS technology can pinpoint location when it is outdoors, typically achieving accuracy of within 10 meters.[8]

B. Types of Government Requests for Mobile Phone Data

Law enforcement agents can request two categories of cell site location information: historical cell site data, which can be used to retrace previous movements, or prospective cell site data, which can be used to track mobile phones in real time. The availability of historical information and the length of time this information is stored depend on the policies of the mobile phone carrier. According to an internal Department of Justice document, obtained by the ACLU through a public records act request, mobile phone carriers store their customers' historical location information for significant periods of time: Verizon stores the cell towers used by a mobile phone for "one rolling year"; T-Mobile keeps this information "officially 4-6 months, really a year or more"; Sprint and Nextel store this data for "18-24 months"; and AT&T/Cingular retains it "from July 2008."[9]

Law enforcement agencies can obtain data regarding the movements of one or more persons over time, or they can obtain data regarding all of the people whose phones were using a particular tower at a particular time. This latter method of obtaining cell site location information is often referred to as a "tower dump."

Because tower dumps obtain the information of everyone whose phone was using a particular cell phone tower, by their nature they sweep in vast quantities of data about innocent people who will never know that their location data was shared with the government.

Mobile carriers have established automated systems to provide location and other customer data to law enforcement agents. For example, Sprint created a website, which was used to transmit 8 million "pings" of location data in a year.[10]

Sprint charges $30 a month per target for use of its L-Site program to track location.[11] Location surveillance is one of the cheapest and easiest, yet most invasive forms of government surveillance.

III. Current Law Is Unclear and Inadequately Protective of Privacy

There is confusion among courts, law enforcement agents and members of the public regarding what legal standard law enforcement agents must meet to obtain mobile phone location data. The principal law that governs law enforcement access to records regarding electronic communications, the Electronic Communications Privacy Act of 1986, does not expressly address law enforcement access to mobile phone location data. In fact, one federal appellate court struggling to apply the law to a government request for historical cell site location information stated that it was "stymied by the failure of Congress to make its intention clear."[12]

The ACLU has documented the resulting patchwork of varied and conflicting legal standards. In August 2011, 35 ACLU affiliates submitted public records requests with state and local law enforcement agencies around the nation seeking information about their policies, procedures, and practices for obtaining mobile phone location data.[13]

Over 200 local law enforcement agencies responded. While the overwhelming majority engaged in at least some cell phone tracking, the legal standards they met varied widely. For example, police in Lincoln, Nebraska obtain even GPS data without a warrant based upon probable cause. Police in Wilson County, North Carolina obtain historical cell site location information by proffering only that the data is "relevant and material" to an ongoing investigation. Yet some police departments, including police in the County of Hawaii, Wichita, and Lexington, Kentucky, do secure warrants based upon probable cause to obtain mobile phone location data.

If these police departments can protect both public safety and privacy by meeting the warrant and probable cause requirements, then surely other agencies can as well.

Moreover, it is not just state and local law enforcement agencies that obtain mobile phone location data under inconsistent standards. The U.S. Attorney's Offices appear to do so as well.

The Department of Justice recommends that law enforcement agents obtain a warrant based upon probable cause to precise access real-time location data.[14] However, not all U.S. Attorneys Offices comply with this recommendation. Litigation by the ACLU and Electronic Frontier Foundation revealed that U.S. Attorney's Offices in the District of New Jersey and the Southern District of Florida have obtained even what the Department of Justice classifies as precise mobile phone location data without obtaining a warrant and showing probable cause.[15]

Unfortunately, today the federal government's policies, procedures and practices for obtaining mobile phone location data are more opaque than ever. In what has been labeled as the most consequential Fourth Amendment decision in a decade, in *United States v. Jones*, the Supreme Court held that attaching a GPS device to a car and tracking its movements is a search under the Fourth Amendment.[16] *Jones*, however, left unresolved whether such GPS tracking is the sort of search that requires a warrant based on probable cause. Moreover, the Court did not discuss how its holding would apply to surveillance performed with other technologies such as mobile phone tracking. While FBI General Counsel Andrew Weissmann has explained that the Department of Justice has issued two guidance memoranda setting out its view of how *Jones* affects the constitutionality of various forms of location tracking, neither has been made public despite an ACLU request for them under the Freedom of Information Act. The ACLU has filed suit in federal court to force the release of these memoranda.

IV. Tracking People's Location Can Invade Their Privacy Because It Reveals A Great Deal About Them

Location tracking enables law enforcement to capture details of someone's movements for months on end, unconstrained by the normal barriers of cost and officer resources.[17] In *United States v. Jones*,[18] the Supreme Court held that a Fourth Amendment search occurred when the government placed a GPS tracking device on the defendant's car and monitored his whereabouts nonstop for 28 days.[19] A majority of the Justices also stated that "the use of longer term GPS monitoring . . . impinges on expectations of privacy" in the location data downloaded from that tracker.[20] As Justice Alito explained, "[s]ociety's expectation has been that law enforcement agents and others would not -- and indeed, in the main, simply could not -- secretly monitor and catalog every single movement of an individual's car, for a very long period."[21]

Justice Sotomayor emphasized the intimate nature of the information that might be collected by the GPS surveillance, including "trips to the psychiatrist, the plastic surgeon, the abortion clinic, the AIDS treatment center, the strip club, the criminal defense attorney, the by-the-hour motel, the union meeting, the mosque, synagogue or church, the gay bar and on and on."[22] While even the limited collection of geolocation information can reveal intimate and detailed facts about a person, the privacy invasion is multiplied many times over when law enforcement agents obtain geolocation information for prolonged periods of time. As the D.C. Circuit Court of Appeals has observed, "[a] person who knows all of another's travels can deduce whether he is a weekly church goer, a heavy drinker, a regular at the gym, an unfaithful husband, an outpatient receiving medical treatment, an associate of particular individuals or political groups—and not just one such fact about a person, but all such facts."[23]

There have always been facets of American life that have been uniquely safeguarded from the intrusive interference and observation of government. Location tracking threatens to make even those aspects of life an open book to government. As Justice Sotomayor pointed out in *Jones*, "Awareness that the Government may be watching chills associational and expressive freedoms. And the Government's unrestrained power to assemble data that reveal private aspects of identity is susceptible to abuse."[24] Further, location information from cell phones can reveal people's locations and movement within their homes and other spaces that receive heightened protection under the Fourth Amendment.[25]

While privacy rights are often conceptualized as belonging to individuals, they are also important because they ensure a specifically calibrated balance between the power of individuals on the one hand and the state on the other. When the sphere of life in which individuals enjoy privacy shrinks, the state becomes all the more powerful:

> The net result is that GPS monitoring--by making available at a relatively low cost such a substantial quantum of intimate information about any person whom the Government, in its unfettered discretion, chooses to track--may alter the relationship between citizen and government in a way that is inimical to democratic society.[26]

Chief Judge Kozinski of the U.S. Court of Appeals for the Ninth Circuit has elaborated on this critical point:

> I don't think that most people in the United States would agree with the panel that someone who leaves his car parked in his driveway outside the door of his home invites people to crawl under it and attach a device that will track the vehicle's every movement and transmit that information to total strangers. There is something creepy and un-American about such clandestine and underhanded behavior. To those of us who have lived under a totalitarian regime, there is an eerie feeling of déjà vu.[27]

Furthermore, while the government routinely argues that records of a person's prior movements deserve less privacy protection than records of where a person travels in real time, this is a meaningless distinction. As one judge has noted, "[t]he picture of [a person]'s life the government seeks to obtain is no less intimate simply because it has already been painted."[28] It is hard to see how daily requests for historical location differ from continuous real-time tracking.

While the *Jones* case dealt with long-term tracking of movements, even single points of mobile phone location data can intrude upon reasonable expectations of privacy – a single GPS data point revealing that someone is in the waiting room of an abortion clinic, a church or at an AA meeting can reveal information that is highly sensitive. The Supreme Court has held that location tracking even using relatively crude "beeper" trackers implicates reasonable expectations of privacy where it "reveals information that could not have been obtained through visual surveillance from a public space."[29] For this reason, and because law enforcement agents often will not know whether a particular piece of mobile phone location data will implicate a person's privacy interest in their location in private spaces, the better rule is an across-the-board requirement that law enforcement agents obtain a warrant based on probable cause for mobile phone location data.

V. Congress Should Act to Protect Americans' Privacy by Imposing a Warrant and Probable Cause Requirement for Mobile Phone Location Data

Congress is in a good position to protect Americans' privacy. In his concurrence in *Jones*, Justice Alito wrote: "In circumstances involving dramatic technological change, the best solution to privacy concerns may be legislative."[30] Given that it will likely take years before the Supreme Court once again considers the constitutionality of location tracking, Congress should not stand by as the privacy of Americans is invaded due to confusion over the rules.

The warrant and probable cause requirements play important roles in safeguarding Americans' privacy. The function of the warrant clause is to safeguard the rights of the innocent by preventing the state from conducting searches solely in its discretion:

> Absent some grave emergency, the Fourth Amendment has interposed a magistrate between the citizen and the police. This was done not to shield criminals nor to make the home a safe haven for illegal activities. It was done so that an objective mind might weigh the need to invade that privacy in order to enforce the law. The right of privacy was deemed too precious to entrust to the discretion of those whose job is the detection of crime and the arrest of criminals. Power is a heady thing; and history shows that the police acting on their own cannot be trusted.[31]

The warrant and probable cause requirements are especially important here given the extraordinary intrusiveness of modern-day electronic surveillance.

The warrant requirement imposes no unreasonable burden on the law enforcement agents – they obtain these regularly and routinely for searches of homes, vehicles and email accounts. Warrants are a clear and familiar standard, requested by law enforcement and issued by judges for hundreds of years. Moreover, under the GPS Act, obtaining warrants for geolocational information would be even less burdensome than the process law enforcement agencies have followed for decades to obtain telephone wiretaps.

VI. Specific Issues

While privacy advocates and law enforcement agents may disagree about many aspects of law enforcement access to mobile phone location data, it is helpful to start out by identifying points of common ground. The Department of Justice already recommends that its agents obtain a warrant based upon probable cause to engage in precise forms of real-time mobile tracking.[32] This is identical to the standard advocated by the ACLU and others pushing for reform, and it is the standard that would be mandated by the GPS Act.

There is disagreement regarding what standard law enforcement should meet to engage in less precise forms of real-time tracking such as cell site location information, but this is an increasingly illusory divide. As Professor Blaze has explained, today cell site location information can be very precise and can place people inside constitutionally protected spaces such as a home. Cell cite location information will only get more precise over time. Unless Congress wishes to revisit this issue every few years in order to evaluate the accuracy of current location tracking technology, the standard for all types of real-time location tracking should be the same. That is the only standard that will have any hope of standing the test of time. There is also disagreement regarding what the standard should be for *historical* location data. Because, as discussed above, people have just as strong a privacy interest in where they have been in the past as they do in where they will go in the future, law enforcement agents should also have to obtain a warrant based upon probable cause to access historical mobile phone location data. Another area of contention is how to handle law enforcement requests for "tower dump" data. These requests have unique features, in particular the way in which they sweep in the location data about vast numbers of innocent individuals. It is important that law enforcement agencies implement strict minimization and notice requirements so that after the investigation is over, the individuals are told that their data was obtained by law enforcement. Also, law enforcement agencies should not indefinitely retain data on innocent people. Finally, the ACLU believes that "emergency" must not become a catch-all phrase that allows police to skirt appropriate standards. While obviously legitimate emergencies must be handled quickly, in every case they should be followed by an explanation filed with the court that describes the circumstance of the emergency and certifies that the facts surrounding it are true to the best of the officers' knowledge.

VII. The ACLU Endorses the GPS Act

The ACLU supports passage of the GPS Act because it would ensure that law enforcement agents obtain a warrant for geolocation information, subject to certain reasonable exceptions.

The heart of Act is the requirement that "[a] governmental entity may intercept geolocation information or require the disclosure by a provider of a covered service of geolocation information only pursuant to a warrant issued using the procedures described in the Federal Rules of Criminal Procedure …"[33] In turn, Federal Rule of Criminal Procedure 41 provides that "a warrant may be issued for any of the following: (1) evidence of a crime; (2) contraband, fruits of crime, or other items illegally possessed; (3) property designed for use, intended for use, or used in committing a crime; or (4) a person to be arrested or a person who is unlawfully restrained."

Thus, through its incorporation of the Rule 41 standard, the GPS Act strikes a reasonable—and constitutionally necessary—balance between privacy and law enforcement interests. Under this provision, for example, when law enforcement agents have a good reason to believe that tracking the location of a cell phone will turn up evidence of a crime, or that a cell phone was used during the commission of a crime, law enforcement agents will have little difficulty persuading magistrate judges to grant them permission to engage in location tracking.

Further, the GPS Act contains a limited number of exceptions, for:

- Emergency access when "it is reasonable to believe that the life or safety of the person is threatened";
- Foreign intelligence surveillance covered by the Foreign Intelligence Surveillance Act of 1978;
- Law enforcement emergencies where there is not time to secure a warrant;
- To retrieve lost or stolen phones;
- To allow parents or guardians to monitor children; and
- When the user has consented.

The GPS Act could be strengthened through the inclusion of reporting requirements regarding law enforcement agencies' collection of geolocation information. To be sure, law enforcement agencies may have a legitimate interest in keeping the details of specific investigations secret, but when it comes to aggregate statistical information about the use of specific surveillance techniques, the public interest is best served through disclosure.

Covert surveillance techniques are by their nature secret, which has important ramifications for the ability of both Congress and the public to engage in oversight. Robust reporting requirements play a valuable role in filling what would otherwise be a void of information regarding the activities of government. For example, each year the administrative office of the courts produces aggregate reports on the use of wiretap authorities by law enforcement agencies nationwide. Without revealing any sensitive investigative details, these reports give Congress and the public meaningful insight into the frequency with which the government uses this surveillance technique and the kinds of crimes that they are used to investigate.

Last year, Congress received some data regarding cell phone surveillance after Congressmen Barton and Markey wrote letters to the wireless carriers. Of the four largest carriers, three provided statistics in their responses (T-Mobile declined), revealing that they received 1.3 million requests from law enforcement agencies each year. However, only one company, Sprint Nextel, provided specific data about the location requests it receives.

Congress cannot perform effective oversight of these invasive surveillance powers with data from only one of the four major wireless carriers. Furthermore, as the disclosures were in response to a specific request by two members of Congress, the wireless carriers are not obligated to provide updated data this year. Congress simply cannot perform effective oversight without data. For this reason, we urge the co-sponsors of the legislation to implement reporting requirements.

CONCLUSION

The ACLU agrees with Justice Alito that, in this time of rapid technological change, it is especially appropriate for Congress to step in and regulate the use of surveillance technology by government. The warrant and probable cause requirements strike the appropriate balance, ensuring that legitimate investigations can go forward without eroding the privacy rights of innocent Americans.

End Notes

[1] CTIA, Wireless Quick Facts, http://www.ctia.org/advocacy/research/index.cfm/aid/10323.

[2] See Decl. of Henry Hodor at 7 n.6, available at http://www.aclu.org/pdfs/freespeech/cellfoia_release_4805_001_20091022.pdf.

[3] Hearing on Electronic Communications Privacy Act Reform and the Revolution in Location Based Technologies and Services Before the Subcomm. on the Constitution, Civil Rights, and Civil Liberties of the H. Comm. on Judiciary, 111th Cong. 5 (2010) (statement of Professor Matt Blaze), available at http://judiciary.house.gov/hearings/pdf/ Blaze 100624.pdf; Thomas Farely & Ken Schmidt, Cellular Telephone Basics: Basic Theory and Operation, Private Line (Jan. 1, 2006), http://www.privateline.com/mt_ cellbasics/ iv_ basic_theory_and_operation/.

[4] Stephanie K. Pell & Christopher Soghoian, Can You See Me Now? Toward Reasonable Standards for Law Enforcement Access to Location Data That Congress Could Enact, 27 Berkeley Tech. L.J. 117, 132 (2012).

[5] Statement of Professor Matt Blaze, supra note 3, at 13-14.

[6] Id. at 13.

[7] Id. at 10. 8Id. at 5.

[9] U.S. Dep't of Justice, Retention Periods of Major Cellular Service Providers (Aug. 2010), available at https://www.aclu.org/cell-phone-location-tracking-request-responsecell-phone-company-data-retention-chart.

[10] Pell & Soghoian, supra note 4, at 121.

[11] Helen A.S. Popkin, Carriers Charge Cops for Cellphone Information, NBCNews.com, http://www.nbcnews.com/technology/technolog/carriers-charge-cops-cellphoneinformation-656559.

[12] In re Application of U.S. for an Order Directing a Provider of Elec. Commc'n Serv. to Disclose Records to Gov't, 620 F.3d 304, 319 (3d Cir. 2010).

[13] Supporting documentation demonstrating the factual assertions throughout this section can be found at ACLU, Cell Phone Location Tracking Public Records Request (Mar. 25, 2013), http://www.aclu.org/protecting-civil-liberties-digital-age/cell-phone-locationtracking-public-records-request.

[14] The Electronic Communications Privacy Act: Government Perspective on Protecting Privacy in the Digital Age: Hearing Before the S. Comm. on Judiciary, 125th Cong. 7 (2011) (statement of James A. Baker, Associate Deputy Att'y Gen., U.S. Dep't of Justice). available at http://1.usa.gov/IsojNy.

[15] ACLU, ACLU v. Department of Justice: ACLU Lawsuit To Uncover Records of Cell Phone Tracking (Sept. 6, 2011), http://www.aclu.org/free-speech/aclu-v-departmentjustice

[16] 132 S. Ct. 945, 949 (2012).

[17] See United States v. Pineda-Moreno, 617 F.3d 1120, 1124 (9th Cir. 2010) (Kozinski, J, dissenting from denial of rehearing en banc) ("The modern devices used in PinedaMoreno's case can record the car's movements without human intervention—quietly, invisibly, with uncanny precision. A small law enforcement team can deploy a dozen, a hundred, a thousand such devices and keep track of their various movements by computer, with far less effort than was previously needed to follow a single vehicle.").

[18] 132 S. Ct. 945, 954 (2012)

[19] Id. at 954.

[20] Id. at 953-64 (Sotomayor, J., concurring); see also id. at 964 (Alito, J., concurring).

[21] Id. at 964 (Alito, J., concurring).

[22] Id. at 955 (quoting People v. Weaver, 12 N.Y.3d 433, 442 (N.Y. 2009)).

[23] United States v. Maynard, 615 F.3d 544, 562 (D.C. Cir. 2010), aff'd sub nom. United States v. Jones, 132 S. Ct. 945 (2012).

[24] Jones, 132 S. Ct. at 956 (Sotomayor, J., concurring) (quotations omitted).

[25] See In re Application of the United States of America for Historical Cell Site Data, 747 F. Supp. 2d 827, 840 (S.D. Tex. 2010) ("[Cell site location information] will also inevitably be more intrusive [than vehicle GPS tracking], because the phone can be monitored indoors where the expectation of privacy is greatest."); see also In the Matter of the Application of the United States of America for an Order Directing a Provider of Electronic Communication Service to Disclose Records to the Government, 620 F.3d 304, 318 (3d Cir. 2010).

[26] Jones, 132 S. Ct. at 956 (Sotomayor, J., concurring) (quotations omitted).

[27] United States v. Pineda-Moreno, 617 F.3d 1120, 1126 (9th Cir. 2010) (Kozinski, C.J., dissenting). See also United States v. Cuevas-Perez, 640 F.3d 272, 286 (7th Cir. 2011) (Wood, J., dissenting) ("The technological devices available for [monitoring a person's movements] have rapidly attained a degree of accuracy that would have been unimaginable to an earlier generation. They make the system that George Orwell depicted in his famous novel, 1984, seem clumsy and easily avoidable by comparison.").

[28] In re Application of the U.S. for Historical Cell Site Data, 747 F. Supp. 2d 827, 840 (S.D.Tex. 2010) (citation omitted).

[29] United States v. Karo, 468 U.S. 705, 707 (1984).

[30] 132 S. Ct. at 964.

[31] McDonald v. United States, 335 U.S. 451, 455 (1948).

[32] See The Electronic Communications Privacy Act: Government Perspective on Protecting Privacy in the Digital Age: Hearing Before the S. Comm. on Judiciary, 125th Cong. 7 (2011) (statement of James A. Baker, Associate Deputy Att'y Gen., U.S. Dep't of Justice). available at http://1.usa.gov/IsojNy.

[33] § 2602(h)(2).

In: Electronic Communications Privacy Act
Editor: Marissa G. Haul
ISBN: 978-1-62948-826-4

Chapter 11

TESTIMONY OF MATT BLAZE, PROFESSOR, UNIVERSITY OF PENNSLYVANIA. HEARING ON "ELECTRONIC COMMUNICATIONS PRIVACY ACT (ECPA) PART 2: GEOLOCATION PRIVACY AND SURVEILLANCE"*

1. INTRODUCTION AND BACKGROUND

Thank you for the opportunity to provide some background about Location technology in current and emerging wireless networking. I hope my remarks will be helpful in understanding how Location information is calculated and the direction that this important and yet rather complex technology is taking. I offer this statement today on my own behalf and do not represent any other party or organization.

As I will discuss below, geolocation is an area that is enjoying a period of rapid technological innovation and competition among different technologies. Many assumptions that might have been true several years ago, such as that GPS satellites always provide higher precision Location information than the cellular network does, are no Longer universally true today. For any legislation that seeks to regulate the use or disclosure of Location tracking

* This is an edited, reformatted and augmented version of a testimony, presented April 25, 2013 before the House Judiciary Committee, Subcommittee on Crime, Terrorism, Homeland Security, and Investigations.

technology to remain meaningful in the years to come, it is critical that it avoid defining terms in ways that are likely to become obsolete soon after it becomes Law.

In sum, my primary messages to policy makers considering how best to legislate in the area of Location tracking are:

> The accuracy and precision with which a cellular telephone handset can be Located by network-based (non-GPS) techniques depends on a range of factors, but has been steadily improving as technology has advanced and as new infrastructure is deployed in cellular networks. Under some circumstances, the Latest generation of this technology permits the network to calculate users' Locations with a precision that approaches that of GPS.
>
> A mobile user, in the course of his or her daily movements, will periodically connect to cell towers serving Large and small geographic sectors. Even if the network only records cell tower data, the precision of that data will vary widely for any given customer over the course of a given day, from the relatively Less precise to the relatively very precise, and neither the user nor the carrier will be able to predict whether the next data Location collected will be relatively more or Less precise. For a typical user, over time, some of that data will inevitably reveal locational precision approaching that of GPS.
>
> Network-based geolocation can often be *more* revealing than GPS tracking, because new and emerging cell Location techniques can work indoors and in places not typically accessible to GPS receivers, and the increasingly high resolution that that cell site tracking can achieve in densely populated areas -- and the ability to provide this data even when the handset is indoors -- can paint an even richer picture of an individual's movements than GPS.

I am currently an associate professor of computer and information science at the University of pennsylvania in philadelphia, where I serve as director of the Distributed Computing Laboratory and conduct research on computer security, cryptography, network communication, and surveillance technology. Prior to joining the faculty at Penn, I was for 12 years a member of the research staff at AT&T Labs (previously known as AT&T bell Labs) in New Jersey. I have a phd in computer science from Princeton University, a Masters degree from columbia, and I completed my undergraduate studies at the City University of New York.

A focus of my research is on the properties and capabilities of surveillance technology (both lawful and illicit) in the context of modern digital systems and communications networks. This research aims to strengthen our critical infrastructure against criminals and other unauthorized eavesdroppers and to help ensure that authorized surveillance systems work as intended in the rapidly changing environments in which they must reliably collect evidence and investigative intelligence. Sometimes, this work has Led to surprising observations about real-world surveillance systems. For example, in 1994, I discovered weaknesses in the NSA's “clipper” key escrow encryption system that Led to that system's abandonment before it was widely deployed. More recently, my graduate students and I found previously undiscovered vulnerabilities in analog telephone wiretaps used by Law enforcement, and we identified ways for Law enforcement agencies to harden their CALEA intercept systems against a variety of surveillance countermeasures.

There is perhaps no more ubiquitous symbol of our highly connected society than the cellular telephone. Over the course of only a few short decades, mobile communication devices have evolved from being little more than an expensive curiosity for the wealthy into a basic necessity for most Americans, transforming the way we communicate with one another, do business, and obtain and manage the increasing volume of information that is available to us.

According to recent estimates, there are today more than 331 million active wireless subscriber accounts in the United States. Many households now forgo traditional “landline” telephone service, opting instead for cellular phones carried by each family member. Wireless carriers have strained to keep up with the explosive demand for cellular service, in many areas deploying new infrastructure (most visibly cellular antenna towers) as quickly as they can find places to put it.

As difficult as it may be to imagine modern Life without the cell phone, it is sometimes easy to forget how rapidly the technology has come about and how quickly new research ideas in wireless communication can advance into products and services that we take for granted. Over the Last 25 years the mobile telephone has transformed from an analog voice-only service (originally available in only a few markets) into a high-bandwidth, always-on Internet access portal. “Smartphones”, such as the Latest iphones and Android devices, act not just as voice telephones, but as personal digital organizers, music players, cameras, email readers, and personal computers, in a package that fits in our pocket. We now carry our phones with us wherever we go, and we expect them to have service wherever we happen to be.

Many of the most important and innovative new applications and services that run on mobile devices take advantage of the ability to quickly and automatically detect the user's Location to provide Location-specific information and advice. At the same time, cellular providers calculate where phones in their networks are Located (and how they move) to manage various network functions and to plan where new infrastructure is required.

2. WIRELESS LOCATION TECHNOLOGIES

Unlike conventional wireline telephones, cellular telephones and cellular data devices use radio to communicate between the users' handsets and the telephone network. Cellular service providers maintain networks of radio base stations (also called "cell sites") spread throughout their geographic coverage areas. Each base station is responsible for making connections between the regular telephone network and nearby cellular phones when they make or receive calls.

Cell phone handsets periodically (and automatically) identify themselves to the nearest base station (that with the strongest radio signal) as they move about the coverage area. If a phone moves away from the base station with which it started a call and nearer to a different base station, the call is "handed off" between base stations without interruption. This process of "registration" between a phone and the nearest cellular base stations happens automatically whenever a cellular handset is turned on; no intervention by the user is required. The effect is that phones will generally work any time they are within radio range of at Least one base station, which allows users to use their phone at any Location in their provider's geographic coverage area.

There are two different technical approaches that can be used for calculating the Location of a cell phone. In the first approach, the user's phone calculates its own Location using special GPS satellite receiver hardware built in to the handset. In the second approach, the cellular system infrastructure calculates the Location of the phones that are active in the network, using the normal cellular radio interfaces and without explicit assistance from the users' handsets.

2.1. Handset-Based GPS

For smartphone applications that run on the user's handset, the most prominent Location technology is GPS. In GPS Location, a user's phone contains special hardware that receives signals from a constellation of global position satellites. This allows a phone handset to calculate its Latitude and Longitude whenever it is in range of the satellites. GPS technology can achieve very high spatial resolution (typically within ten meters). In the Latest phone models that incorporate GPS chipset hardware, GPS Location features are integrated into applications for mapping, street directions, and to obtain information about local services and merchants.

Whether or not the calculated GPS Location of a handset is sent to the network (or any other third party) depends on the application software that the phone is running. Some applications, as a matter of course, may periodically transmit their Location to external services. For example, a mapping application might send its current GPS-calculated Location to a network-based service in order to discover, say, the Locations of nearby businesses that might be of interest to the user. Network-based services that make use of a phone's GPS Location might be offered by the cellular carrier or by a third party, internet-based entity.

Unfortunately, GPS, for all its promise, has a number of fundamental Limitations. It relies on special hardware in the phone (particularly a GPS receiver chip) that is currently included only in the Latest handset models and that generally is enabled for Location tracking only when the phone user is explicitly using it to run a Location-based application on the phone. Perhaps most importantly, GPS works reliably only outdoors, when the handset is in "view" of several GPS satellites in the sky above.

2.2. Network-Based Location

GPS is only one technology for cell Location, and while it is the most visible to the end user, GPS is neither the most pervasive nor the most generally applicable cellular phone Location system, especially in the surveillance context. More ubiquitously available are techniques that (unlike GPS) do not depend on satellites or special hardware in the handset, but rather on radio signal data collected and analyzed at the cellular providers' towers and base stations. These "network-based" Location techniques can give the position of virtually every handset active in the network at any time, regardless of whether the mobile devices are equipped with GPS chips and without the explicit knowledge or active cooperation of the phone users.

The accuracy and precision with which a handset can be Located by network-based (non-GPS) techniques depends on a range of factors, but has been steadily improving as technology has advanced and as new infrastructure is deployed in cellular networks. Under some circumstances, the Latest generation of this technology permits the network to calculate users' Locations with a precision that approaches that of GPS.

Network-based Location techniques work by exploiting the cellular radio infrastructure that communicates between the network and the users' phones. ALL cellular systems have an extensive network of base stations ("towers") spread throughout their areas of service such that a cell phone in any Locations in the coverage area is within radio range of at Least one base station. This arrangement essentially divides the carrier's coverage area into a mosaic of local "sectors", each served by an antenna at a local cellular base station. Network-based Location enables a cellular provider to identify the sector in which a user's phone is Located, and, in some cases, to further pinpoint their Location within a sector.

2.2.1. Sector Identification

At a minimum, cellular providers record the identity of the particular base station (or sector) with which a cellular phone was communicating every time it makes or receives a call and whenever it moves from one sector to another. How precisely this information by itself allows a phone to be Located depends on the size of the sector; phones in smaller sectors can be Located with better accuracy than those in Larger sectors.

Historically, in the first cellular systems, base stations were generally placed as far apart from one another as possible while still providing adequate radio coverage across the area terrain (effectively making the sector areas they cover as Large as technically possible). In early cellular systems, a base station might have covered an area several miles or more in diameter (and in sparsely populated, rural areas, this may still be true today). But as cellular phones have become more popular and as users expect their devices to do more and to work in more Locations, the size of the "typical" cell sector has been steadily shrinking.

The reason for this trend toward smaller cell sectors is the explosive growth in the demand for wireless technology. A sector base station can handle only a Limited number of simultaneous call connections given the amount of radio spectrum "bandwidth" allocated to the wireless carrier. As the density of cellular users grows in a given area, the only way for a carrier to accommodate more customers is to divide the coverage area into smaller and smaller sectors, each served by their own base stations and antennas. New services such as 3G and LTE/4G Internet create additional pressure on the available spectrum bandwidth, usually requiring, again, that the area covered by each sector be made smaller and smaller. At the same time, users increasingly rely on their mobile devices to work wherever they happen to be, indoors and out, on the street, in offices and residences, even in basements and elevators. The only way to make service more reliable in more places under varying radio conditions is to add base stations that cover "dead spots". Adding base stations to eliminate dead spots further reduces the area of a typical sector's coverage.

As a result of these pressures, the number of cellular base stations has been growing steadily, with a corresponding decrease in the geographic area served by each. According to a recent cellular telecommunications Industry Association (CTIA) study, the number of cellular base stations in the United States tripled over the most recent ten year period. Indeed, this trend has been accelerating rapidly, with the deployment of the Latest generation of smaller and smaller-scale cellular base stations (called, variously, "microcells", "picocells" and "femtocells"). These small cells are designed to serve very small areas, such as particular floors of buildings or even individual homes and offices. By some estimates, the number of these small-scale cellular base stations equaled or outstripped the number of conventional cells in the US in 2010, and their deployment continues to grow at a very fast rate.

The effect of this trend toward smaller cell sectors is that knowing the identity of the base station (or sector ID) that handled a call is tantamount to knowing a phone's Location to within a relatively small geographic area. In relatively unpopulated areas with open terrain, a sector might cover an area miles in diameter. But In urban areas and other environments that use microcells, a sector's coverage area can be quite small indeed, sometimes effectively identifying individual floors and rooms within buildings.

2.2.2. Enhanced Location with Time- and Angle- of Arrival

The decreasing size of cell sectors is not the only factor making cellular network-based Location more accurate. New technology allows cellular network providers to Locate not just the sector in which the users' wireless device is Located, but its position *within* the sector. By correlating the precise time and angle at which a given device's signal arrives at multiple sector base stations, new technology now makes it practical for a network operator to pinpoint a phone's Latitude and Longitude at a level of accuracy that can approach that of GPS.

A variety of "off-the-shelf" products and system upgrades have recently become available to cellular providers that use enhanced time- and/or angle- of arrival calculations to collect precise Location information about users' devices as they move around the network. Current commercially available versions of this technology can pinpoint a phone's Location to an accuracy of within 50 meters or Less under many circumstances, and emerging versions of the technology can increase accuracy even beyond that. This is accomplished without requiring any new or special hardware (such as GPS chips) to be installed on the end-users' phones. Accurate Locations can be tracked with this technology even when no calls are being made or received, as Long as the User's phone is turned on and is within a coverage area. (whether locations are routinely tracked and recorded at times other than when calls are made or received depends on the policy of the particular carrier).

Although these enhanced location technologies are not yet universally available in every network, wireless carriers are deploying them because they provide information that is extremely valuable in managing their networks and Businesses. By tracking more precisely where mobile devices are located within sectors (and their patterns of movement), a carrier can better identify where new infrastructure might be required, where old infrastructure might be redundant, and how and where their customers use different service offerings.

While each carrier has its own data collection and retention practices, carriers typically create "call detail records" that can include the most accurate location information available to them. Historically, before more advanced location techniques were available, carrier call detail records typically have included only the cell sector or base station identifier that handled the call. As discussed in the previous section, the base station or sector identifier now carries with it far more locational precision than it once did.

As even more precise location information becomes available, cellular records increasingly (now and in the future) can effectively include what amounts to the customer's latitude and longitude along with the sector ids traditionally used in cellular carrier databases. Some carriers will also store this location information not just when calls are made or received, but also about "idle" Phones as they move about the network. Creating and maintaining detailed records about the locations of phones as they move from place to place makes good engineering sense, and we should expect the trend toward more, and more precise, location data collection to continue as part of the natural progression of commercial wireless technology. Once the infrastructure to collect it is installed, the marginal cost of collecting and storing high-resolution location data about every customer is relatively small. Such information will be collected because it is extraordinarily valuable for network management, for marketing, and for developing new services.

3. CELL PHONE LOCATION AND LAW ENFORCEMENT SURVEILLANCE

As noted above, even on networks that do not employ time-of-arrival or angleof-arrival Location enhancements, the base station or sector Location now identifies the Location of a surveillance target with increasing specificity as cellular sectors become smaller and smaller and as microcells, picocells, and femtocells are being deployed to provide denser coverage. In Legacy systems or in rural areas, a sector ID might currently specify only a radius of several miles, while in a dense urban environment with microcells, it could identify an individual floor or even a room within a building. How precisely the sector ID Locates a target depends on the Layout of the particular carrier's network and where in the network the target is Located, but the industry trend is moving inexorably toward sectors that cover smaller and smaller areas.

Most carriers' systems use a variety of Large and small sector configurations that vary based on the different terrain and densities they must cover. A mobile user, in the course of his or her daily movements, will periodically move in and out of Large and small sectors. Even if the network only records cell tower data, the precision of that data will vary widely for any given customer over the course of a given day, from the relatively Less precise to the relatively very precise, and neither the user nor the carrier will be able to predict whether the next data Location collected will be relatively more or Less precise. For a typical user, over time, some of that data will inevitably reveal locational precision approaching that of GPS.

As cellular carriers roll out better Location technologies in the course of their business, the Location information sent to Law enforcement (as transmitted from the carrier's call database in (near) real time in response to a wiretap order) is, inherently, becoming more and more precise. As sectors become smaller, the locational information they reveal becomes more intrinsically precise. And as networks improve, sector data is increasingly being Linked to or supplanted by even more accurately calculated position information about each customer’s handset.

In the past, when cell sectors were widely spaced and before the availability of the enhanced network-based Location technologies now being deployed by wireless carriers, it may have been technically sound to distinguish between Location based on the cellular network (at presumably Low accuracy) and that based on GPS (at higher accuracy). Today, however, this distinction is increasingly obsolete, and as cellular networking technology evolves, it is becoming effectively meaningless. As microcell technology and enhanced Location techniques become more widely deployed in cellular networks, the information revealed by the cell sector identifier pinpoints, under many circumstances, a user's Location to a degree once possible only with dedicated GPS tracking devices. It is no Longer valid to assume that the cell sector recorded by the network will give only an approximate indication of a user's Location. The gap between the Location precision in today's cellular call detail records and that of a GPS tracker is closing, especially as carriers incorporate the Latest technologies into their networks.

Because the precision provided by cellular network-based Location techniques approaches that of GPS-based tracking technology, cellular Location tracking has significant advantages for Law enforcement surveillance operations over traditional GPS trackers. New and emerging cell Location techniques can work indoors and in places not typically accessible to GPS receivers. Cellular Location information is routinely and automatically calculated by the network, without triggering any suspicious or alerting behavior on the handset that might be noticed by the subject. And the "tracking device" is no Longer a hidden box that must be surreptitiously installed and that might be discovered, but a benign object that is deliberately carried by the target: his or her own telephone, computer, or tablet.

These characteristics -- ubiquitous and continuous availability, Lack of alerting, and high precision -- make network-based cellular tracking an extremely attractive and powerful tool for Law enforcement surveillance. The increasingly high resolution that that cell site tracking can achieve in densely populated areas — and the ability to provide this data even when the handset is indoors — can paint an even richer picture of an individual's movements than can vehiclebased GPS devices.

INDEX

D

E

I

J

K

L

M

N

O

P

Q

R

S

T